Microelectronics Laboratory

Using Software Tools: PSpice, OrCAD, Multisim

Muhammad H. Rashid, Ph.D.

Fellow IET (UK), Life Fellow IEEE (USA)

Presently, Professor
Electrical and Computer Engineering
Florida Polytechnic University
Previously, University of West Florida

Cengage

Australia • Brazil • Canada • India • Mexico • Singapore • United Kingdom • United States

Cengage

Microelectronics Laboratory Using Software Tools: PSpice, OrCAD, Multisim

Muhammad H. Rashid

ISBN-13: 978-81-3152-958-4
ISBN-10: 81-315-2958-4

Cengage Learning India Pvt. Ltd.
T-303, 3rd Floor
DAV Complex, Plot 3
Mayur Vihar Phase 1
Delhi-110091

TRADEMARK INFORMATION

PSpice, Probe and OrCAD are registered trademarks of MicroSim Corporation and Cadence Design Systems; Multisim is the trademark of National Instruments. LT-Spice is the trademark of Linear Technology Corporation.

Printed by:
Saurabh Printers Pvt Ltd
67A-68 Ecotech Ext-I Greater Noida
Tel-0120-2341180

Printed in India
Print Number: 03 Print Year: 2025

To

my parents,

my wife, Fatema,

my children, Faez, Farzana, and Hasan,

my grandchildren, Hannah, Laith, Laila, Nora, Amal, Issac, and Inara.

Contents

PART III Field-Effect Transistors (FETs) and Applications

PART IV Operational Amplifiers (Op-Amps) and Applications

Preface

Due to the advancement of many available integrated circuit (IC) packages for analog and digital circuits, the emphasis of electronics lab has shifted from the traditional lab manual, which described the procedures for the measurements of device characteristics and verifications of theoretical results by practical measurements. With the rapidly changing technology and the job descriptions of engineering graduates, the engineering curriculum is undergoing major changes in order to introduce specific life-long learning skills for survival in the rapidly changing professional environment.

The mathematical derivations are kept minimum by using approximate circuit models of operational amplifiers, transistors, and diodes. However, the significance of these approximations are established by computer-aided analysis. Due to the complexity of electronic circuits, computer-aided simulation has also become an integral part of an assignment involving design, development, and analysis. For example, simulation is essential for evaluating the performance of a proposed circuit under various conditions and for making any adjustments in order to meet certain design specifications. A laboratory is the ideal place to verify the theoretical development and to understand the effects of practical limitations. Computer simulation cannot substitute the practical lab experience. It is very highly desirable to include open-ended labs to meet certain design requirements/specifications rather than traditional labs with lab procedures. The open-ended labs help students develop skills in problem-solving, critical thinking, reasoning, analysis, and evaluations. Since engineering often involves innovation or invention, creativity is very important.

Current ABET (Accreditation Board of Engineering and Technology; http://www.abet.org) criteria and other engineering criteria under the Washington Accord (http://www.washingtonaccord.org/) require developing the ability (a) to use the techniques, skills, and modern engineering tools necessary for engineering practice, and (b) to design and conduct experiments, as well as to analyze and interpret data. A well-designed labs should be able to document and demonstrate the achievement of these student learning outcomes.

An electronic lab can introduce many of the desirable skills such as

- To reinforce the basic techniques for analyzing electronic circuits.
- To reinforce the understanding of the characteristics of semiconductor devices.
- To reinforce the applications of electronic devices and to illustrate the applications of commonly used integrated circuits.
- To develop skills for analysis and design of electronic circuits.
- The use of computer software tools for design verifications and performance evaluations including evaluating the effects of parametric variations.
- To develop the ability of developing procedures and instrumentation setup for testing prototype for design and development purposes.

Therefore, carefully designed lab experiments should include device characteristics, device applications, analysis, design to meet certain specifications, cost estimate, procedural development for design verifications, and computer-aided simulation. This lab book has 47 experiments to cover these areas. An instructor can choose the experiments to complement the theoretical lectures over one semester or two semesters or even three semesters. The introduction covers the laboratory safety guidelines and lists the practical values of passive components. The labs are divided into four parts: Part I—Semiconductor Diodes and Applications, Part II—Bipolar Junction Transistors (BJTs) and Applications, Part III—Field-Effect Transistors (FETs) and Applications, and Part IV—Operational Amplifiers (Op-Amps) and Applications.

Although the book makes references to the chapters of the book [1] by the author, it can be used with any other books in electrical, electronics and communication engineering, or engineering technology. References [3], [4], and [5] are the split versions of Ref. [2].

1. Rashid, M.H. *Microelectronic Circuits: Analysis and Design*, 3/e. Cengage Publishing: Boston, MA, 2017.
2. Rashid, M.H. *Microelectronic Circuits: Analysis and Design*, 2/e. Cengage Publishing: Boston, MA, 2011.
3. Rashid, M.H. *Electronic Devices and Circuits*, 1/e. Cengage Learning India: New Delhi, 2014.
4. Rashid, M.H. *Electronic Circuits and Applications*, 1/e. Cengage Learning India: New Delhi, 2014.
5. Rashid, M.H. *Linear Integrated Circuits*, 1/e. Cengage Learning India: New Delhi, 2014.
6. Rashid, M.H. *Microelectronic Circuits: Analysis and Design*. PWS Publishing, 1999.
7. Rashid, M.H. *Introduction to PSpice Using OrCAD for Circuits and Electronics*, 3/e. Prentice-Hall Inc., 2003.

SUPPLEMENTS

Students and instructors are strongly encouraged to explore the electronic concepts through the lab exercises in the lab book. The student learning outcomes (SLOs) are listed at the beginning of each lab. PSpice and OrCAD schematic files are provided in **Cengage Digital App** for ready use of the reader. Please refer to **Appendix** at the end of the book for "Instructions for using the Accompanied Software."

Notes:

- Schematics in the text were drawn in PSpice schematics. However, these schematics can be drawn and run in OrCAD, Multisim, LTSpice, or any electronic circuit simulator. Running the simulation in Multisim or LTSpice would need some changes and adjustment to the files.
- **Appendix A:** Introduction to OrCAD of Ref. [1] covers drawing schematics and running the simulation files. For more details, see Ref. [7] by the author.

LTSpice: PSpice and OrCAD schematics generate LTSpice netlist. LTspice can import this netlist file and run the simulation.

Multisim: It can import OrCAD files (*.dsn) and SPICE netlist files (.cir) to run the simulation.

The student version PSpice schematics, OrCAD capture, or Multisim software can be obtained or downloaded from the following sources:

OrCAD	**Multisim**
Cadence Design Systems, Inc. 2655 Seely Avenue San Jose, CA 95134, USA *websites*: http://www.cadence.com http://www.orcad.com http://www.ema-eda.com	National Instruments Corporation 11500 N Mopac Expy Austin, TX 78759-3504 *website*: http://www.ni.com/multisim/try/

ASSESSMENT OF STUDENT LEARNING OUTCOMES

Laboratory courses are generally integrated within an engineering curriculum. The question always arises what are the objectives and expected course learning outcomes for laboratory experiences? Labs are traditionally conducted through hardware type of equipment. Can these be achieved through computer simulations, virtual labs, on-line labs, multimedia, or any other means? An ABET committee[1] has identified 13 objectives, and descriptions of each objective can be found in Table A.1. These can be used as student surveys to assess the course learning outcomes. Preferably at the end of each lab. One could also set up as a multiple-choice type online survey at the end of end of each course.

1. **Instrumentation:** Apply appropriate sensors, instrumentation, and/or software tools.
2. **Models:** Identify the strengths and limitations of theoretical models.
3. **Experiment:** Devise an experimental approach, and specify appropriate equipment and procedures.
4. **Data analysis:** Demonstrate the ability to collect, analyze, and interpret data, and to form and support conclusions.
5. **Design:** Design, build, or assemble a part, product, or system.
6. **Learn from failure:** Recognize unsuccessful outcomes due to faulty equipment.
7. **Creativity:** Demonstrate appropriate levels of independent thought, creativity, and capability.
8. **Psychomotor:** Demonstrate competence in selection, modification, and operation of appropriate engineering tools and resources.
9. **Safety:** Recognize health, safety, and environmental issues.
10. **Communication:** Communicate effectively about laboratory work.
11. **Teamwork:** Work effectively in teams, including structure individual and joint accountability.
12. **Ethics in the lab:** Behave with highest ethical standards.
13. **Sensory awareness:** Use the human senses to gather information and to make sound engineering judgments.

Table A.1 Objectives and Course Learning Outcomes for Laboratory Experiences

Department: ________________ University/College: ________________
Student Name ________________ Laboratory Course: ________________
Semester: ________ Year: ________

Using the following scales, please rate each applicable Lab Experiment which lead to the Student Learning Outcomes (SLOs): 5 = Excellent (exceeding expectation), 4 = Very Good (above expectation), 3 = Good (met expectation), 2 = Fair (below expectation), and 1 = Poor

By completing the laboratory experiments, students will be able to

Lab Objective	Course Learning Outcomes (CLOs)	Laboratory Experiment Nos.									
		1	2	3	4	5	6	7	8	9	10
# 1 *Instrumentation*	Apply appropriate sensors, instrumentation, and/or software tools to make measurements of physical quantities.										

(Continued)

[1] Feisel, L.D., Peterson, G.D., and Feisel, L.D. *A Colloquy on Learning Objectives for Engineering Education Laboratories*. In: Proceedings of the American Society for Engineering Education Annual Conference & Exposition, 2002.

Table A.1 Continued

Lab Objective	Course Learning Outcomes (CLOs)	Laboratory Experiment Nos.									
		1	2	3	4	5	6	7	8	9	10
# 2 *Models*	Identify the strengths and limitations of theoretical models as predictors of real world behaviors. This may include evaluating whether a theory adequately describes a physical event and establishing or validating a relationship between measured data and underlying physical principles.										
# 3 *Experiment*	Devise an experimental approach, specify appropriate equipment and procedures, implement these procedures, and interpret the resulting data to characterize an engineering material, component, or system.										
# 4 *Data Analysis*	Demonstrate the ability to collect, analyze, and interpret data, and to form and support conclusions. Make order of magnitude judgments, and know measurement unit systems and conversions.										
# 5 *Design*	Design, build, or assemble a part, product, or system, including using specific methodologies, equipment, or materials; meeting client requirements; developing system specifications from requirements; and testing and debugging a prototype, system, or process using appropriate tools to satisfy requirements.										
# 6 *Learn from Failure*	Recognize unsuccessful outcomes due to faulty equipment, parts, code, construction, process, or design, and then re-engineer effective solutions.										
# 7 *Creativity*	Demonstrate appropriate levels of independent thought, creativity, and capability in real-world problem solving.										
# 8 *Psychomotor*	Demonstrate competence in selection, modification, and operation of appropriate engineering tools and resources.										

(Continued)

Table A.1 Continued

Lab Objective	Course Learning Outcomes (CLOs)	Laboratory Experiment Nos.									
		1	2	3	4	5	6	7	8	9	10
# 9 *Safety*	Recognize health, safety, and environmental issues related to technological processes and activities, and deal with them responsibly.										
# 10 *Communication*	Communicate effectively about laboratory work with a specific audience, both orally and in writing, at levels ranging from executive summaries to comprehensive technical reports.										
# 11 *Teamwork*	Work effectively in teams, including structure individual and joint accountability; assign roles, responsibilities, and tasks; monitor progress; meet deadlines; and integrate individual contributions into a final deliverable.										
# 12 *Ethics in the Lab*	Behave with highest ethical standards, including reporting information objectively and interacting with integrity.										
# 13 *Sensory Awareness*	Use the human senses to gather information and to make sound engineering judgments in formulating conclusions about real-world problems.										

Acknowledgments

Thanks are due to the editorial team at Cengage Learning, and also to Dr M. Farooq at West Virginia University Institute of Technology for his comments and suggestions.

Finally, thanks to my family for their patience while I was occupied with this and other projects.

Any comments and suggestions regarding this book are welcome. They should be sent to the author

Dr Muhammad H. Rashid
Professor
Electrical and Computer Engineering

About the Author

Muhammad H. Rashid is currently employed by the Florida Polytechnic University as a *Professor of Electrical and Computer Engineering*. Previously, he was employed by the University of Florida as *Professor and Director of UF/UWF Joint Program*. Rashid received B.Sc. degree in Electrical Engineering from the Bangladesh University of Engineering and Technology, and M.Sc. and Ph.D. degrees from the University of Birmingham, UK. Previously, he worked as Professor of Electrical Engineering and the Chair of the Engineering Department at Indiana University-Purdue University at Fort Wayne. He also worked as Visiting Assistant Professor of Electrical Engineering at the University of Connecticut, Associate Professor of Electrical Engineering at Concordia University (Montreal, Canada), Professor of Electrical Engineering at Purdue University Calumet, and Visiting Professor of Electrical Engineering at King Fahd University of Petroleum and Minerals (Saudi Arabia), as a design and development engineer with Brush Electrical Machines Ltd. (England, UK), a Research Engineer with Lucas Group Research Centre (England, UK), a Lecturer and Head of Control Engineering Department at the Higher Institute of Electronics (in Libya and Malta).

Dr Rashid is actively involved in teaching, researching, and lecturing in electronics, power electronics, and professional ethics. He has published 18 books listed in the US Library of Congress and more than 160 technical papers. His books are adopted as textbooks all over the world. His book *Power Electronics* has translations in Spanish, Portuguese, Indonesian, Korean, Italian, Chinese, Persian, and Indian edition. His book *Microelectronics* has translations in Spanish in Mexico and in Spain, Italian, and Chinese.

He has received many invitations from foreign governments and agencies to give keynote lectures and consult, by foreign universities to serve as an external examiner for undergraduate, master's, and Ph.D. examinations, by funding agencies to review research proposals, and by USA and foreign universities to evaluate promotion cases for professorship. Dr Rashid has worked as a regular employee or consultant in Canada, Korea, United Kingdom, Singapore, Malta, Libya, Malaysia, Saudi Arabia, Pakistan, and Bangladesh. Dr Rashid has traveled to almost all States in USA and many countries to lecture and present papers (Japan, China, Hong Kong, Indonesia, Taiwan, Malaysia, Thailand, Singapore, India, Pakistan, Turkey, Saudi Arabia, United Arab Emirates, Qatar, Libya, Jordan, Egypt, Morocco, Malta, Italy, Greece, United Kingdom, Brazil, and Mexico).

He is a *Fellow* of the Institution of Engineering and Technology (IET, UK) and a *Life Fellow* of the Institute of Electrical and Electronics Engineers (IEEE, USA). He was elected as an IEEE Fellow with the citation "*Leadership in power electronics education and contributions to the analysis and design methodologies of solid-state power converters.*" Dr Rashid is the recipient of the *1991 Outstanding Engineer Award* from the Institute of Electrical and Electronics Engineers (IEEE). He received the 2002 IEEE Educational Activity Award (EAB) Meritorious Achievement Award in Continuing Education with the following citation *"for contributions to the design and delivery of continuing education in power electronics and computer-aided-simulation."* He is the recipient of the 2008 IEEE Undergraduate Teaching Award with citation "*For his distinguished leadership and dedication to quality undergraduate electrical engineering education, motivating students and publication of outstanding textbooks.*" He is also the recipient of the IEEE 2013 Industry Applications Society *Outstanding Achievement Award.*

Dr Rashid is an ABET program evaluator for electrical and computer engineering (and also from 1995-2000) and was an engineering evaluator for the Southern Association of Colleges and Schools (SACS, USA). He is also an ABET program evaluator for (general) engineering program. He is the Series Editors of *Power Electronics and Applications* and *Nanotechnology and Applications* with the CRC Press. He serves as the Editorial Advisor of *Electric Power and Energy* with Elsevier Publishing. He lectures and conducts workshops on Outcome-Based Education (OBE) and its implementations including assessments.

Dr Rashid is a Distinguished Lecturer for the IEEE Education Society and a Regional Speaker (previously Distinguished Lecture) for the IEEE Industrial Applications Society. He also authored a book on *The Process of Outcome-Based Education—Implementation, Assessment and Evaluations*, UiTM Press, Malaysia, 2012.

Introduction

Learning Objectives

To introduce to the lab safety guidelines and the format of lab reports.
After the end of this experiment, you should be able to

- List the lab safety guidelines.
- Apply the lab report format.
- Select the standard values of passive components.

GUIDELINES FOR LABORATORY SAFETY

It is mandatory that the safety guidelines be read carefully before starting any of the laboratory experiments. Electrical shock can kill or maim an individual instantaneously. Therefore, extreme care must be taken when working in an electrical or electronics laboratory.

The following guidelines must be strictly followed to assure personal safety. You must read each guideline and put a check mark (✓) against it.

Personal Safety Instructions	Check (✓)
• Never energize your circuit until you have completed building it and rechecked your wiring connection.	
• Disconnect all power sources before making any modifications to your circuit.	
• No part of your body, hair, or clothing be in direct contact with any components of an energized circuit.	

(*Continued*)

Continued

Personal Safety Instructions	Check (✓)
• Make sure your hands are dry.	
• Always wear rubber soled, or good electrically insulated, shoes in the laboratory, and do not stand on damp or any other electrically conductive surface while performing an experiment.	
• When taking meter readings of an energized circuit, use only one hand. This eliminates an arm–chest–arm path for the current to flow. Current levels of a few milliamperes flowing through the heart can be lethal.	
• Never work alone in the laboratory so that in the event of an emergency there will be someone nearby to disconnect the power supply of your station or even for the entire laboratory.	
• Be familiar with the lab layout.	
• Be familiar with the locations and uses of the emergency power supply switches.	
• Be familiar with the locations and uses of fire extinguishers.	
• Be familiar with the exits in case of emergency.	
• On the very first day of the laboratory meeting, ask your instructor to show you the emergency switches and their uses.	
• Always discharge a capacitor, or a bank of capacitor, before touching it.	
• No lab instructor will allow horseplay in the laboratory.	
• Use common sense at all times. If you are not sure about touching any wire or component, do not do it.	
• Ask your instructor for advice. If he is not around, find him or wait for him.	

To avoid lethal electrical hazards in the laboratory, the above guidelines (and others as deemed appropriate by your instructor) must be strictly adhered to and practiced. If you have any doubts or are unsure of anything, ask your instructor. You will probably be asked to sign a statement that verifies that you have read these safety guidelines.

COVER PAGE OF LAB REPORTS

DEPARTMENT OF ______________________ ENGINEERING

UNIVERSITY/COLLEGE OF ______________________

LAB COURSE NUMBER: ______________________

TITLE OF EXPERIMENT: ______________________

STUDENT NAME: ______________________

DATE OF LAB PERFORMED: ______________________

DATE OF REPORT SUBMITTED: ______________________

NAME OF PARTNERS (IF ANY): ______________________

____

(Your signature after the statement)

I/We certify that this assignment is the result of my/our own efforts.

- Signature(s): ______________________ Date: ______________________
- University or College e-mail(s): ______________________

Lab Course Number: ______________________

Course Title: ______________________

Department: ______________________

University/College: ______________________

This statement as follows may be required by your instructor from each student.

I, the undersigned, have read the safety guidelines and am aware of any consequences for not adhering to them. Neither my instructor nor my university will be legally liable for any accidents due to any negligence on my part. I have also read the template/or the format of the cover page for the lab reports and understand the requirement for including the cover page for each lab report.

Student Signature: ______________ Date: ______________ Student Name: ______________

EQUIPMENT

Be familiar with the use of the following lab equipment:

- Dual Trace scope
- Function generator and sweeper
- Digital multimeter
- Dual power supply

Passive Components

Table 1 Standard values (in ohms) for metal film resistors (tolerance ±1%) and carbon resistors (tolerance ±5% and ±10%)

1%	5%	10%	1%	5%	10%	1%	5%	10%	1%	5%	10%
10.0	10	10	20.0	20		40.2			61.9	62	
10.2			20.5			41.2			63.4		
10.5			21.0			42.2			64.9		
10.7			21.5			43.2	43		66.5		
11.0	11		22.1	22	22	44.2			68.1	68	68
11.3			22.6			45.3			69.8		
11.5			23.2			46.4			71.5		
11.8	12	12	23.7			47.5	47	47	73.2		
12.1			24.3	24		48.7			75.0	75	
12.4			24.9			49.9			76.8		
12.7			25.5			51.1	51		78.7		
13.0	13		26.1			52.3			80.6		
13.3			26.7	27	27	53.6			82.5	82	82
13.7			27.4			54.9			84.5		
14.0			28.0			56.2	56	56	86.6		
14.3			28.7			57.6			88.7		
14.7			29.4			59.0			90.9	91	
15.0	15	15	30.1	30		60.4			93.1		
15.4			30.9						95.3		
15.8			31.6						97.6		

(*Continued*)

Table 1 Continued

1%	5%	10%	1%	5%	10%	1%	5%	10%	1%	5%	10%
16.2	16		32.4	33	33						
16.5			33.2								
16.9			34.0								
17.4			34.8								
17.8			35.7	36							
18.2	18	18	36.5								
18.7			37.4								
19.1			38.3								
19.6			39.2	39	39						

Note: The available values for carbon are $1\ \Omega \leq R \leq 100\ \text{M}\Omega$ and for metal film are $10\ \Omega \leq R \leq 10\ \text{M}\Omega$. The available values are obtained by multiplying the sequence number by a power of 10 (i.e., 10^{-1}, 10^{0}, 10^{1}, 10^{2}, 10^{3}, etc.)

Table 2 Standard values (in ohms) for wire-wound resistors (tolerance ± 5%)

0.008	0.75	7.5	27	62	180	450	1 k	4 k
0.01	1.0	8	30	70	200	470	1.2 k	5 k
0.02	1.5	10	33	75	220	500	1.3 k	10 k
0.03	2.0	12	35	80	250	560	1.5 k	15 k
0.05	2.5	15	40	82	270	600	1.8 k	20 k
0.1	3.0	16	45	100	300	680	2 k	25 k
0.15	3.3	20	47	110	330	700	2.2 k	40 k
0.2	4.0	22	50	120	390	750	2.5 k	50 k
0.26	5.0	22.5	56	150	400	910	3 k	100 k
0.3	6	25	60	160	430		3.5 k	150 k
0.5	7							

Table 3 Power ratings for resistors

Type	Tolerance	Power ratings
Carbon resistors	5% and 10%	$\frac{1}{8}$ W

(*Continued*)

Table 3 Continued

Type	Tolerance	Power ratings
		$\frac{1}{4}$ W
		$\frac{1}{2}$ W
		1 W
		2 W
Metal film resistors	1%	$\frac{1}{8}$ W
		$\frac{1}{4}$ W
		$\frac{1}{2}$ W
Wire-wound resistors 5%	5%	5 W
		12 W
		25 W
		50 W
		100 W
		225 W

Table 4 Color code for resistors

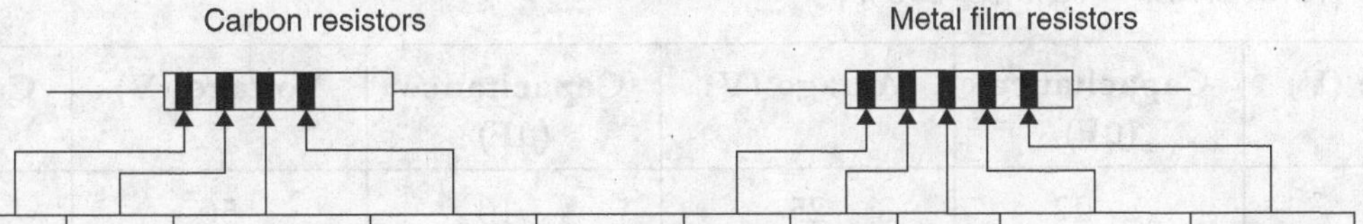

1st Digit	2nd Digit	Multiplier	Tolerance	Color	1st Digit	2nd Digit	3rd Digit	Multiplier	Tolerance
0	0	$10^0 = 1$	—	Black	0	0	0	$10^0 = 1$	—
1	1	$10^1 = 10$	—	Brown	1	1	1	$10^1 = 10$	±1%
2	2	$10^2 = 100$	—	Red	2	2	2	$10^2 = 100$	—
3	3	$10^3 = 1$ k	—	Orange	3	3	3	$10^3 = 1$ k	—
4	4	$10^4 = 10$ k	—	Yellow	4	4	4	$10^4 = 10$ k	—
5	5	$10^5 = 100$ k	—	Green	5	5	5	$10^5 = 100$ k	—
6	6	$10^6 = 1$ M	—	Blue	6	6	6	$10^6 = 1$ M	—
7	7	$10^7 = 10$ M	—	Violet	7	7	7	$10^7 = 10$ M	—
8	8		—	Grey	8	8	8		—
9	9		—	White	9	9	9		—
—	—		± 5%	Gold	—	—	—		—
—	—		± 10%	Silver	—	—	—		—
—	—		± 20%	No band	—	—	—		—

Table 5 Standard values (in Ohms) for carbon composition, linear taper potentiometers (tolerance ±10%: power ratings 2.25 W)

50	1 k	10 k	100 k	1 M
150	1.5 k	15 k	150 k	1.5 M
200	2 k	20 k	200 k	2 M
250	2.5 k	25 k	250 k	2.5 M
350	3.5 k	35 k	350 k	3.5 M
500	5 k	50 k	500 k	5 M
750	7.5 k	75 k	750 k	

Table 6 Standard values (in ohms) for conductive plastic potentiometers (tolerance ±10% power rating $\frac{1}{2}$ W)

250			
1 k	10 k	100 k	1 M
2.5 k	25 k	250 k	2.5 M
5 k	50 k	500 k	5 M

Table 7 Standard values (in ohms) for CERMET potentiometers (tolerance ±10%: power rating $\frac{1}{2}$ W)

50				
100	1 k	10 k	100 k	1 M
200	2 k	20 k	200 k	2 M
500	5 k	50 k	500 k	

Table 8 Standard values for polarized alumminum electrolytic capacitors (tolerance – 10% to +50%)

Voltage (V)	Capacitance (μF)	Voltage (V)	Capacitance (μF)	Voltage (V)	Capacitance (μF)
10	22	25	10	50	0.1
	33		22		0.22
	47		33		0.33
	100		47		0.47
	220		100		1.0
	330		220		2.2
	470		330		3.3
	1000		470		4.7

(Continued)

Table 8 Continued

Voltage (V)	Capacitance (µF)	Voltage (V)	Capacitance (µF)	Voltage (V)	Capacitance (µF)
	2200		1000		10
	3300		2200		22
	4700		3300		33
	6800		4700		47
	10000				100
					220
					330
					470
					1000
					2200

Table 9 Standard values for ceramic disc capacitors (tolerance ±10%)

Voltage (V)	Capacitance (pF)
200	10
	15
	22
	33
	47
	68
	100
	150
	220
	330
	470
	680
	1000
	1500

(*Continued*)

Table 9 Continued

Voltage (V)	Capacitance (pF)
	2200
	3300
	4700
	6800
	10000
	15000

Table 10 Standard values for mylar polyester capacitors (tolerance ± 10%)

Voltage (V)	Capacitance (μF)
100	0.001
	0.0015
	0.0022
	0.0033
	0.0047
	0.0068
	0.0082
	0.01
	0.015
	0.022
	0.027
	0.033
	0.039
	0.047
	0.056
	0.068
	0.082
	0.1
	0.12

(Continued)

Table 10 Continued

Voltage (V)	Capacitance (μF)
	0.15
	0.18
	0.22
	0.27
	0.33
	0.39
	0.47
	0.56
	0.68
	0.82
	1

Table 11 Standard values for ceramic variable capacitors (tolerance ± 10%)

Voltage (V)	Capacitance (pF)	
	min	max
250	1	4.5
	2.5	10
	4	18
	6	35
	7	40
	8	50

CHAPTER 1

Oscilloscope Measurements

Learning Objectives

To take measurements of waveforms by oscilloscope.

PRE-LAB ASSIGNMENT

Read on *Understanding Oscilloscope Functions* from pages 21 to 29 of the Tektronix User Manual for TDS2000B Series Digital Oscilloscopes. Alternatively, you can use any other oscilloscope that is available.

EXPERIMENTS

Students are strongly encouraged and recommended to build the circuits to validate the theoretical results.

The times associated with an output signal are defined as follows:

- Delay time t_d is the time before the circuit can respond to any input signal.
- Rise time t_r is the time required for the output to rise from 10% to 90% of its final (high) value.
- On time t_{on} is the time during which the circuit is fully turned on and functions in its normal mode.
- Fall time t_f is the time required for the output to decrease from 90% to 10% of its initial (high) value.
- Off time t_{off} is the time during which the circuit is completely off, not operating. Thus, the switching period T is

$$T = t_d + t_r + t_{on} + t_f + t_{off}$$

Part I: Measurements of pulse wave signal (see pages 31–33 of the Tektronix User Manual)

1. Turn on the function generator and connect a pulse signal of unknown amplitude and a frequency to the oscilloscope input.
2. Measure the minimum and maximum amplitudes, the frequency, and the peak-to-peak voltage of the input signal.

$V_{i(min)}$ = ________V; $V_{i(max)}$ = ________V; f = ________ Hz; $V_{i(pk-pk)}$ = ________V

Part II: Measurements of sinewave signal (see pages 31–33 of the Tektronix User Manual)

3. Turn on the function generator and connect a sine wave signal of unknown amplitude and f frequency to the oscilloscope input.
4. Measure the minimum and maximum amplitudes, the frequency, and the peak-to-peak voltage of the input signal.

$V_{i(min)} =$ ________ V; $V_{i(max)} =$ ________ V; $f =$ ________ Hz; $V_{i(pk-pk)} =$ ______ V

Part III: Measurements of voltage gain and phase shift of a simple RC circuit (see pages 34–36 of the Tektronix User Manual).

5. Turn on the function generator and connect a sine wave signal of 1 V amplitude (peak) at a frequency of 1 kHz to the RC circuit shown in Fig. 1-1. Measure the peak amplitude of the input voltage and the output voltage, and determine the voltage gain.

$V_{i(pk)} =$ ________ V; $V_{o(pk)} =$ ________ V; $A_v = \dfrac{V_{o(pk)}}{V_{i(pk)}} =$ ________

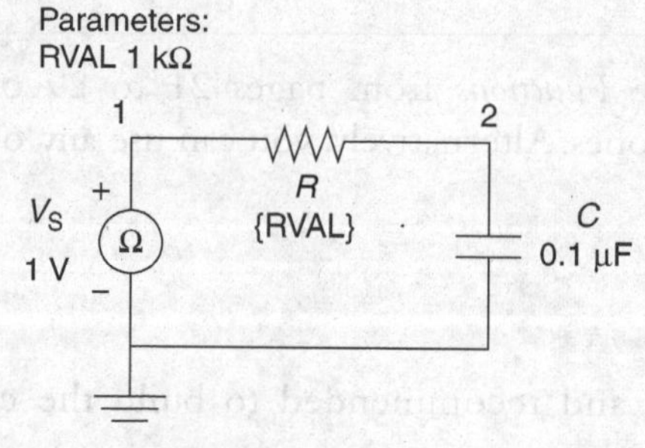

Figure 1-1 RC circuit

Part IV: Measurement of pulsed response of a simple CR circuit (see pages 37–40 of the Tektronix User Manual). A typical pulse response is shown in Fig. 1-2, where in time constant τ = RC and T is the period.

6. Turn on the function generator and connect a pulse wave signal of −1 to +1 V amplitude at a frequency of 1 kHz to the RC circuit shown in Fig. 1-1. Measure the delay time, rise time, fall time, on-line, off-time, and the period.

$t_d =$ ________ μs; $t_r =$ ________ μs; $t_f =$ ________ μs

$t_{on} =$ ________ μs; $t_{off} =$ ________ μs

$T = t_d + t_r + t_f + t_{on} + t_{off} =$ ________ μs; $f = \dfrac{1}{T_f} =$ ________ μs

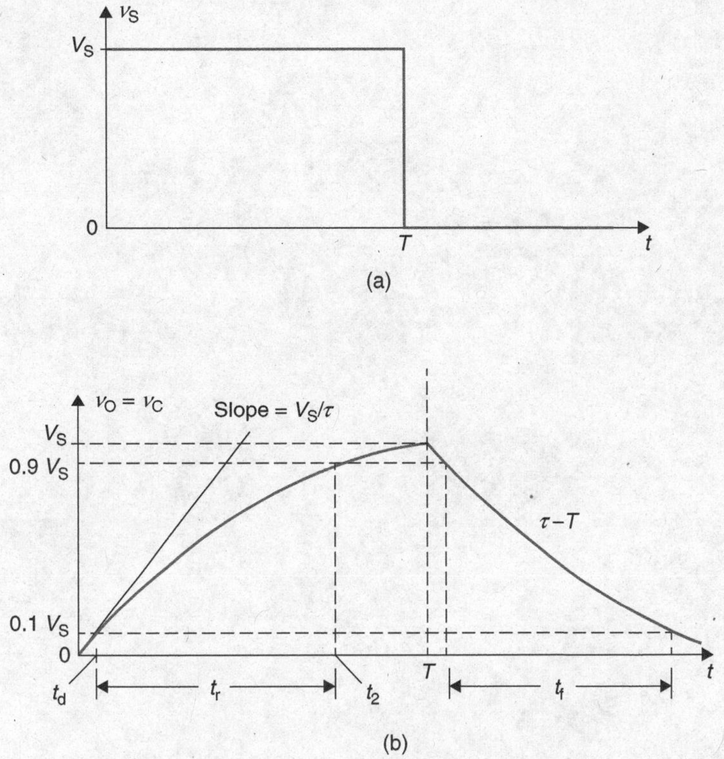

Figure 1-2 Pulse response of an RC circuit: (a) input and (b) output for τ−T

REPORT

1. Describe the safety issues considered while conducting the experiment.

____

____

____

2. Conclusion and comment on achieving goals or objectives of this experiment.

____

____

____

ATTACH ALL PLOTS/GRAPHS OF PULSE RESPONSES TO YOUR REPORT

PART I

SEMICONDUCTOR DIODES AND APPLICATIONS

CHAPTER

2 Diode Characteristics

Learning Objectives

To investigate diode characteristic and determine diode model parameters. We will use computer simulation to plot the diode characteristic and to derive the small-signal diode parameters of a specific diode.

After the end of this experiment, you will be able to

- Describe the voltage–current characteristic of a small-signal semiconductor diode.
- Derive approximate model parameters of a diode.

PRE-LAB ASSIGNMENT

Read on *Characteristics of Diodes* (e.g., Rashid's Section 4.4: Characteristics of Practical Diodes).

COMPUTER SIMULATION

Software tools: PSpice, OrCAD, Multisim, LTSpice, or any electronic circuit simulator.

1. Simulate the circuit as shown in Fig. 2-1 using computer simulation to plot the v–i characteristic of the diode D1N4148. The dc voltage source V_{DD} has a nominal value of 2 V, and it varies from 0 to 3 V with an increment of 0.01 V.

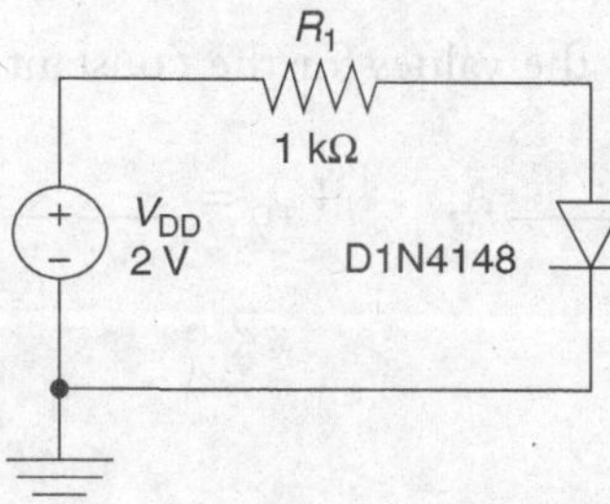

Figure 2-1 A diode simulation circuit

2. Using the i–v data sheet, relate the diode current i_D to the anode–cathode voltage v_D by Shockley equation as follows:

$$i_D = i_S(1 - e^{-v_D/(\eta V_T)}) \qquad (2.1)$$

where I_S is the leakage (or reverse saturation) current, n is the empirical constant known as the emission coefficient or ideality factor, and V_T is a constant called the thermal voltage (25.8 mV) at the room temperature.

I_S = ________ A; n = ________

3. From the computer simulation plot of the v–i forward characteristic, find the small-signal diode model so that the diode voltage v_D can be related to the diode current i_D by

$$v_D = V_{TD} + r_d i_D$$

where V_{TD} is the threshold diode voltage and r_d is the small-signal diode resistance.

V_{TD} = ________ V; r_d = ________ Ω

4. Using the diode equation (2.1) and the load line $(-1/R_1)$, calculate the operating or Q-point defined by V_D and I_D.

V_D = ________ V; I_D = ________ mA

5. Calculate the diode parameters in step 3 using V_D and I_D in step 4.

$r_d = \dfrac{25.8\text{ mV}}{I_D}$ = ________ = ________ Ω; $V_{TD} = V_D - r_d I_D$ = ________ V

Compare these values of r_d and V_{TD} with those in step 3, and explain the reasons for any discrepancies.

____

____

____

____

6. From the simulation output file, write the values for the constant value of V_{DD} = 2V.

V_D = ________ V; I_D = ________ A; V_{TD} = ________ V; r_d = ________ Ω

EXPERIMENTS

The students are strongly encouraged and recommended to build and test the diode circuit to validate the theoretical and computer simulation results.

Procedure

Part 1

1. Set up the circuit as shown in Fig. 2-2 with a silicon diode (lN4148). Connect an ammeter (in series with the diode) and a voltmeter (across the diode) to measure the diode current i_D and diode voltage v_D, respectively.
2. Vary the dc voltage V_{DD} and record V_{DD}, v_D, and $i_D = (V_{DD} - v_D)/R_1$. Do not exceed 5 mA in the forward direction and 10 V in the reverse direction. Complete Table 2-1. Plot between v_D and i_D gives the v–i characteristic of the diode.

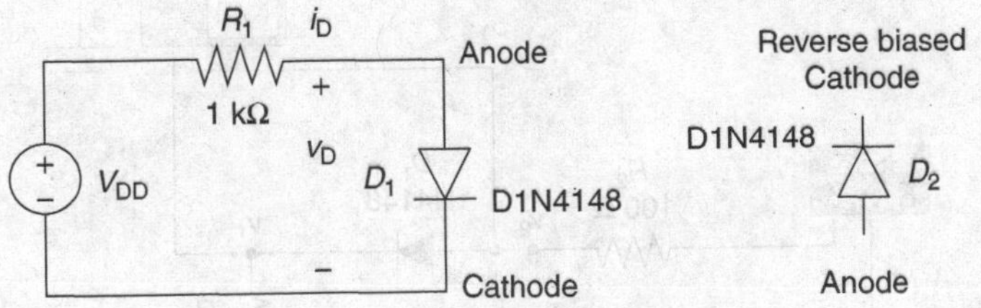

Figure 2-2 Diode test circuit

Table 2-1 Diode data

V_{DD} (V)	Diode voltage, v_D (V)	$V_{R1} = V_{DD} - v_D$ (V)	$i_D = V_{R1t}/R_1$ (mA)
1			
2			
3			
4			
5			
6			
7			
8			
9			
10			

Note: Use a multimeter to measure the actual value of R_1 = _____________ Ω.

Part 2

1. Set up the circuit shown in Fig. 2-3 with the input frequency set for 1 kHz and the amplitude set at minimum setting with a silicon diode. Resistance R_1 measures the diode current i_D, and its voltage drop is $v_1 = R_1 i_D$.

2. Center the scope beam in the bottom left quadrant and adjust the horizontal (HOR) and vertical (VERT) gain controls in order to be able to display 5 mA vertically and 1 V horizontally.
3. Increase the output of the function generator to give the diode characteristic. The diode current should be limited to 5 mA. Record the diode forward characteristic.
4. To determine the reverse characteristic, center the beam in the upper right quadrant. The currents will be in the microampere range. Thus, the vertical amplifier gain setting will have to be changed. Record the diode reverse characteristic.
5. Record the reverse characteristic to a maximum reverse voltage of 10 V.

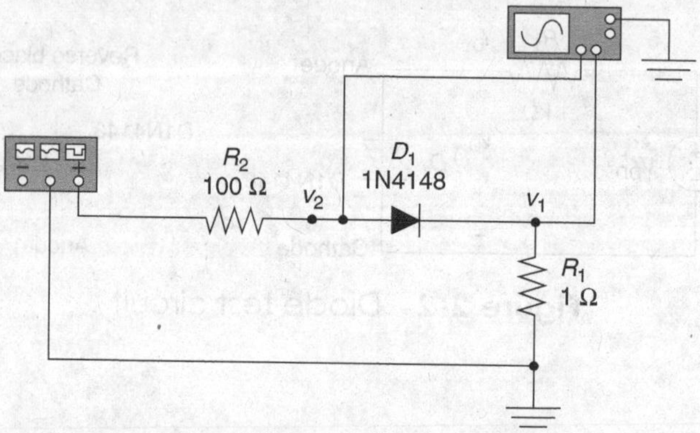

Figure 2-3 Diode test circuit with instruments

REPORT

1. The data obtained for silicon diode (in Part I, step 2) is to be plotted accurately with diode voltage on the abscissa and diode current on the ordinate of the graph. Compare the results with those obtained by using oscilloscope and comment.

____

____

____

____

2. Plot the data for the forward characteristics of the silicon diodes on semi-logarithmic graph paper (at least 3 cycles) and determine

Saturation current, I_S = ________ A; Empirical constant, n = ________

3. If the silicon diode is connected in series with a resistance of $R = 200$ and a dc source of $V_{DD} = 10$ V, determine the operating point (V_D, i_D) and the model parameters.

V_D = ________ V; i_D = ________ A; V_{TD} = ________ V

4. Analyze and interpret the data caused by any variations and practical limitations.

5. Describe the safety issues considered while conducting the experiment.

6. Describe the process to design and conduct experiments.

7. Conclusion and comment on achieving goals or objectives of this experiment.

ATTACH ALL PLOTS/GRAPHS TO YOUR REPORT

CHAPTER

3 Diode Rectifiers

Learning Objectives

To study the operation of half- and full-wave rectifier circuits. We will use computer simulation to plot the output waveforms of rectifier circuits.

After the end of this experiment, you will be able to

- Describe the operation of diode rectifiers that can convert an ac voltage into a dc voltage.
- Evaluate the effects of output filter in reducing the ripple content of the output voltage.

PRE-LAB ASSIGNMENT

Read on *Diode Rectifiers* (e.g. Rashid's Section 4.8: Diode Rectifiers; Section 4.9: C–Filters).

COMPUTER SIMULATION

Software Tools: PSpice, OrCAD, Multisim, LTSpice, or any electronic circuit simulator.

A rectifier is a device that is capable of producing a direct current from an alternating current source. Rectifiers find important applications. Depending upon the type of rectifiers, the rms value is related to the maximum value of the waveform by an appropriate constant.

1. Simulate the half-wave rectifier as shown in Fig. 3-1 by using computer simulation to plot the output voltage across the load resistance R_L. Use a 60 Hz, 120 V ac source, a step-down transformer of 115 V to 6.3 V filament type, a load resistance R_L of 100 Ω, 1 kΩ, 10 kΩ, and a source resistance of $R_3 = 1\ \text{m}\Omega$.

Notes:

- The transformer inductors and turns ratios are related by

$$\frac{N_1}{N_2} = \sqrt{\frac{L_1}{L_2}}$$

where L_1 and N_1 are the primary inductances and the number of turns, respectively, and L_2 and N_2 are the secondary inductances and the number of turns, respectively.

- In case of any difficulties in simulating a coiled transformer, use a voltage-controlled voltage-source (VCVS) with a gain of 0.0525.

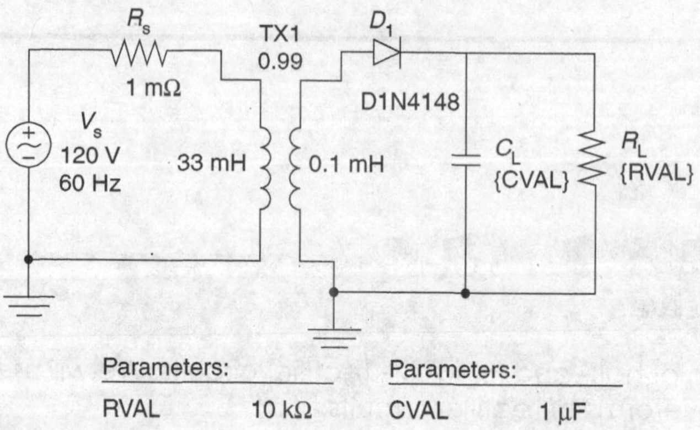

Figure 3-1 Half-wave rectifier

2. Disconnect C_L or set C_L to a very small value, say C_L = 1 pF. Observe the output voltage $v_O(t)$ and its peak value V_m. Record $v_o(t)$ for each R_L.

   What is the effect of the load resistance R_L on the output voltage, and why? Explain.

   ___

   ___

   ___

   What is the purpose of the small resistance R_s in Fig. 3-1? Explain.

   ___

   ___

   ___

   With a 1 μF capacitor across the 10 kΩ load, observe and record $v_o(t)$, the cut-in point (minimum voltage), the cut-out point (maximum voltage), and the peak-to-peak amplitude of ripple voltage. Complete Table 3-1. Repeat with a 200 μF capacitor.

Table 3-1 Effect of filter capacitance on the output voltage for R_L = 10 kΩ (halfwave)

Filter capacitance	Peak input voltage, V_m	Minimum output voltage, $V_{o(min)}$	Maximum output voltage, $V_{o(max)}$	Peak-to-peak output ripple voltage, ΔV_o
C_L = 1 μF				
C_L = 200 μF				

3. Repeat step 2 for $R_L = 1\ k\Omega$ and complete Table 3-2.

Table 3-2 Effect of filter capacitance on the output voltage for $R_L = 1\ k\Omega$ (halfwave)

Filter capacitance	Peak input voltage, V_m	Minimum output voltage, $V_{o(min)}$	Maximum output voltage, $V_{o(max)}$	Peak-to-peak output ripple voltage, ΔV_o
$C_L = 1\ \mu F$				
$C_L = 200\ \mu F$				

What is the effect of the filter capacitor C_L on the output voltage, and why? Explain.

4. The second rectifier is the full-wave rectifier shown in Fig. 3-2. This circuit is composed of two half-wave rectifier circuits so that conduction occurs in one diode during one half of the cycle and through the other diode during the opposite half of the cycle. The output dc voltage of this circuit is twice that of the half-wave circuit. Repeat steps 1 and 2 and complete Table 3-3 for $R_L = 10\ k\Omega$.

Table 3-3 Effect of filter capacitance on the output voltage for $R_L = 10\ k\Omega$ (fullwave)

Filter capacitance	Peak input voltage, V_m	Minimum output voltage, $V_{o(min)}$	Maximum output voltage, $V_{o(max)}$	Peak-to-peak output ripple voltage, ΔV_o
$C_L = 1\ \mu F$				
$C_L = 200\ \mu F$				

5. Repeat step 4 for $R_L = 1\ k\Omega$ and complete Table 3-4.

Table 3-4 Effect of filter capacitance on the output voltage for $R_L = 1\ k\Omega$ (fullwave)

Filter capacitance	Peak input voltage, V_m	Minimum output voltage, $V_{o(min)}$	Maximum output voltage, $V_{o(max)}$	Peak-to-peak output ripple voltage, ΔV_o
$C_L = 1\ \mu F$				
$C_L = 200\ \mu F$				

Comment on the performance of the full-wave rectifier compared to that of the half-wave rectifier.

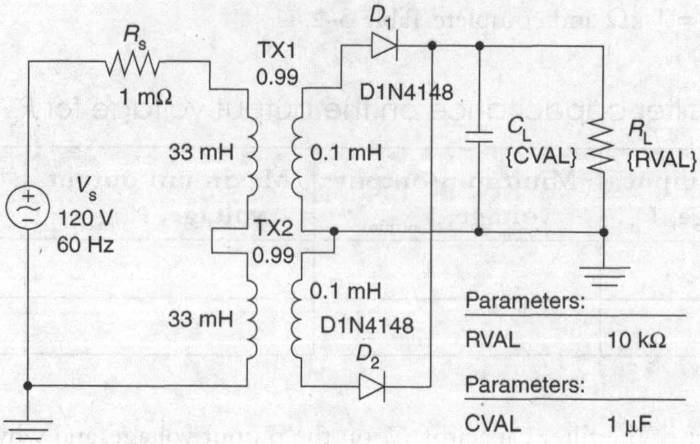

Figure 3-2 Full-wave rectifier

6. The third rectifier is the full-wave bridge rectifier shown in Fig. 3-3. Repeat step 4 and complete Table 3-5 for $R_L = 10$ kΩ.

Table 3-5 Effect of filter capacitance on the output voltage for $R_L = 10$ kΩ (bridge rectifier)

Filter capacitance	Peak input voltage, V_m	Minimum output voltage, $V_{o(min)}$	Maximum output voltage, $V_{o(max)}$	Peak-to-peak output ripple voltage, ΔV_o
$C_L = 1$ μF				
$C_L = 200$ μF				

7. Repeat step 5 for $R_L = 1$ kΩ and complete Table 3-6.

Table 3-6 Effect of filter capacitance on the output voltage for $R_L = 1$ kΩ

Filter capacitance	Peak input voltage, V_m	Minimum output voltage, $V_{o(min)}$	Maximum output voltage, $V_{o(max)}$	Peak-to-peak output ripple voltage, ΔV_o
$C_L = 1$ μF				
$C_L = 200$ μF				

Comment on the performance of the full-wave bridge rectifier compared to those of the full-wave rectifier in step 4.

___

___

___

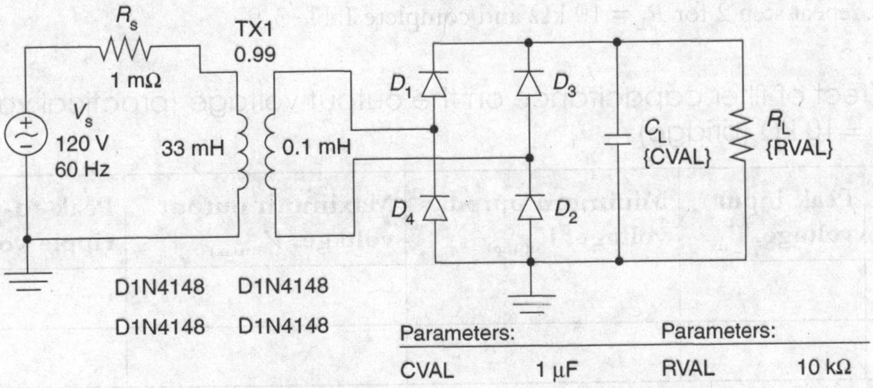

Figure 3-3 Full-wave bridge rectifier

EXPERIMENTS

The students are strongly encouraged and recommended to build and test the diode circuit to validate the theoretical and computer simulation results.

Procedure

1. Set up the circuit shown in Fig. 3-1. Use a 60 Hz, 120 V ac source, a step-down transformer of 115 V to 6.3 V filament type, a load resistance R_L of 10 kΩ, and R_s = 10 Ω. Observe the output voltage $v_O(t)$ and its peak value V_m. Record $v_O(t)$.
2. Place one 1 μF capacitor across the 10 kΩ load. Observe and record $v_O(t)$, cut-in point (minimum voltage) and cut-out point (maximum voltage), and the peak-to-peak amplitude of ripple voltage. Complete Table 3-7. Repeat with a 200 μF capacitor.

Table 3-7 Effect of filter capacitance on the output voltage (practical values) for R_L = 10 kΩ (halfwave)

Filter capacitance	Peak input voltage, V_m	Minimum output voltage, $V_{o(min)}$	Maximum output voltage, $V_{o(max)}$	Peak-to-peak output ripple voltage, ΔV_o
C_L = 1 μF				
C_L = 200 μF				

3. Repeat step 2 for R_L = 1 kΩ and complete Table 3-8.

Table 3-8 Effect of load resistance on the output voltage (practical values) for R_L = 1 kΩ (fullwave)

Filter capacitance	Peak input voltage, V_m	Minimum output voltage, $V_{o(min)}$	Maximum output voltage, $V_{o(max)}$	Peak-to-peak output ripple voltage, ΔV_o
C_L = 1 μF				
C_L = 200 μF				

4. For Fig. 3-2, repeat step 2 for $R_L = 10\ k\Omega$ and complete Table 3-9.

Table 3-9 Effect of filter capacitance on the output voltage (practical values) for $R_L = 10\ k\Omega$ (bridge)

Filter capacitance	Peak input voltage, V_m	Minimum output voltage, $V_{o(min)}$	Maximum output voltage, $V_{o(max)}$	Peak-to-peak output ripple voltage, ΔV_o
$C_L = 1\ \mu F$				
$C_L = 200\ \mu F$				

5. For Fig. 3-3, repeat step 2 for $R_L = 10\ k\Omega$ and complete Table 3-10.

Table 3-10 Effect of load resistance on the output voltage (measured values) for $R_L = 1\ k\Omega$

Filter capacitance	Peak input voltage, V_m	Minimum output voltage, $V_{o(min)}$	Maximum output voltage, $V_{o(max)}$	Peak-to-peak output ripple voltage, ΔV_o
$C_L = 1\ \mu F$				
$C_L = 200\ \mu F$				

REPORT

1. For each circuit, determine the output resistance R_o of the power supply.

Hint: Consider the % regulation equation, $R_o = \text{LRG} \times R_L$.

$$\text{LRG} = \frac{V_{o(\text{no-load})} - V_{o(\text{full-load})}}{V_{o(\text{full-load})}} \times 100 = \_\_\_\_\_\_ \times 100 = \_\_\_\_\_\_\ \% \tag{3.1}$$

2. What is the peak inverse voltage (PIV) that appears across a diode in all the three circuits given in Figs. 3.1–3.3?

PIV (for circuit in Fig. 3-1) = ________V; PIV (for circuit in Fig. 3-2) = ________V;

PIV (for circuit in Fig. 3-3) = ______V.

3. Which is the best circuit for a given capacitor and a load resistor? Comment.

____

____

____

4. Find the optimal capacitor $C_L = 1/(4fR_o)$ for the three circuits given in Figs. 3.1–3.3.

   C_L (for circuit in Fig. 3-1) = ________; C_L (for circuit in Fig. 3-2) = ________;

   C_L (for circuit in Fig. 3-3) = ________

5. Calculate the rms value of the ripple voltage V_r for a given capacitor C_L = 200 μF and R_L = 1 kΩ. Compare this with the measured data for each circuit and complete Table 3-11.
6. Calculate the efficiency of rectification for each circuit and compare this with the measured data.

   η(for circuit in Fig. 3-1) = ________ %; η(for circuit in Fig. 3-2) = ________ %;

   η(for circuit in Fig. 3-3) = ________ %

Table 3-11 Ripple voltage and efficiency of rectification

Filter circuit	Ripple voltage, V_r (calculated)	Ripple voltage, V_r (practical)	Efficiency of rectification, η (calculated) %	Efficiency of rectification, η (measured) %
Figure 3-1				
Figure 3-2				
Figure 3-3				

7. Analyze and interpret the data due to any variations and practical limitations.

   ____

   ____

   ____

8. Describe the safety issues considered while conducting the experiment.

   ____

   ____

   ____

9. Describe the process to design and conduct experiments.

   ____

   ____

10. Conclusion and comment on achieving goals or objectives of this experiment.

   ____

   ____

   ____

ATTACH ALL PLOTS/GRAPHS TO YOUR REPORT

CHAPTER 4

Design of a Zener Diode Regulator

Learning Objectives

To design a Zener diode regulator to give a specified output voltage even though the input voltage and the load current may vary widely. We will use computer simulation to verify the design and evaluate the performance of the regulator.

After the end of this experiment, you will be able to

- Describe the voltage–current characteristic of a Zener diode and derive its small-signal model.
- Design and analyze a Zener regulator to meet certain specifications.

PRE-LAB ASSIGNMENT

Read on *Zener Diodes* (e.g., Rashid's Section 4.7: Zener Diodes).

COMPUTER SIMULATION

Software Tools: PSpice, OrCAD, Multisim, LTSpice, or any electronic circuit simulator.

A Zener diode is a silicon pn-junction device that is optimized by internal design for operation in the breakdown region. It maintains an essentially constant voltage across its terminal over a specified range of current values. Therefore, a minimum value of reverse current must be maintained in order to keep the diode in regulation. There is also a maximum current above which the diode will be damaged due to excessive power dissipation. In the forward direction, it exhibits the characteristic of a normal diode.

Characteristic of Zener Diode

1. Simulate the circuit as shown in Fig. 4-1 using computer simulation to plot the v–i characteristic of the Zener diode D1N750 whose specifications are $V_Z = 4.7$ V at $I_Z = 20$ mA, Zener resistance $r_Z = 2.6\ \Omega$, and $I_{Z\,(max)} = 70$ mA. The dc voltage source V_{DD} has a nominal value of 10 V, and it is varied from 2 to −20 V with an increment of 0.01 V. Note that in the forward direction, it behaves as a normal diode.
   Note: If the Zener diode D1N750 is not available, use any other diode that is available.
2. From the computer simulation plot of the reverse v–i characteristic, find the Zener voltage:

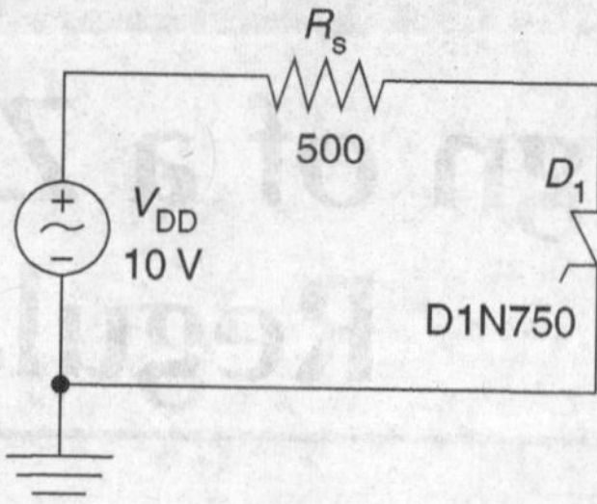

Figure 4-1 A Zener diode test circuit

$V_Z =$ ________ @ $I_Z = 20$ mA

Find the small-signal Zener model so that the Zener voltage can be related to the diode current i_D by

$$v_Z = V_{TZ} + r_Z\, i_D$$

where V_{TZ} is the threshold Zener voltage and r_d is the small-signal Zener resistance.

$V_Z =$ ________ @ $I_Z = 20$ mA; $V_{TZ} =$ ________ V; $r_Z =$ ________ Ω

3. Calculate the values of r_Z and V_{TZ} from the specifications.

$V_{TZ} = v_Z - r_Z\, i_D = 4.7 - 2.6 \times 20$ mA $=$ ________ V; $r_Z = 2.6\ \Omega$

4. Compare these values of r_Z and V_{TZ} with those in step 2, and explain the reason(s) for any discrepancies.

____

____

____

____

DESIGN SPECIFICATIONS

Zener Diode Regulator

One of the common applications of Zener diodes is in voltage regulator, which can maintain a constant output voltage while both the input voltage and the load conditions may vary. This is shown in Fig. 4-2. If the input voltage is less than the Zener voltage, then the Zener diode will offer a high resistance and the output voltage will follow the potential divider rule. Thus,

$$V_o = \frac{R_L}{R_L + R_S} V_{DD}, \quad \text{for } V_{DD} < V_Z \tag{4.1}$$

If the input voltage is more than the Zener voltage, the Zener diode acts as a variable resistance such that the output voltage is kept constant due to Zener action. Load resistance R_L may vary from infinity (open circuit) to a minimum value for a specified maximum load current. The supply voltage V_{DD} may also vary from its nominal value. The value of R_S should be selected such that the Zener current must not exceed the maximum current rating when the load is disconnected and the supply voltage reaches its maximum value. Also, the Zener current must not go below the knee value when the supply voltage becomes minimum and the load current is maximum. This will ensure that the Zener operates in regulation. Ideally, the output voltage is supposed to remain constant at the Zener voltage. However, the output voltage V_o changes with the load current and the dc input voltage.

Design a Zener regulator of Fig. 4-2 (by finding the value of R_s) so that the output voltage is $V_L = 5\,V \pm 5\%$. The load resistance R_L can vary from 1 kΩ to ∞, and the dc input voltage V_{DD} can vary from 10 to 20 V.

Note: Select the component values closest to the practical values.

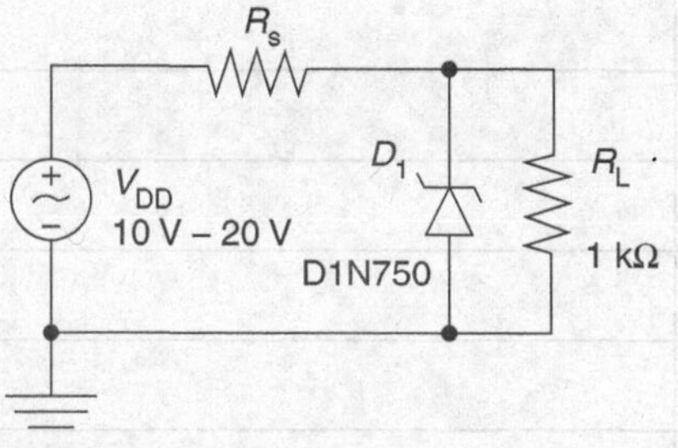

Figure 4-2 Zener diode regulator

EXPERIMENTS

The students are strongly encouraged and recommended to build and test the diode circuit to validate the theoretical and computer simulation results.

Procedure

Part 1

1. Set up the circuit as shown in Fig. 4-3 with a Zener diode (lN750). Connect an ammeter and a voltmeter to measure the Zener current i_Z and the zener voltage v_Z, respectively.
2. Vary the dc voltage V_{DD} in increments of 0.5 V. Record V_{DD}, and $v_Z = V_{DD} - R_1 i_Z$. Do not exceed 70 mA in the reverse direction. Complete Table 4-1. Plot of v_Z against i_Z will give the v–i Zener characteristic.

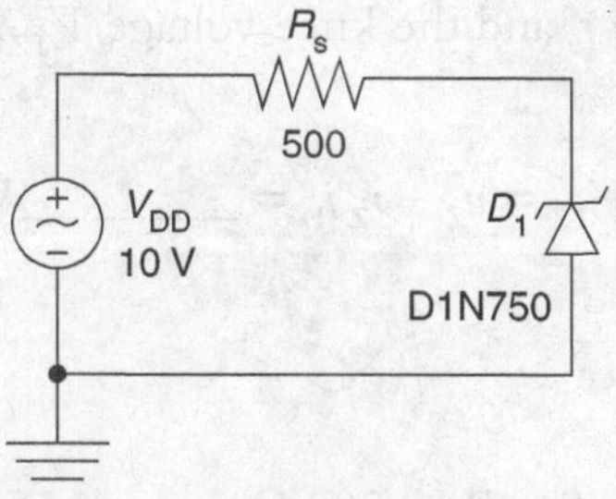

Figure 4-3 Zener diode test circuit

Table 4-1 Zener data

V_{DD}	v_Z	i_Z
0		
0.5		
1		
1.5		
2		
2.5		
3		
3.5		
4		
4.5		
5		
5.5		
6		

Part 2

1. Set up the circuit shown in Fig. 4-4 with the input frequency set for 100 Hz and the amplitude set at a minimum setting. Resistance R_L measures the Zener current i_Z, and its voltage drop is $v_1 = R_L i_Z$. You use Zener diode 1N750 or 1N751.
2. To determine the reverse (Zener) characteristic, center the oscilloscope beam in the upper right quadrant. Increase the output of the function generator to give the Zener characteristic. Adjust the HOR and VERT gain controls of the oscilloscope. The Zener current should be limited to 50 mA. The reverse characteristic is to be limited to a maximum voltage of 10 V.
3. Zoom the oscilloscope display. Read the v-i values at the knee point at which the Zener action begins. Take two other values in the linear range.

V_{Z1} = ________V; I_{Z1} = ________ mA; V_{Z2} = ________V; I_{Z2} = ________ mA

4. Calculate the small-signal resistance r_z and the knee voltage V_{TZ}.

$$r_Z = \frac{\Delta V_Z}{\Delta I_Z} = \_\_\_\_\_\_\_\_\ \Omega; \qquad V_{TZ} = v_Z - r_Z\, i_D = \_\_\_\_\_\_\_\_\ \text{V}$$

Part 3

1. Set up the circuit shown in Fig. 4-5. Set $R_L = 500\ \Omega$ to ∞.
2. Complete Table 4-2 by calculating the percentage (%) regulation defined by

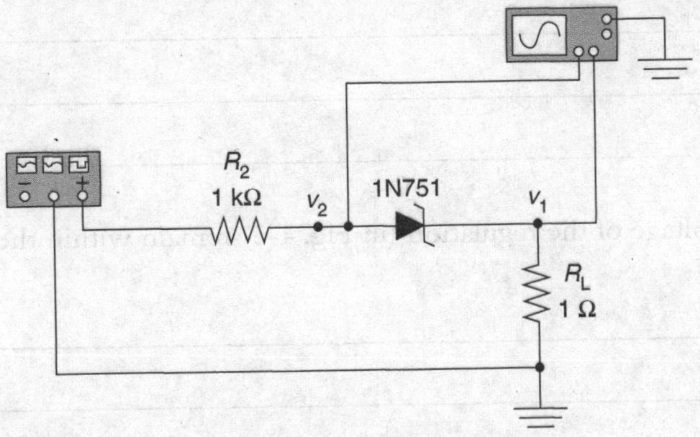

Figure 4-4 Zener diode test circuit

$$\text{Load regulation (LRG)} = \frac{V_{o\,(\text{no-load})} - V_{o\,(\text{load})}}{V_{o\,(\text{no-load})}}$$

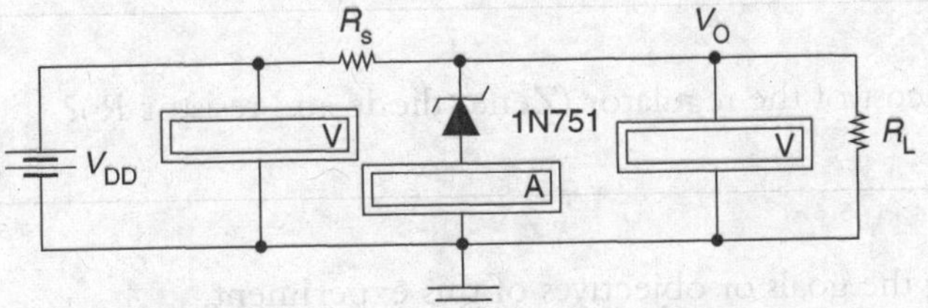

Figure 4-5 Zener diode regulator

Table 4-2 Zener experimental data

	Calculated				Simulated				Experimental			
	V_{DD}		V_{DD}		V_{DD}		V_{DD}		V_{DD}		V_{DD}	
	10	10	20	20	10	10	20	20	10	10	20	20
R_L	∞	500	∞	500	∞	500	∞	500	∞	500	∞	500
V_L												
I_L												
I_Z												
% LGR												

REPORT

1. The data obtained for Zener diode (in Part I in Experiment, step 2) is to be plotted accurately with Zener voltage on the abscissa and Zener current on the ordinate of the graph. Compare the results with those obtained by using oscilloscope and comment.

2. Does the load voltage of the regulation (in Fig. 4-5) remain within the specifications? If not, explain the reasons.

3. Does the load regulation (in Fig. 4-5) depend upon the supply voltage, V_{DD}? Explain.

4. What is the estimated cost of the regulator (Zener diode and resistor R_s)?

5. Comment on meeting the goals or objectives of this experiment.

6. Analyze and interpret the data due to any variations and practical limitations.

7. Describe the safety issues considered while conducting the experiment.

8. Describe the process to design and conduct experiments.

9. Conclusion and comment on achieving goals or objectives of this experiment.

ATTACH ALL PLOTS/GRAPHS TO YOUR REPORT

CHAPTER 5

Design of a Diode Power Supply

Learning Objectives

To design a diode power supply in order to give a specified dc output voltage within a certain ripple voltage. You will use computer simulation to verify the design and evaluate the performance of the rectifier.

After the end of this experiment, you will be able to

- Analyze and design a diode rectifier circuit to meet the given specifications.

PRE-LAB ASSIGNMENT

Read on *Diode Rectifiers* (e.g., Rashid's Section 4.8: Diode Rectifiers).

DESIGN SPECIFICATIONS

Design a power supply using diodes to meet the following specifications:

- dc output power, $P_O = 500$ mW
- dc output voltage, $V_{o(avg)} = 5\text{ V} \pm 5\%$ ripple voltage
- ac main supply, $V_S = 115\text{–}120$ V (rms), 60 Hz
- Fundamental frequency of the output ripple voltage, $f_{o(ripple)} = 120$ Hz

Note: Select the component values closest to the practical values.

Hint: In order to meet the specifications, one could choose either the center-tapped rectifier or the bridge rectifier. The bridge rectifier is available commercially in a module and there is no need to build from discrete devices. The design includes (1) finding the specifications of the input transformer, (2) selecting the diode bridge, and (3) finding the values of the output filter.

COMPUTER SIMULATION

Software Tools: **PSpice, OrCAD, Multisim, LTSpice, or any electronic circuit simulator.**

1. Simulate the power supply by using computer simulation to plot the output voltage across the load resistance R_L. Use a 60 Hz, 120 V ac source, a step-down transformer. Observe and record $v_o(t)$, the cut-in point (minimum voltage), the cut-out point (maximum voltage), and the peak-to-peak amplitude of ripple voltage. Complete Table 5-1.
2. Repeat step 1 for a 60 Hz, 120 V ac source.

Table 5-1 Nominal output voltage

ac supply voltage (rms)	Peak input voltage, V_m	Minimum output voltage, $V_{o(min)}$	Maximum output voltage, $V_{o(max)}$	Peak-to-peak output ripple voltage, ΔV_o
$V_s = 120$ V				
$V_s = 115$ V				

3. Assign ±5% tolerances to all filter elements such as capacitors and resistors. Run the simulation for the worst-case maximum output voltage and complete Table 5-2.

Table 5-2 Worst-case maximum output voltage

ac supply voltage (rms)	Peak input voltage, V_m	Minimum output voltage, $V_{o(min)}$	Maximum output voltage, $V_{o(max)}$	Worst-case peak-to-peak output ripple voltage, ΔV_o
$V_s = 120$ V				
$V_s = 115$ V				

4. Does your design meet the specifications under the worst-case conditions? If not, modify the component values so that the specifications are met. Note these components values.

_______________ _______________ _______________

5. Run the computer simulation with your suggested values in step 4 and complete the computer values in Table 5-2.
6. Comment on the effects of the component tolerances on the design.

____

____

____

REPORT

1. Compare the results in Tables 5-1 and 5-2. Comment on any discrepancies.

____

2. Does the ripples on the output voltage remain within the specifications? If not, explain the reasons.

3. What are the parameters that influence the output resistance R_o of the power supply? Explain.

4. What is the estimated cost of the power supply?

5. Analyze and interpret the data due to any variations and practical limitations.

6. Describe the safety issues considered while conducting the experiment.

7. Describe the process to design and conduct experiments.

8. Conclusion and comment on achieving goals or objectives of this experiment.

ATTACH ALL PLOTS/GRAPHS TO YOUR REPORT

PART II

BIPOLAR JUNCTION TRANSISTORS (BJTs) AND APPLICATIONS

CHAPTER 6

Characteristics and Biasing of Bipolar Junction Transistors

Learning Objectives

To investigate the characteristics of bipolar junction transistors (BJTs) and to determine the BJT model parameters. You will use computer simulation to plot the BJT characteristics and to derive the small-signal BJT parameters of a specific BJT.

After the end of this experiment, you should be able to

- Describe the voltage–current characteristics of BJTs.
- Derive the approximate model parameters of a BJT.

PRE-LAB ASSIGNMENT

Read on *Characteristics of BJTs* (e.g., Rashid's Section 5.10: Characteristics; Section 5.11: Circuit Models).

COMPUTER SIMULATION

Software Tools: **PSpice, OrCAD, Multisim, LTSpice, or any electronic circuit simulator.**

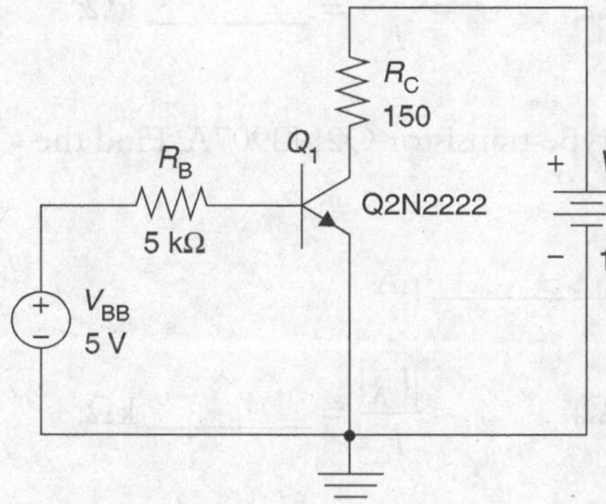

Figure 6-1 A BJT test circuit

If transistor 2N2222 is not available, use any other transistor that is available.

1. Simulate the circuit shown in Fig. 6-1 using computer simulation to plot the output characteristics of the BJT Q2N2222. The dc collector voltage source V_{CC} has a nominal value of 12 V and is varied from 0 to 15 V with an increment of 0.1 V. The dc base voltage source V_{BB} has a nominal value of 5 V, and it is varied from 1 to 6 V with an increment of 0.5 V.
   Note: V_{BB} is a VSRC part. In the dc sweep setup, make V_{BB} as the nested sweep variable and V_{CC} as the main sweep variable. Also, make sure that nested sweep is enabled.
2. Plot the output characteristics i_C versus v_{CE} for various values of V_{BB} (i.e., the base current i_B) as shown in Fig. 6-2. Add the load line for V_{CC} = 12 V and R_C = 150 W. This is shown in Fig. 6-2.

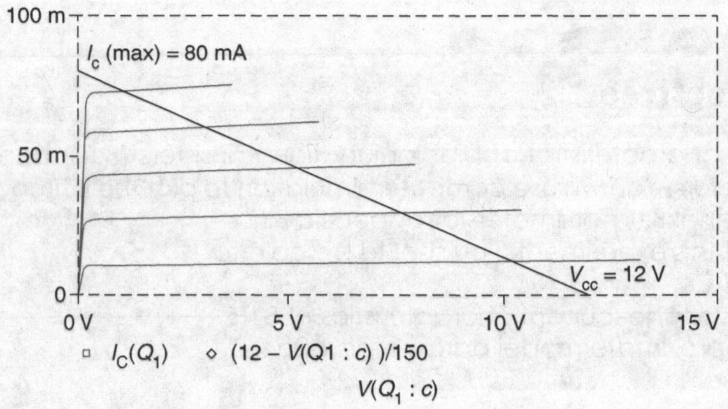

Figure 6-2 BJT characteristics

3. For the Q-point for V_{CE} = 5 V, find

   I_C = ________ mA; I_B = ________ µA

4. From the Q-point, calculate the small-signal BJT model parameters.

   $r_\pi = \dfrac{25.8\text{ mV}}{I_B}$ = ________ kΩ; $r_o = \dfrac{|V_A|}{I_C}$ = ________ kΩ; $g_m = \dfrac{\beta_F}{r_\pi}$ = ________ mA/V

5. Repeat steps 1 to 4 for the PNP-type transistor Q2N2907A. Find the Q-point and the model parameters for V_{CE} = –5 V.

   I_C = ________ mA; I_B = ________ µA

   $r_\pi = \dfrac{25.8\text{ mV}}{I_B}$ = ________ kΩ; $r_o = \dfrac{|V_A|}{I_C}$ = ________ kΩ; $g_m = \dfrac{\beta_F}{r_\pi}$ = ________ mA/V

6. Simulate the biasing circuit in Fig. 6-3 and complete the simulation values in Table 6-1.

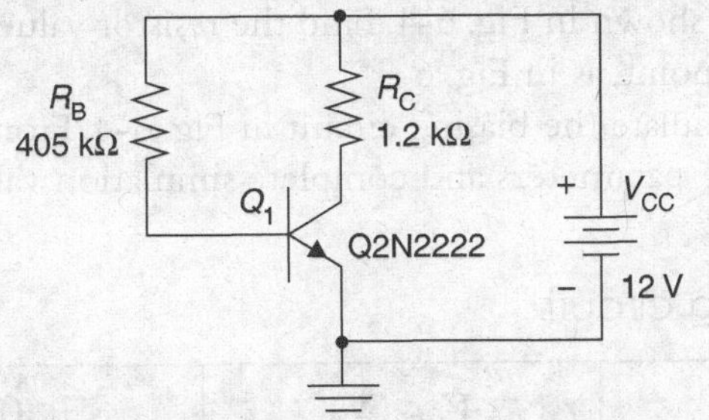

Figure 6-3 A self-biasing circuit

Table 6-1 Self-biasing circuit

	V_{BE} (V)		V_{CE} (V)		I_B (μA)		I_C (mA)	
Transistor	2N2222	2N3904	2N2222	2N3904	2N2222	2N3904	2N2222	2N3904
Calculated								
Simulation								
Experimental								

7. Repeat step 6 with the NPN transistor 2N3904. Find the percentage change in the collector current and the collector-emitter voltage when you changed 2N2222 to 2N3904.

   $\Delta I_C =$ ________%; $\Delta V_{CE} =$________%.

   What causes a change in the Q-point? Explain.

   ____

   ____

   ____

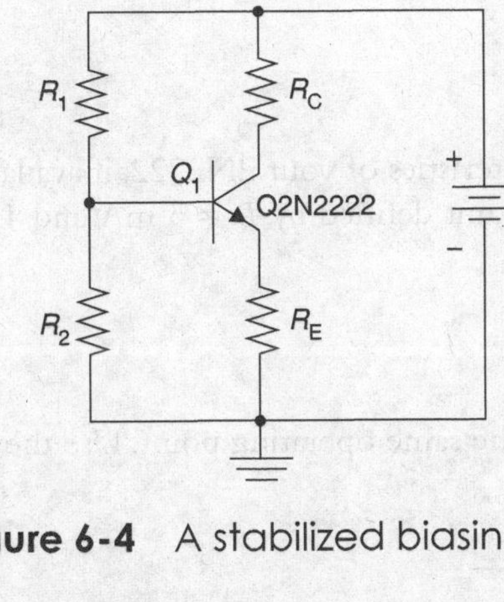

Figure 6-4 A stabilized biasing circuit

8. A stabilized biasing circuit is shown in Fig. 6-4. Find the resistor values so that I_C and V_{CE} have the same (calculated) values at the Q-point, as in Fig. 6-3.
9. With the values in step 8, simulate the biasing circuit in Fig. 6-4. From the computer simulation output file, find the small-signal BJT parameters and complete simulation values in Table 6-2.

Table 6-2 Stabilized biasing circuit

	V_{BE} (V)		V_{CE} (V)		I_B (μA)		I_C (mA)	
Transistor	**2N2222**	**2N3904**	**2N2222**	**2N3904**	**2N2222**	**2N3904**	**2N2222**	**2N3904**
Calculated								
Simulated								
Experimental								

10. Repeat step 9 with the NPN transistor 2N3904. Find the percentage change in the collector current and the collector-emitter voltage when you changed 2N2222 to 2N3904.

$\Delta I_C =$ ________%; $\Delta V_{CE} =$ ________%

You should notice that the amount of change in the Q-point is much less compared to the circuit in Fig. 6-3. Why? Explain.

____

____

____

EXPERIMENTS

The students are strongly encouraged and recommended to build and test the diode circuit to validate the theoretical and computer simulation results.

Procedure

Part 1

1. Use a curve tracer to plot the characteristics of your 2N2222, if available. Otherwise skip Part 1.
2. Record the dc β_F at the operating point defined by $I_C = 5$ mA and $V_{CE} = 5$ V. The dc β_F is displayed at the lower left side of the screen as h_{fe}.

$\beta_F =$ ________

3. Measure the small-signal β_f around the same operating point. Use the two nearest curves available.

$$\beta_f = \frac{\Delta i_C}{\Delta i_B} = \_\_\_\_\_\_\_\_ = \_\_\_\_\_\_\_\_$$

4. Use the cursors to measure the small-signal output resistance r_o at the same operating point. Note that r_o is the resistance proportional to the slope of the i_C–v_{CE} curve, i.e., $1/r_o = \Delta i_C/\Delta v_{CE}$.

$$r_o = \frac{\Delta i_C}{\Delta v_{CE}} = \_\_\_\_\_\_\_\_ = \_\_\_\_\_\_\_\_ \text{ k}\Omega$$

5. Measure the small-signal input resistance r_π (= 25.8 mV/I_B) at the same operating point.

$$r_\pi = \frac{25.8 \text{ mV}}{I_B} = \_\_\_\_\_\_\_\_ = \_\_\_\_\_\_\_\_ \text{ k}\Omega$$

6. Complete the curve-tracer values in Table 6-3.

Table 6-3 Transistor parameters

From	I_C (mA)	I_B (μA)	V_{CE} (V)	β_F	β_f	r_o (kΩ)	r_B (Ω)
Curve tracer							
Simulated							
Data sheet							
Experimental							

Part 2

1. Set up the circuit shown in Fig. 6-3. Measure the biasing currents and voltages to complete the practical values in Table 6-1.
2. Set up the circuit shown in Fig. 6-4. Measure the biasing currents and voltages to complete the practical values in Table 6-2. Also, find the small-signal parameters to complete the practical values in Table 6-3.

REPORT

1. What design conditions have you assumed in finding the resistor values in Fig. 6.4?

____

____

Are the resistor values unique to satisfy the specified biasing values of I_B, I_C, and V_{CE} in Fig. 6-4? Explain.

____

____

____

What are the recommended design guidelines?

____

____

2. Run the simulation for sensitivity and compare the sensitivity of the collector current i_C with respect to the transistor beta.

   Sensitivity: __________ % for Fig. 6-3; Sensitivity: __________ % for Fig. 6-4

3. As shown in Table 6-3, you can find the parameters by different methods. Which one will you recommend? Why? Explain.

4. If you perform this experiment with a different transistor of the same type 2N2222, do you think you will get the same results? Explain your answer.

5. Analyze and interpret the data due to any variations and practical limitations.

6. Describe the safety issues considered while conducting the experiment.

7. Describe the process to design and conduct experiments.

8. Conclusion and comment on achieving goals or objectives of this experiment.

ATTACH ALL PLOTS/GRAPHS TO YOUR REPORT

CHAPTER

7

Design of a BJT Common-Emitter Amplifier

Learning Objectives

To design a common-emitter amplifier to give a specified voltage gain. You will use computer simulation to verify the design and evaluate the performance of the amplifier.

After the end of this experiment, you will be able to

- Describe the operation of a common-emitter amplifier and its small-signal equivalent circuit.
- Analyze and design a common-emitter amplifier to meet the given specifications.

PRE-LAB ASSIGNMENT

Read on *Common-Emitter Amplifiers* (e.g., Rashid's Section 5.15: Common-Emitter Amplifiers).

DESIGN SPECIFICATIONS

Design the common-emitter amplifier (as shown in Fig. 7-1) to meet the following specifications:

- Voltage gain, $|A_v| = v_o/v_s = 20 \pm 5\%$
- Input resistance, $R_i = v_i/i_s \geq 15\ \text{k}\Omega$
- Load resistance, $R_L = 10\ \text{k}\Omega$
- Source resistance, $R_s = 200\ \Omega$
- dc supply, $V_{CC} = 12\text{V}$
- Input signal, $v_s = 0$–10 mV (peak sinusoidal)
- Use NPN transistor 2N2222. Assume $\beta_F = 255$ for 2N2222 and $\beta_F = 231$ for 2N2907A (if not available, use any other BJT that is available).
- Quiescent collector current, $I_C = 5$ mA (assumed)

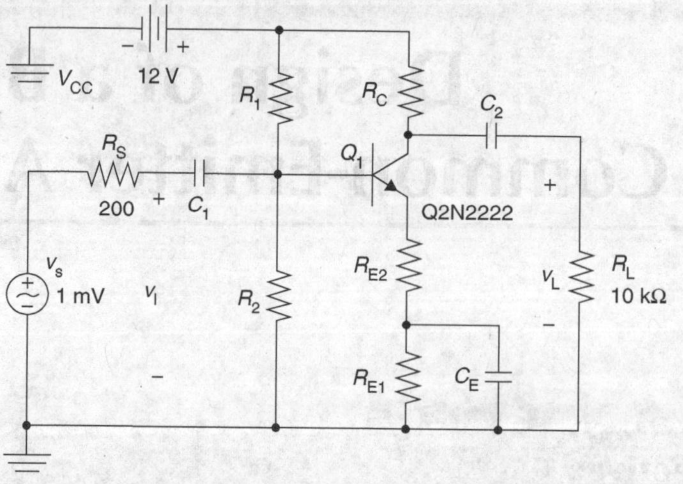

Figure 7-1 A BJT amplifier

PAPER–PENCIL DESIGN

1. After completing your paper–pencil design, write the circuit values.

   R_C = ________ kΩ; R_1 = ________ kΩ, R_2 = ________ kΩ

   R_E (= $R_{E1} + R_{E2}$) = ________ kΩ; R_{E1} = ________ Ω; R_{E2} = ________ Ω

   C_1 = ________ μF; C_2 = ________ μF; C_E = ________ μF

2. Complete the calculated values in Table 7-1.
   Note: Select the component values closest to the practical values.

Table 7-1 Biasing values and transistor parameters

	I_C (mA)	I_B (μA)	V_{CE} (V)	V_E	V_B	r_o (kΩ)	r_π (Ω)
Calculated							
Simulated							
Experimental							

COMPUTER SIMULATION

Software Tools: PSpice, OrCAD, Multisim, LTSpice, or any electronic circuit simulator.

1. Simulate the amplifier circuit shown in Fig. 7-1 by using a computer simulation to find the dc biasing information. Assume v_s as a sinusoidal voltage. From the simulation output file, complete the simulated values in Table 7-1.
2. Simulate the amplifier by using a computer simulation to plot the output voltage $v_L(t)$ across the load resistance R_L.

Note: Since your input signal v_s is sinusoidal, the output voltage v_L should ideally be sinusoidal. If your output is distorted significantly, then your dc operating point is not set properly and you need to redesign your biasing circuit. A properly designed biasing circuit should allow the maximum swing of the collector current and the collector–emitter voltage without introducing any significant amount of signal distortion.

3. Plot the input signal voltage $v_s(t)$, output voltage $v_L(t)$, voltage gain $A_v = v_L/v_s$, input resistance $R_i = v_i/i_s$. Record.

$v_{L(peak)}$ = ________ mV; $v_{s(peak)}$ = ________ mV; $A_v = \dfrac{v_{L(peak)}}{v_{s(peak)}}$ = ________ V/V

$R_i = \dfrac{v_{i(peak)}}{i_{s(peak)}}$ = ________ kΩ

4. Assign ±5% tolerance to all capacitors and resistors. Run the simulation for the worst-case maximum output voltage and record.

$v_{L(peak)}$ = ________ mV; $v_{s(peak)}$ = ________ mV; $A_v = \dfrac{v_{o(peak)}}{v_{s(peak)}}$ = ________ V/V

$R_i = \dfrac{v_{i(peak)}}{i_{s(peak)}}$ = ________ kΩ

5. Does your design meet the specifications under the worst-case conditions? If not, which resistance would you adjust to get the desired gain? Why? Explain.

____

____

Change the component values so that the specifications are met. Note these values.

____________ ____________ ____________

6. Reduce R_{E2} to zero, and find the maximum voltage gain.

$A_{v(max)} = \dfrac{v_{L(peak)}}{v_{s(peak)}}$ = ________ V/V

7. If you find that the maximum voltage gain $A_{v(max)}$ is less than the desired value, what should you do? How would you meet the gain specifications? Explain.

____

____

____

8. Run the computer simulation with your suggested values in step 5 (try adjusting R_{E1} and R_{E2}), and complete the simulated values in Table 7-2.

Table 7-2 Amplifier parameters

	$R_i = v_{i(peak)}/i_{s(peak)}$ (kΩ)	$R_{in} = v_{s(peak)}/i_{s(peak)}$ (kΩ)	R_o (Ω)	$A_v = v_{L(peak)}/v_{s(peak)}$
Calculated				
Simulated				
Practical				

9. To find the output resistance R_o, run the simulation for $R_L = \infty$ (or say 10 MΩ), 10 kΩ. Calculate the output resistance R_o of the amplifier from the equation.

$$R_o = R_L\left[\frac{V_{L(\text{no-load})} - V_{L(\text{full-load})}}{V_{L(\text{full-load})}}\right] = \_\_\_\_\_\_\_\_\ \Omega \tag{7.1}$$

10. Comment on the effects of the component tolerance on the design.

____

____

EXPERIMENTS

The students are strongly encouraged and recommended to build and test the amplifier circuit to validate the theoretical and computer simulation results.

1. Set up your final amplifier circuit. Observe the output voltage $v_L(t)$ and its peak value V_m.
2. Take dc biasing measurements to complete the practical values in Table 7-1.

3. Measure: $v_{L(peak)}$ = ________ mV; $v_{s(peak)}$ = ________ mV; $A_v = \dfrac{v_{L(peak)}}{v_{s(peak)}}$ = ________ V/V

   $R_i = \dfrac{v_{i(peak)}}{i_{s(peak)}}$ = ________ kΩ; $R_{in} = \dfrac{v_{s(peak)}}{i_{s(peak)}}$ ________ kΩ

4. Measure the output resistance R_o of the amplifier.

   V_L(no load) = ________ mV; V_L(full load) = ________ mV; R_o = ________ Ω

5. Complete the practical values in Table 7-2.

REPORT

1. Compare the results in Tables 7.2 and comment on any discrepancies.

____

____

____

2. Does the voltage gain remain within the specifications? If not, explain the reasons.

3. What are the parameters that influence the output resistance R_o of the amplifier? Explain.

4. What is the estimated cost of the amplifier?

5. Analyze and interpret the data due to any variations and practical limitations.

6. Describe the safety issues considered while conducting the experiment.

7. Describe the process to design and conduct experiments.

8. Conclusion and comment on achieving goals or objectives of this experiment.

ATTACH ALL PLOTS/GRAPHS TO YOUR REPORT

CHAPTER

8

Design of a BJT Common-Collector Amplifier

Learning Objectives

To design BJT common-collector amplifiers to give a unity voltage gain and a low output resistance. We will use computer simulation to verify the design and evaluate the performance of the amplifiers.

After the end of this experiment, you will be able to

- Describe the operation and characteristics of a common-collector amplifier.
- Analyze and design a common-collector amplifier to meet the given specifications.

PRE-LAB ASSIGNMENT

Read on *Common-Collector Amplifiers* (e.g., Rashid's Section 5.18: Emitter Follower).

DESIGN SPECIFICATIONS

Design the common-collector amplifier (emitter follower) as shown in Fig. 8-1 to meet the following specifications:

- Voltage gain, $|A_v| = v_o/v_s \approx 1 \pm 5\%$
- Input resistance, $R_i = v_i/i_s \geq 5\ k\Omega$
- Output resistance, $R_o \leq 250\ \Omega$
- Load resistance, $R_L = 10\ k\Omega$
- Source resistance, $R_s = 200\ \Omega$
- dc supply, $V_{CC} = 12\ V$
- Input signal, $v_s = 0–2\ mV$ (peak sinusoidal), 1 kHz
- Use NPN transistor 2N2222. Assume $\beta_F = 255$ for 2N2222 and $\beta_F = 231$ for 2N2907A (if not available, use any other BJT that is available).
- Quiescent collector current, $I_C = 5\ mA$ (assumed)

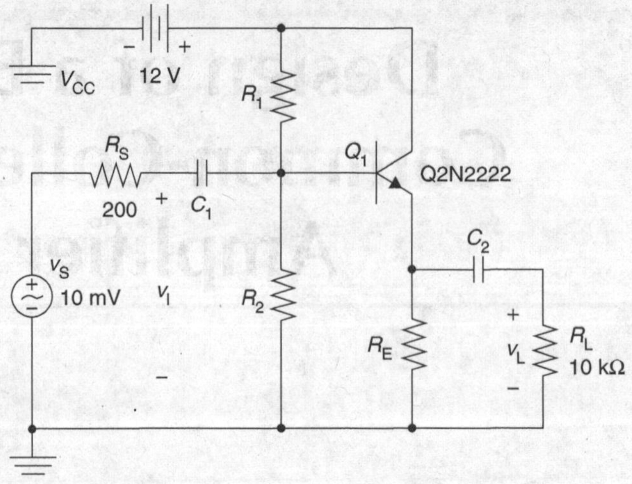

Figure 8-1 A BJT emitter follower

PAPER–PENCIL DESIGN

1. After completing your paper–pencil design, write the circuit values.

   R_1 = ________ kΩ; R_2 = ________ kΩ; R_E = ________ kΩ

   C_1 = ________ μF; C_2 = ________ μF

2. Complete the calculated values in Table 8-1.
   Note: Select the component values closest to the practical values.

Table 8-1 Biasing values of emitter follower

	I_C (mA)	I_B (μA)	V_{CE} (V)	V_E	V_B	r_o (kΩ)	r_π (Ω)
Calculated							
Simulated							
Experimental							

COMPUTER SIMULATION

Software tools: PSpice, OrCAD, Multisim, LTSpice, or any electronic circuit simulator.

1. Simulate the emitter-follower circuit shown in Fig. 8-1 by using computer simulation to find the dc biasing information. From the simulation output file, complete simulated values in Table 8-1.
2. Simulate the amplifier by using computer simulation to plot the output voltage $v_L(t)$ across the load resistance R_L.
   Note: Since your input signal v_s is sinusoidal, the output voltage v_L should ideally be sinusoidal. If your output is distorted significantly, then your dc operating point is not set properly and you need to

redesign your biasing circuit. A properly designed biasing circuit should allow the maximum swing of the collector current and the collector–emitter voltage without introducing any significant amount of signal distortion.

3. Plot the input signal voltage $v_s(t)$, output voltage $v_L(t)$, voltage gain $A_v = v_L/v_s$, and input resistance $R_i = v_i/i_s$. Record.

$v_{L\,(peak)}$ ________ mV; $v_{s\,(peak)}$ ________ mV; $A_v = \dfrac{V_{L\,(peak)}}{V_{s\,(peak)}}$ ________ V/V

$R_i = \dfrac{v_{i(peak)}}{i_{s(peak)}} =$ ________ kΩ

4. Assign ±5% tolerance to all capacitors and resistors. Run the simulation for the worst-case maximum output voltage and record.

$v_{L\,(peak)} =$ ________ mV; $v_{s\,(peak)} =$ ________ mV; $A_v = \dfrac{v_{o\,(peak)}}{v_{s\,(peak)}} =$ ________

$R_i = \dfrac{v_{i\,(peak)}}{i_{s\,(peak)}} =$ ________ kΩ

5. To find the output resistance R_o, run the simulation for $R_L = \infty$ (or say 10 MΩ), 10 kΩ. Calculate the output resistance R_o of the amplifier from the equation.

$$R_o = R_L\left[\frac{V_{L\,(no\text{-}load)} - V_{L\,(full\text{-}load)}}{V_{L\,(full\text{-}load)}}\right] = \_\_\_\_\_\_\_\_\ \Omega \tag{8.1}$$

6. Does your design meet the specifications under the worst-case conditions? If not, which resistance would you adjust to get the desired gain? Why?

____

____

Change the component values so that the specifications are met. Note these values.

____________ ____________ ____________

7. Run the computer simulation with your suggested values in step 6 (try adjusting RE), and complete the simulated values in Table 8-2.

Table 8-2 Emitter-follower parameters

	$R_i = v_{i\,(peak)}/i_{s\,(peak)}$ (kΩ)	$R_{in} = v_{s\,(peak)}/i_{s\,(peak)}$ (kΩ)	R_o (Ω)	$A_v = v_{L\,(peak)}/v_{s\,(peak)}$
Calculated				
Simulated				
Experimental				

8. Comment on the effects of the component tolerance on the design.

____

____

EXPERIMENTS

The students are strongly encouraged and recommended to build and test the amplifier circuit to validate the theoretical and computer simulation results.

1. Set up your final emitter-follower circuit in Fig. 8-1. Take dc biasing measurements to complete the experimental values in Table 8-1.
2. Observe the output voltage $v_L(t)$ and its peak value V_m.
3. Measure: $v_{L\,(peak)}$ = ________ mV; $v_{s\,(peak)}$ = ________ mV; $A_v = \frac{v_{L\,(peak)}}{v_{s\,(peak)}}$ = ________ V/V

   $R_i = \frac{v_{i\,(peak)}}{i_{s\,(peak)}}$ = ________ kΩ; $R_{in} = \frac{v_{s\,(peak)}}{i_{s\,(peak)}}$ = ________ kΩ

4. Measure the output resistance R_o of the amplifier.

   $V_{L(no\ load)}$ = ________ mV; $V_{L(full\ load)}$ = ________ mV; R_o = ________ Ω

5. Complete the experimental values in Table 8-2.

REPORT

1. Compare the results in Tables 8.2 and comment on any discrepancies.

____

____

____

2. Does the output resistance remain within the specifications? If not, explain the reasons.

____

____

____

3. What are the parameters that influence the output resistance R_o of the amplifier? Explain.

____

4. What is the estimated cost of the amplifier?

5. Analyze and interpret the data due to any variations and practical limitations.

6. Describe the safety issues considered while conducting the experiment.

7. Describe the process to design and conduct experiments.

8. Conclusion and comment on achieving goals or objectives of this experiment.

ATTACH ALL PLOTS/GRAPHS TO YOUR REPORT

CHAPTER 9

Design of a Multistage BJT Amplifier

Learning Objectives

To design a multistage BJT amplifier to give a specified voltage gain. You will use computer simulation to verify the design and evaluate the performance of the amplifier.

After the end of this experiment, you should be able to

- Describe the operation of a multistage amplifier.
- Analyze and design a multistage amplifier to meet the given specifications.

PRE-LAB ASSIGNMENT

Read on *Multistage BJT Amplifiers* (e.g., Rashid's Section 5.20: Multistage Amplifiers).

DESIGN SPECIFICATIONS

Design the multi-stage BJT amplifier as shown in Fig. 9-1 to meet the following specifications:

- Voltage gain, $|A_v| = v_L/v_s = 200 \pm 5\%$
- Input resistance, $R_i = v_i/i_s \geq 20\ k\Omega$
- Output resistance, $R_o \leq 250\ \Omega$
- Load resistance, $R_L = 10\ k\Omega$
- Source resistance, $R_s = 200\ \Omega$
- dc supply voltage, $V_{CC} = 12\,V$
- Input signal, $v_s = 0-10$ mV (peak sinusoidal), 1 kHz
- Use NPN transistors of type 2N2222. Assume $\beta_F = 255$ for 2N2222 and $\beta_F = 231$ for 2N2907A (if not available, use any other BJT that is available).
- Quiescent collector current, $I_C = 5$ mA (assumed)

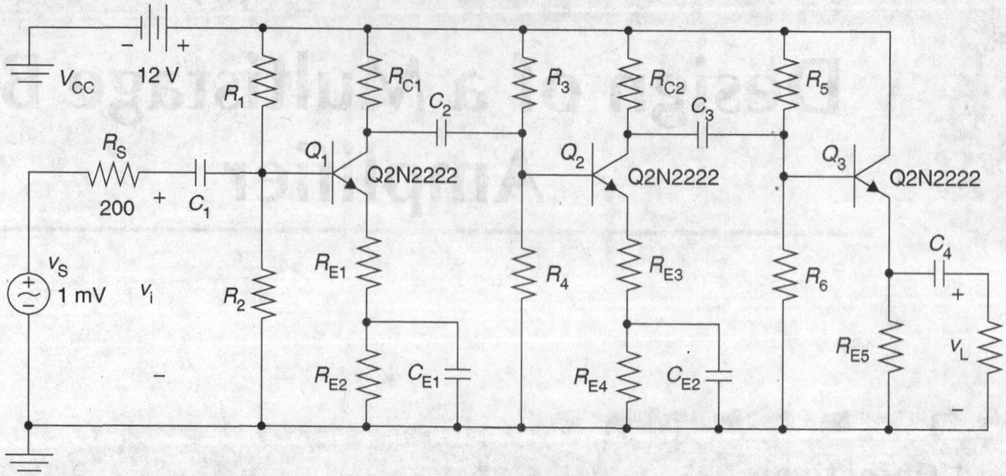

Figure 9-1 A multistage BJT amplifier

PAPER–PENCIL DESIGN

1. After completing your paper–pencil design, write the circuit values.

R_{C1} = ________ kΩ; R_{C2} = ________ kΩ

R_1 = ________ kΩ; R_2 = ________ kΩ; R_3 = ________ kΩ; R_4 = ________ kΩ

R_5 = ________ kΩ; R_6 = ________ kΩ

R_{E1} = ________ Ω; R_{E2} = ________ Ω; R_{E3} = ________ Ω; R_{E4} = ________ Ω

R_{E5} = ________ Ω

C_1 = ________ μF; C_2 = ________ μF; C_3 = ________ μF; C_4 = ________ μF

C_{E1} = ________ μF; C_{E2} = ________ μF

2. Complete the calculated values in Table 9-1.
Note: Select the component values closest to the practical values.

Table 9-1 Multistage amplifier parameters

	$R_i = v_{i(peak)}/i_{s(peak)}$ (kΩ)	$R_{in} = v_{s(peak)}/i_{s(peak)}$ (kΩ)	R_o (Ω)	$A_v = v_{L(peak)}/v_{s(peak)}$
Calculated				
Simulated				
Experimental				

COMPUTER SIMULATION

Software Tools: PSpice, OrCAD, Multisim, LTSpice, or any electronic circuit simulator.

1. Simulate the amplifier by using computer simulation to plot the output voltage $v_L(t)$ across the load resistance R_L.
   Note: Since your input signal v_s is sinusoidal, the output voltage v_L should ideally be sinusoidal. If your output is distorted significantly, then your dc operating point is not set properly and you need to redesign your biasing circuit. A properly designed biasing circuit should allow the maximum swing of the collector currents and the collector−emitter voltages without introducing any significant amount of signal distortion.
2. Plot the input signal voltage $v_s(t)$, output voltage $v_L(t)$, voltage gain $A_v = v_L/v_s$, and input resistance $R_i = v_i/i_s$. Record.

   $v_{L(peak)} =$ ________ mV; $v_{s(peak)} =$ ________ mV; $A_v = \dfrac{v_{L(peak)}}{v_{s(peak)}} =$ ________

   $R_i = \dfrac{v_{i(peak)}}{i_{s(peak)}} =$ ________ kΩ

3. Assign ±5% tolerance to all capacitors and resistors. Run the simulation for the worst-case maximum output voltage and record.

   $v_{L(peak)} =$ ________ mV; $v_{s(peak)} =$ ________ mV; $A_v = \dfrac{v_{o(peak)}}{v_{s(peak)}} =$ ________;

   $R_i = \dfrac{v_{i(peak)}}{i_{s(peak)}} =$ ________ kΩ

4. Does your design meet the specifications under the worst-case conditions? If not, which resistance would you adjust to get the desired gain? Why? Explain.

   ____

   ____

   Change the component values so that the specifications are met. Note these values.

   ________ ________ ________ ________

5. Reduce R_{E1} and R_{E3} to zero (while increasing R_{E2} and R_{E4} by the same amount) and find the maximum voltage gain.

   $A_{v(max)} = \dfrac{v_{L(peak)}}{v_{s(peak)}} =$ ________ V/V

6. If you find that the maximum voltage gain $A_{v(max)}$ is less than your desired value, what should you do? How would you meet the gain specifications? Explain.

   ____

   ____

7. Run the simulation with your suggested values in step 4 and complete the simulated values in Table 9-1.
8. To find the output resistance R_o, run the simulation for $R_L = \infty$ (or say 10 MΩ), 10 kΩ. Calculate the output resistance R_o of the amplifier from the equation.

$$R_o = R_L\left[\frac{V_{L(\text{no-load})} - V_{L(\text{full-load})}}{V_{L(\text{full-load})}}\right] = \_\_\_\_\_\_\_\_ \Omega \tag{9.1}$$

9. Comment on the effects of the component tolerance on the design.

____

____

EXPERIMENTS

The students are strongly encouraged and recommended to build and test the amplifier circuit to validate the theoretical and computer simulation results.

1. Set up your final amplifier circuit. Observe the output voltage $v_L(t)$ and its peak value V_m.
2. Measure: $v_{L(\text{peak})} =$ ________ mV; $v_{s(\text{peak})} =$ ________ mV; $A_v = \dfrac{v_{L(\text{peak})}}{v_{s(\text{peak})}} =$ ________ V/V

   $R_i = \dfrac{v_{i(\text{peak})}}{i_{s(\text{peak})}} =$ ________ kΩ; $R_{in} = \dfrac{v_{s(\text{peak})}}{i_{s(\text{peak})}} =$ ________ kΩ

3. Measure the output resistance R_o of the amplifier.

   $V_{L(\text{no load})} =$ ________ mV; $V_{L(\text{full load})} =$ ________ mV; $R_o =$ ________ Ω

4. Complete the experimental values in Table 9-1.

REPORT

1. Compare the results in Tables 9-1 and comment on any discrepancies.

____

____

____

2. Does the voltage gain remain within the specifications? If not, explain the reasons.

____

____

____

3. What are the parameters that influence the voltage gain A_v of the amplifier? Explain.

4. What is the estimated cost of the amplifier?

5. Analyze and interpret the data due to any variations and practical limitations.

6. Describe the safety issues considered while conducting the experiment.

7. Describe the process to design and conduct experiments.

8. Conclusion and comment on achieving goals or objectives of this experiment.

ATTACH ALL PLOTS/GRAPHS TO YOUR REPORT

CHAPTER 10

Design of a BJT CE-Amplifier for Frequency Response

Learning Objectives

To design a BJT common-emitter amplifier to give a specified voltage gain. You will use computer simulation to verify the design and evaluate the performance of the amplifier.

After the end of this experiment, you should be able to

- Describe the frequency characteristics of common-emitter amplifiers and the circuit elements that contribute to the frequency response.
- Analyze and design common-emitter amplifiers to meet certain frequency specifications.

PRE-LAB ASSIGNMENT

Read on *Frequency Response of BJT Amplifiers* (e.g., Rashid's Section 8.9: Frequency Response of Common-Emitter Amplifiers).

DESIGN SPECIFICATIONS

Design the common-emitter amplifier as shown in Fig. 10-1 to meet the following specifications:

- Mid-band voltage gain, $|A_{v(mid)}| = v_o/v_s = 20 \pm 5\%$
- Low cut-off frequency, $f_L = 1$ kHz $\pm$ 5%
- High cut-off frequency, $f_H = 250$ kHz $\pm$ 5%
- Input resistance, $R_i = v_i/i_s \geq 5$ kΩ
- Load resistance, $R_L = 10$ kΩ
- Source resistance, $R_s = 200\ \Omega$
- dc supply voltage, $V_{CC} = 12$V
- Input signal, $v_s = 0-1$ mV (peak sinusoidal), 100 Hz to 300 kHz
- Use NPN transistor 2N2222. Assume $\beta_F = 255$ for 2N2222 and $\beta_F = 231$ for 2N2907A (if not available, use any other BJT that is available).
- Quiescent collector current, $I_C = 5$ mA (assumed)

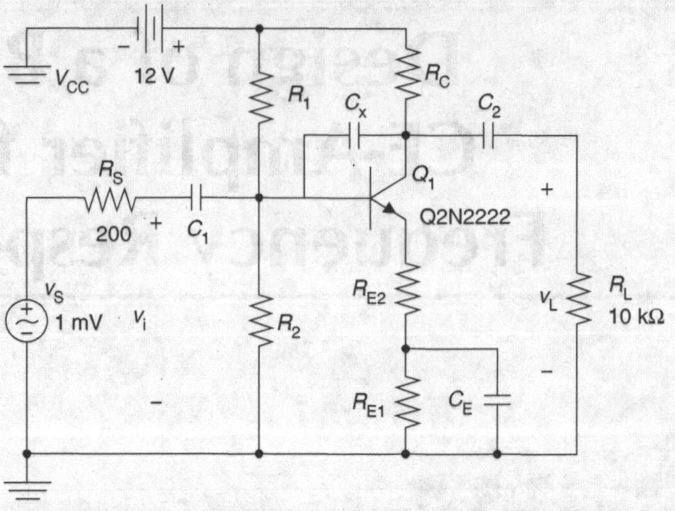

Figure 10-1 A BJT common-emitter amplifier

PAPER–PENCIL DESIGN

1. After completing your design, write the circuit values.

R_C = ________ kΩ; R_1 = ________ kΩ; R_2 = ________ kΩ; R_{E1} = ________ Ω

R_{E2} = ________ Ω

C_1 = ________ μF; C_2 = ________ μF; C_E = ________ μF; C_x = ________ nF

2. Complete the calculated values in Table 10-1.
   Note: Select the component values closest to the practical values.

Table 10.1 Frequency response of BJT amplifiers

	Calculated	Simulated	Experimental
f_L (kHz)			
f_L (kHz)			
$A_{v(mid)}$			

COMPUTER SIMULATION

Software Tools: PSpice, OrCAD, Multisim, LTSpice, or any electronic circuit simulator.

1. To find the frequency response (ac analysis), simulate the amplifier circuit shown in Fig. 10-1 by using computer simulation.

$A_{v(mid)} = \frac{v_{o\,(peak)}}{v_{s\,(peak)}}$ = ________ V/V; f_L = ________ kHz; f_H = ________ kHz

2. Assign ±5% tolerance to all capacitors and resistors. Run the simulation for the worst-case maximum gain and record.

$A_{v(mid)} = \frac{v_{o(peak)}}{v_{s(peak)}} =$ ________; $f_L =$ ________ kHz; $f_H =$ ________ kHz

3. Does your design meet the specifications under the worst-case conditions? If not, which resistance(s) would you adjust to get the desired gain? Which capacitor(s) would you adjust to get the desired cut-off frequencies? Why? Explain.

____

____

Change the component values so that the specifications are met. Note these values.

________________ ________________ ________________

4. Run the computer simulation with your suggested values in step 3 and complete the simulated values in Table 10-1.

   Comment on the effects of the component tolerance on the design.

____

____

EXPERIMENTS

The students are strongly encouraged and recommended to build and test the amplifier circuit to validate the theoretical and computer simulation results.

1. Set up your final amplifier circuit. Observe the output voltage $v_L(t)$ and its peak value V_m.

2. Measure: $v_{L(peak)} =$ ________ mV; $v_{s(peak)} =$ ________ mV; $A_v = \frac{v_{L(peak)}}{v_{s(peak)}} =$ ________ V/V

   $R_i = \frac{v_{i(peak)}}{i_{s(peak)}} =$ ________ kΩ; $R_{in} = \frac{v_{s(peak)}}{i_{s(peak)}} =$ ________ kΩ

3. Measure the output resistance R_o of the amplifier.

   $V_{L(no\ load)} =$ ________ mV; $V_{L(full\ load)} =$ ________ mV; $R_o =$ ________ Ω

4. Complete the experimental values in Table 10-1.

REPORT

1. Compare the results in Table 10-1 and comment on any discrepancies.

2. Does the frequency limits remain within the specifications? If not, explain the reasons.

3. What are the parameters that influence the high and low frequencies? Explain.

4. What is the estimated cost of the amplifier?

5. Analyze and interpret the data due to any variations and practical limitations.

6. Describe the safety issues considered while conducting the experiment.

7. Describe the process to design and conduct experiments.

8. Conclusion and comment on achieving goals or objectives of this experiment.

ATTACH ALL PLOTS/GRAPHS TO YOUR REPORT

CHAPTER 11

Actively Biased BJT Common-Emitter Amplifier

Learning Objectives

To investigate the characteristic of a common-emitter amplifier biased by a BJT current source. You will use computer simulation to evaluate the performance of the common-emitter amplifier.

After the end of this experiment, you should be able to

- Describe the operation of a BJT current source and its small-signal equivalent circuit.
- Describe the transfer characteristic of an actively biased common-emitter amplifier.
- Analyze an actively biased common-emitter amplifiers.

PRE-LAB ASSIGNMENT

Read on *Active-Biased CE-amplifiers* (e.g., Rashid's Section 5.17: Active-Biased CE-Amplifiers).

PAPER–PENCIL ANALYSIS

An emitter follower as shown in Fig. 11-1 is biased by a BJT current source. Assume $\beta_F = 255$ for 2N2222 and $\beta_F = 231$ for 2N2907A (if not available, use any other BJT that is available).

1. Find the dc collector and base biasing currents.

   $I_{C1} = I_{C2} =$ ________ mA; $I_{B1} =$ ________ μA

2. Calculate the output resistances of the transistors: r_{o1} for Q_1 and r_{o2} for Q_2.

   $r_{o1} =$ ________ kΩ; $r_{o2} =$ ________ kΩ

3. Calculate the small-signal parameters of the emitter follower.

   $A_v = \dfrac{v_{L\,(peak)}}{v_{i\,(peak)}} =$ ________ V/V; $R_i = \dfrac{v_{i\,(peak)}}{i_{i\,(peak)}} =$ ________ kΩ; $R_o =$ ________ Ω

4. Complete the calculated values in Table 11-1.

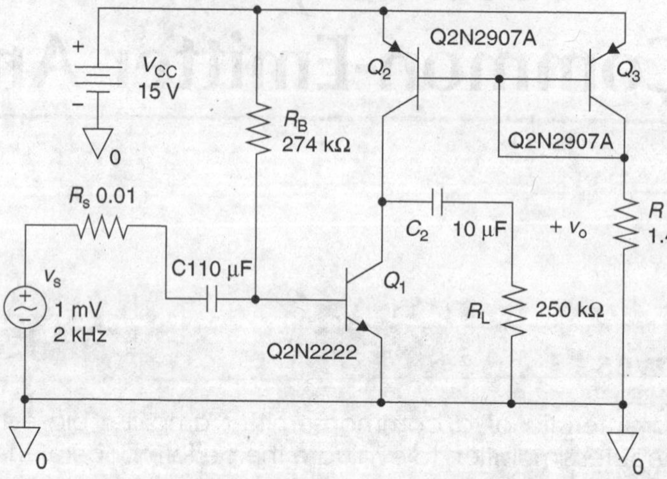

Figure 11-1 An active-biased common-emitter amplifier

Table 11-1 Biasing values and amplifier parameters

	I_{C1} (mA)	I_{B1} (μA)	r_{01} (kΩ)	r_{02} (kΩ)	A_v	R_i (kΩ)	R_o (Ω)
Calculated							
Simulated							
Experimental							

COMPUTER SIMULATION

Software Tools: PSpice, OrCAD, Multisim, LTSpice, or any electronic circuit simulator.

1. Simulate the emitter-follower circuit shown in Fig. 11-1 by using computer simulation to find the dc biasing information. From the simulation output file, complete the simulated values in Table 11-1.
2. Simulate the amplifier by using computer simulation to plot the output voltage $v_L(t)$ across the load resistance R_L. Since your input signal v_i is sinusoidal, the output voltage v_L should ideally be sinusoidal. Is the output voltage v_L sinusoidal?

____

Compare the output voltage with the input voltage. Explain any differences or deviations.

____

____

3. From the plots of the input signal voltage $v_i(t)$ and the output voltage $v_L(t)$, find the voltage gain A_v and the input resistance R_i. Record.

$v_{L(peak)}$ = ________ mV; $v_{i(peak)}$ = ________ mV; $A_v = \dfrac{v_{L\,(peak)}}{v_{i\,(peak)}}$ = ________

$R_i = \dfrac{v_{i\,(peak)}}{i_{i\,(peak)}}$ = ________ kΩ

4. To find the output resistance R_o, run the simulation for $R_L = \infty$ (or say 10 MΩ), 10 kΩ. Calculate the output resistance R_o of the amplifier from the equation.

$$R_o = R_L\left[\frac{V_{L(no\text{-}load)} - V_{L(full\text{-}load)}}{V_{L(full\text{-}load)}}\right] = \_\_\_\_\_\_\_\_ \ \Omega \qquad (11.1)$$

5. Complete the simulated values in Table 11-1.

EXPERIMENTS

The students are strongly encouraged and recommended to build and test the amplifier circuit to validate the theoretical and computer simulation results.

1. Set up your final amplifier circuit shown in Fig. 11-1. Observe the output voltage $v_L(t)$ and its peak value V_m.
2. Take dc biasing measurements to complete the experimental values in Table 11-1.
3. Measure: $v_{L(peak)}$ = ________ mV; $v_{i(peak)}$ = ________ mV

$A_v = \dfrac{v_{L\,(peak)}}{v_{i\,(peak)}}$ = ________ V/V; $R_i = \dfrac{v_{i\,(peak)}}{i_{i\,(peak)}}$ = ________ kΩ

4. Measure the output resistance R_o of the amplifier.

$V_{L(no\ load)}$ = ________ V; $V_{L(full\ load)}$ = ________ V; R_o = ________ Ω

5. Complete the experimental values in Table 11-1.

REPORT

1. Compare the results in Table 11-1 and comment on any discrepancies.

____

____

2. You will notice that the output voltage is shifted up or down. What causes this shift? Explain.

3. How would you reduce the dc biasing current I_{C1} of Q_1? Explain.

4. If you change the dc supply voltage ($V_{CC} = 10\,V$), what would you do to keep the dc biasing current I_{C1} the same as the values for $V_{CC} = 15\,V$. Explain.

5. What are the advantages of an active biasing?

6. What are the disadvantages of an active biasing?

7. What is the estimated cost of the amplifier?

8. Analyze and interpret the data due to any variations and practical limitations.

9. Describe the safety issues considered while conducting the experiment.

10. Describe the process to design and conduct experiments.

11. Conclusion and comment on achieving goals or objectives of this experiment.

ATTACH ALL PLOTS/GRAPHS TO YOUR REPORT

CHAPTER

12

Design of BJT-Active Current Sources

Learning Objectives

To design BJT-active current sources to give a specified constant current. You will use computer simulation to verify the design and evaluate the performance of current sources.

After the end of this experiment, you should be able to

- Describe the operation of BJT constant current sources and their small-signal equivalent circuit.
- Analyze and design BJT current sources to meet the given specifications.

PRE-LAB ASSIGNMENT

Read on *BJ-Active Current Sources* (e.g., Rashid's Section 14.6: BJT Current Sources).

DESIGN SPECIFICATIONS

Part I: Wilson Current Source

Design a Wilson current source to bias an emitter follower (as shown in Fig. 12-1) to meet the following specifications:

- Quiescent biasing current, $I_Q = 190\ \mu A \pm 5\%$
- Voltage gain, $|A_v| = v_L/v_s \approx 1 \pm 5\%$
- Load resistance, $R_L = 22\ k\Omega$
- dc supply voltage, $V_{CC} = V_{EE} = 12\ V$
- Input signal, $v_i = 0–4$ V (peak sinusoidal), 1 kHz
- Use NPN transistors of type 2N2222 (assume $\beta_F = 255$ (if not available, use any other BJT that is available).

Part II: Cascoded Current Source

Design a cascoded current source to bias an emitter follower (as shown in Fig. 12-2) to meet the following specifications:

- Quiescent biasing current, I_Q = 190 μA ± 5%
- Voltage gain, $|A_v| = v_L/v_s \approx 1 \pm 5\%$
- Load resistance, R_L = 22 kΩ
- dc supply voltage, $V_{CC} = V_{EE}$ = 12 V
- Input signal, v_i = 0–4 V (peak sinusoidal), 1 kHz
- Use NPN transistors of type 2N2222 (assume β_F = 255)

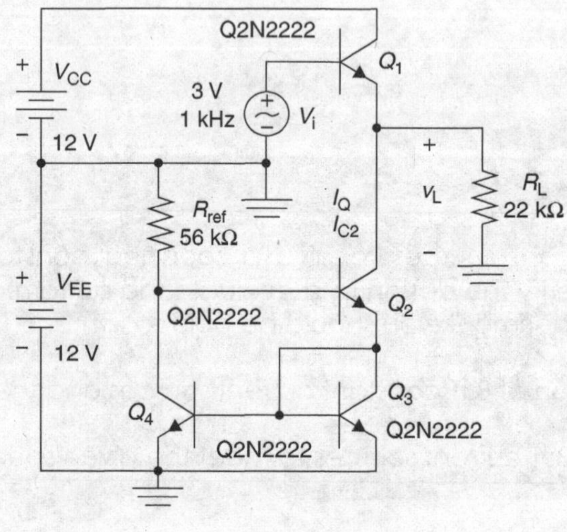

Figure 12-1 Wilson current source

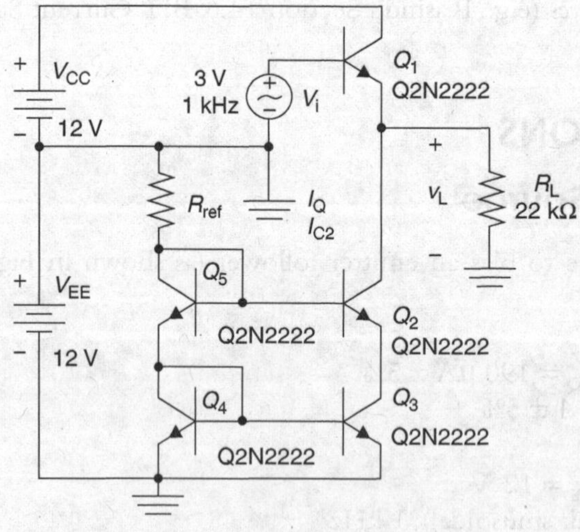

Figure 12-2 Cascoded current source

PAPER–PENCIL DESIGN

Note: Select the component values closest to the practical values.

Part I: Wilson Current Source

1. After completing your paper–pencil design, write the circuit value.

R_{ref} = ________ kΩ

2. Find the dc biasing currents.

I_{C1} = ________ mA; I_{B1} = ________ μA

3. Calculate the output resistance r_{o1} for Q_1 and the output resistance r_{o2} for Q_2.

r_{o1} = ________ kΩ; r_{o2} = ________ kΩ

4. Calculate the small-signal parameters of the emitter follower.

$A_v = \frac{v_{L\,(peak)}}{v_{i\,(peak)}}$ = ________ V/V; $R_i = \frac{v_{i\,(peak)}}{i_{i\,(peak)}}$ = ________ kΩ; R_o = ________ Ω

5. Complete the calculated values in Table 12-1.

Table 12-1 Emitter follower with a Wilson current source

	I_Q (mA)	I_{B1} (μA)	r_{01} (kΩ)	r_{02} (kΩ)	A_v	R_i (kΩ)	R_o (Ω)
Calculated							
Simulated							
Experimental							

Part II: Cascode Current Source

1. After completing your paper–pencil design, write the circuit value.

R_{ref} = ________ kΩ

2. Find the dc biasing currents.

I_{C1} = ________ mA; I_{B1} = ________ μA

3. Calculate the output resistance r_{o1} for Q_1 and the output resistance r_{o2} for Q_2.

r_{o1} = ________ kΩ; r_{o2} = ________ kΩ

4. Calculate the small-signal parameters of the emitter follower.

$$A_v = \frac{v_{L\,(peak)}}{v_{i\,(peak)}} = \_\_\_\_\_\_\_\_ \text{V/V}; \quad R_i = \frac{v_{i\,(peak)}}{i_{i\,(peak)}} = \_\_\_\_\_\_\_\_ \text{k}\Omega; \quad R_o = \_\_\_\_\_\_\_\_ \Omega$$

5. Complete the calculated values in Table 12-2.

Table 12-2 Emitter follower with a cascoded current source

	I_Q (mA)	I_{B1} (μA)	r_{o1} (kΩ)	r_{o2} (kΩ)	A_v	R_i (kΩ)	R_o (Ω)
Calculated							
Simulated							
Experimental							

COMPUTER SIMULATION

Software Tools: PSpice, OrCAD, Multisim, LTSpice, or any electronic circuit simulator.

Part I: Wilson Current Source

1. Simulate the emitter-follower circuit shown in Fig. 12-1 by using computer simulation to find the dc biasing information. From the simulation output file, complete the simulated values in Table 12-1.
2. Simulate the amplifier by using computer simulation to plot the output voltage $v_L(t)$ across the load resistance R_L. Since your input signal v_i is sinusoidal, the output voltage v_L should ideally be sinusoidal. Is the output voltage v_L sinusoidal?

____

____

Compare the output voltage with the input voltage. Explain any differences or deviations.

____

____

3. From the plots of the input signal voltage $v_i(t)$ and the output voltage $v_L(t)$, find the voltage gain A_v and the input resistance R_i. Record.

$$v_{L(peak)} = \_\_\_\_\_\_\_\_ \text{mV}; \quad v_{i(peak)} = \_\_\_\_\_\_\_\_ \text{mV}; \quad A_v = \frac{v_{L\,(peak)}}{v_{i\,(peak)}} = \_\_\_\_\_\_\_\_$$

$$R_i = \frac{v_{i\,(peak)}}{i_{i\,(peak)}} = \_\_\_\_\_\_\_\_ \text{k}\Omega$$

4. To find the output resistance R_o, run the simulation for $R_L = \infty$ (or say 10 MΩ), 10 kΩ. Calculate the output resistance R_o of the amplifier from the equation.

$$R_o = R_L \left[\frac{V_{L(\text{no-load})} - V_{L(\text{full-load})}}{V_{L(\text{full-load})}} \right] = \_\_\_\_\_\_\_\_ \Omega \qquad (12.1)$$

5. Complete the simulated values in Table 12-1.
6. Plot the voltage transfer characteristic (v_L versus v_i). Record v_L = ________ V at $v_i = 0$ V. Is $v_L = 0$ V at $v_i = 0$ V? If not, why? Explain.

____

____

If you apply an input voltage at $v_i = 2\sin(2000\pi t)$, what will be the expression for the output load?

v_L = ________

Part II: Cascoded Current Source

1. Simulate the emitter-follower circuit shown in Fig. 12-2 by using computer simulation to find the dc biasing information. From the simulation output file, complete the simulated values in Table 12-2.
2. Simulate the amplifier by using computer simulation to plot the output voltage $v_L(t)$ across the load resistance R_L. Since your input signal v_i is sinusoidal, the output voltage v_L should ideally be sinusoidal. Is the output voltage v_L sinusoidal?

____

Compare the output voltage with the input voltage. Explain any differences or deviations.

____

____

3. From the plots of the input signal voltage $v_i(t)$ and the output voltage $v_L(t)$, find the voltage gain A_v and the input resistance R_i. Record.

$v_{L(\text{peak})}$ = ________ mV; $v_{i(\text{peak})}$ = ________ mV; $A_v = \frac{v_{L\,(\text{peak})}}{v_{i\,(\text{peak})}}$ = ________

$R_i = \frac{v_{i\,(\text{peak})}}{i_{i\,(\text{peak})}}$ = ________ kΩ

4. To find the output resistance R_o, run the simulation for $R_L = \infty$ (or say 10 MΩ), 10 kΩ. Calculate the output resistance R_o of the amplifier from the equation.

$$R_o = R_L \left[\frac{V_{L(\text{no-load})} - V_{L(\text{full-load})}}{V_{L(\text{full-load})}} \right] = \_\_\_\_\_\_\_\_ \Omega \qquad (12.2)$$

5. Complete the simulated values in Table 12-2.

6. Plot the voltage transfer characteristic (v_L versus v_i). Record v_L = ________ V at $v_i = 0$ V. Is $v_L = 0$ V at $v_i = 0$ V? If not, why? Explain.

____

____

____

If you apply an input voltage at $v_i = 2\sin(2000\pi t)$, what will be the expression for the output load?

v_L = ________

EXPERIMENTS

The students are strongly encouraged and recommended to build and test the amplifier circuit to validate the theoretical and computer simulation results.

Part I: Wilson Current Source

1. Set up your final amplifier circuit shown in Fig. 12-1. Observe the output voltage $v_L(t)$ and its peak value V_m.
2. Take dc biasing measurements to complete the experimental values in Table 12-1.
3. Measure: $v_{L(peak)}$ = ________ V; $v_{i(peak)}$ = ________ mV

$$A_v = \frac{v_{L\,(peak)}}{v_{i\,(peak)}} = \text{\_\_\_\_\_\_\_\_ V/V}; \qquad R_i = \frac{v_{i\,(peak)}}{i_{i\,(peak)}} = \text{\_\_\_\_\_\_\_\_ k}\Omega$$

4. Measure the output resistance R_o of the amplifier.

$V_{L(no\ load)}$ = ________ V; $V_{L(full\ load)}$ = ________ V; R_o = ________ Ω

5. Complete the experimental values in Table 12-1.

Part II: Cascode Current Source

1. Set up your final amplifier circuit shown in Fig. 12.2. Observe the output voltage $v_L(t)$ and its peak value V_m.
2. Take dc biasing measurements to complete the experimental values in Table 12-2.
3. Measure: $v_{L(peak)}$ = ________ V; $v_{i(peak)}$ = ________ mV

$$A_v = \frac{v_{L\,(peak)}}{v_{i\,(peak)}} = \text{\_\_\_\_\_\_\_\_ V/V}; \qquad R_i = \frac{v_{i\,(peak)}}{i_{i\,(peak)}} = \text{\_\_\_\_\_\_\_\_ k}\Omega$$

4. Measure the output resistance R_o of the amplifier.

$V_{L(no\ load)}$ = ________ V; $V_{L(full\ load)}$ = ________ V; R_o = ________ Ω

5. Complete the experimental values in Table 12-2.

REPORT

1. Compare the results in Tables 12-1 and 12-2. Comment on any discrepancies.

2. Does the design meet the specifications? If not, explain the reasons.

3. What are the parameters that influence the input and output resistances of the amplifier? Explain.

4. What is the estimated cost of the amplifier?

5. Analyze and interpret the data due to any variations and practical limitations.

6. Describe the safety issues considered while conducting the experiment.

7. Describe the process to design and conduct experiments.

8. Conclusion and comment on achieving goals or objectives of this experiment.

ATTACH ALL PLOTS/GRAPHS TO YOUR REPORT

CHAPTER 13

Characteristics of BJT Differential Amplifiers

Learning Objectives

To investigate the characteristics of differential amplifiers with a current source biasing. You will use computer simulation to evaluate the performance of differential amplifiers.

After the end of this experiment, you should be able to

- Describe the operation and characteristics of differential amplifiers and its small-signal equivalent circuit.
- Analyze differential pairs with a constant current source biasing.

PRE-LAB ASSIGNMENT

Read on *Differential Amplifiers* (e.g., Rashid's Section 15.6: BJT Differential Amplifiers).

PAPER–PENCIL ANALYSIS

A BJT differential pair as shown in Fig. 13-1 is biased by a BJT current source. Assume $\beta_F = 255$ for 2N2222 (if not available, use any other BJT that is available).

1. Find the dc biasing currents.

$I_Q =$ ________ mA; $I_{C1} =$ ________ mA; $I_{B1} =$ ________ µA

2. Calculate the output resistances for Q_1, Q_2, Q_3, and Q_4. Also, the equivalent output resistance of the current source, R_{EE}.

$r_{o1} =$ ________ kΩ; $r_{o2} =$ ________ kΩ; $r_{o3} =$ ________ kΩ

$r_{o4} =$ ________ kΩ; $R_{EE} =$ ________ kΩ

3. Calculate the differential-mode small-signal parameters of the amplifier, i.e., for $v_{s1} = v_{id}/2$ and $v_{s2} = -v_{id}/2$. Assume the output is taken as $v_{od} = v_{O1} - v_{O2}$.

$$A_d = \frac{v_{od}}{v_{id}} = \_\_\_\_\_\_\_\_\_\text{V/V}; \qquad R_{id} = \frac{v_{id}}{i_{id}} = \_\_\_\_\_\_\_\_\_\ \text{k}\Omega$$

4. Calculate the common-mode small-signal parameters of the amplifier, i.e., for $v_{s1} = v_{ic}$ and $v_{s2} = v_{ic}$.

$$A_c = \frac{v_{oc}}{v_{ic}} = \_\_\_\_\_\_\_\_\_\text{V/V}; \qquad R_{ic} = \frac{v_{ic}}{i_{id}} = \_\_\_\_\_\_\_\_\_\ \text{k}\Omega$$

5. Complete the calculated values in Table 13-1.

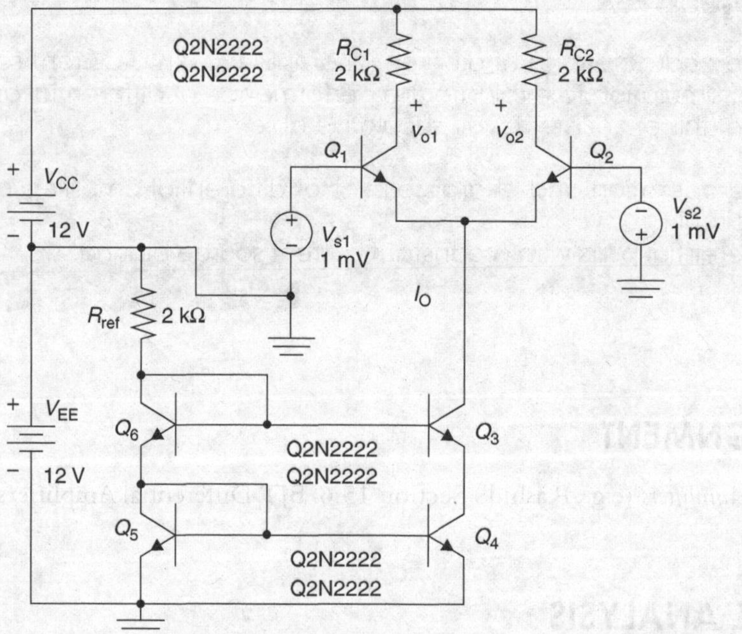

Figure 13-1 BJT differential amplifier with current source biasing

Table 13-1 Parameters of BJT differential amplifier

	I_Q (mA)	I_{C1} (mA)	A_d	R_{id} (kΩ)	A_c	R_{ic} (kΩ)	CMRR
Calculated							
Simulated							
Experimental							

COMPUTER SIMULATION

Software Tools: **PSpice, OrCAD, Multisim, LTSpice, or any electronic circuit simulator.**

1. Simulate the differential amplifier circuit shown in Fig. 13-1 by using computer simulation to find the dc biasing information. From the simulation output file, complete the simulated values in Table 13-1.
2. Apply a differential-mode voltage: $v_{s1} = v_{id}/2 = 1$ mA and $v_{s2} = -v_{id}/2 = 1$ mV. Simulate and record.

$v_{O1} =$ ________ mV; $v_{O2} =$ ________ mV; $v_{od} =$ ________ mV

$A_d = \frac{v_{od}}{v_{id}} =$ ________; $R_{id} = \frac{v_{id}}{i_{id}} =$ ________ kΩ

3. Apply a common-mode voltage: $v_{s1} = v_{ic} = 10$ mV and $v_{s2} = v_{ic} = 10$ mV. Simulate and record.

$v_{O1} =$ ________ mV; $v_{O2} =$ ________ mV; $v_{oc} =$ ________ mV

$A_c = \frac{v_{oc}}{v_{ic}} =$ ________; $R_{ic} = \frac{v_{ic}}{i_{id}} =$ ________ kΩ

4. Complete the simulated values in Table 13-1.
5. Set $v_{s1} = v_{id}/2 = 1$ mV and $v_{s2} = 0$ V. Use dc analysis and plot the voltage transfer characteristic (v_{o1} versus v_{s1}). Record the slope of the plot, i.e., the voltage gain, $A_d =$ ________ V/V.
   Compare this gain with that in step 2. Explain any differences or deviations.

____

____

EXPERIMENTS

The students are strongly encouraged and recommended to build and test the amplifier circuit to validate the theoretical and computer simulation results.

1. Set up the circuit shown in Fig. 13-1.
2. Take dc biasing measurements to complete the experimental values in Table 13-1.
3. Apply a differential-mode voltage: $v_{s1} = v_{id}/2 = 1$ mV and $v_{s2} = -v_{id}/2 = 1$ mV. Measure

$v_{O1} =$ ________ mV; $v_{O2} =$ ________ mV; $v_{od} =$ ________ mV

$A_d = \frac{v_{od}}{v_{id}} =$ ________ V/V; $R_{id} = \frac{v_{id}}{i_{id}} =$ ________ kΩ

4. Apply a common-mode voltage: $v_{s1} = v_{ic} = 10$ mV and $v_{s2} = v_{ic} = 10$ mV. Measure

$v_{O1} =$ ________ mV; $v_{O2} =$ ________ mV; $v_{oc} =$ ________ mV

$A_c = \frac{v_{oc}}{v_{ic}} =$ ________ V/V; $R_{ic} = \frac{v_{ic}}{i_{id}} =$ ________ kΩ

5. Complete the experimental values in Table 13-1.

REPORT

1. Compare the results in Tables 13-1 and comment on any discrepancies.

2. If you increase v_{s1} by a small amount, v_{O1} will decrease and v_{O2} will increase. Why? Explain.

3. How would you increase the differential-mode gain? Explain.

4. How would you reduce the common-mode gain? Explain.

5. What should be the characteristics of an ideal differential amplifier? Explain.

6. What is the estimated cost of the amplifier?

7. Analyze and interpret the data due to any variations and practical limitations.

8. Describe the safety issues considered while conducting the experiment.

9. Describe the process to design and conduct experiments.

10. Conclusion and comment on achieving goals or objectives of this experiment.

ATTACH ALL PLOTS/GRAPHS TO YOUR REPORT

CHAPTER 14

Design of a BJT Differential Amplifier

Learning Objectives

To design a BJT differential amplifier with an active current load and an active current source biasing to give a specified differential gain. You will use computer simulation to verify the design and evaluate the performance of the amplifier.

After the end of this experiment, you should be able to

- Describe the operation of a BJT differential amplifier with an active load and its small-signal equivalent circuit.
- Analyze and design a BJT differential amplifier with an active load to meet the given specifications.

PRE-LAB ASSIGNMENT

Read on *Differential Amplifiers* (e.g., Rashid's Section 15.6: BJT Differential Amplifiers).

DESIGN SPECIFICATIONS

Design a BJT differential amplifier as shown in Fig. 14-1 to meet the following specifications. The output is taken across the collectors of Q_1 and Q_2.

- Differential voltage gain, $A_d = v_{od}/v_{id} = 450 \pm 5\%$
- dc supply voltage of $V_{CC} = V_{EE} = 12$ V
- Use NPN transistors of type 2N2222 and PNP transistors of type 2N2907A. Assume $\beta_F = 255$ for 2N2222 and $\beta_F = 231$ for 2N2907A (if not available, use any other BJT that is available).

PAPER–PENCIL DESIGN

Note: Select the component values closest to the practical values. The component values shown are for illustrations only.

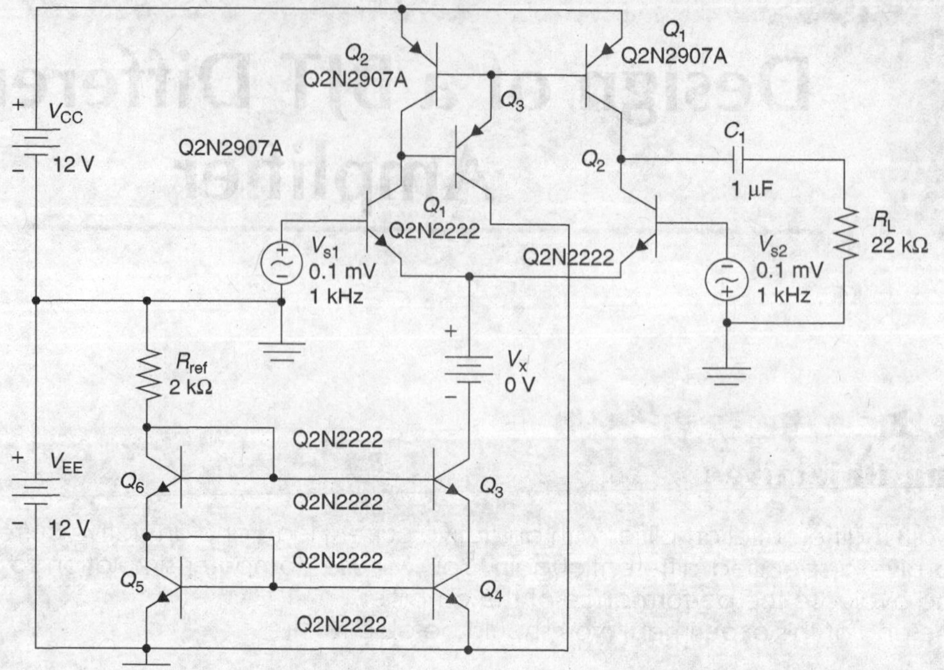

Figure 14-1 BJT differential amplifier with an active load

1. After completing your paper–pencil design, write the circuit value.

   R_{ref} = ________ kΩ

2. Find the dc biasing currents.

   I_Q = ________ mA; I_{C1} = ________ mA; I_{C2} = ________ mA; I_{C7} = ________ mA

   I_{C8} = ________ mA

3. Calculate the output resistances for Q_1, Q_2, Q_3, Q_4, Q_7, and Q_8. Also, calculate the equivalent output resistance of the current source, R_{EE}.

   r_{o1} = ________ kΩ; r_{o2} = ________ kΩ; r_{o3} = ________ kΩ; r_{o4} = ________ kΩ

   r_{o7} = ________ kΩ; r_{o8} = ________ kΩ; R_{EE} = ________ kΩ

4. Calculate the differential-mode small-signal parameters of the amplifier, i.e., for $v_{s1} = v_{id}/2$ and $v_{s2} = -v_{id}/2$. Assume the output is taken as $v_{od} = v_{O2} - v_{O1}$.

   $A_d = \frac{v_{od}}{v_{id}}$ = ________; $R_{id} = \frac{v_{id}}{i_{id}}$ = ________ kΩ

5. Calculate the common-mode small-signal parameters of the amplifier, i.e., for $v_{s1} = v_{ic}$ and $v_{s2} = v_{ic}$.

$$A_c = \frac{v_{oc}}{v_{ic}} = \_\_\_\_\_\_\_\_ \text{V/V}; \quad R_{ic} = \frac{v_{ic}}{i_{id}} = \_\_\_\_\_\_\_\_ \text{k}\Omega$$

6. Complete the calculated values in Table 14-1.

Table 14-1 Parameters of BJT differential amplifier

	I_Q (mA)	I_{C1} (mA)	A_d	R_{id} (kΩ)	A_c	R_{ic} (kΩ)	CMRR
Calculated							
Simulated							
Experimental							

COMPUTER SIMULATION

Software Tools: PSpice, OrCAD, Multisim, LTSpice, or any electronic circuit simulator.

1. Simulate the amplifier circuit shown in Fig. 14-1 by using computer simulation to find the dc biasing information. From the simulation output file, complete the simulated values in Table 14-1.
2. Apply a differential mode voltage: $v_{s1} = v_{id}/2 = 1$ mV and $v_{s2} = -v_{id}/2 = 1$ mV. Simulate and record.

$$v_{O1} = \_\_\_\_\_\_\_\_ \text{mV}; \quad v_{O2} = \_\_\_\_\_\_\_\_ \text{mV}; \quad v_{od} = \_\_\_\_\_\_\_\_ \text{mV}$$

$$A_d = \frac{v_{od}}{v_{id}} = \_\_\_\_\_\_\_\_ \text{V/V}; \quad R_{id} = \frac{v_{id}}{i_{id}} = \_\_\_\_\_\_\_\_ \text{k}\Omega$$

3. Apply a common-mode voltage: $v_{s1} = v_{ic} = 10$ mV and $v_{s2} = v_{ic} = 10$ mV. Simulate and record.

$$v_{O1} = \_\_\_\_\_\_\_\_ \text{mV}; \quad v_{O2} = \_\_\_\_\_\_\_\_ \text{mV}; \quad v_{oc} = \_\_\_\_\_\_\_\_ \text{mV}$$

$$A_c = \frac{v_{oc}}{v_{ic}} = \_\_\_\_\_\_\_\_; \quad R_{ic} = \frac{v_{ic}}{i_{ic}} = \_\_\_\_\_\_\_\_ \text{k}\Omega$$

4. Set $v_{s1} = v_{id}/2 = 1$ mV and $v_{s2} = 0$ V. Use dc analysis and plot the voltage transfer characteristic (v_{O2}–v_{O1} versus v_{s1}). Record the slope of the plot, i.e., the voltage gain, A_d = ________ V/V.
   Compare this gain with that in step 2. Explain any differences or deviations.

____

____

5. Does your design meet the specification under worst-case conditions? If not, change the value of R_{ref} so that the gain specification is met. Note this value.

$$R_{ref} = \_\_\_\_\_\_\_\_ \text{k}\Omega$$

6. Run the computer simulation with your suggested values in step 3 and complete the simulated values in Table 14-1.

   Comment on the effects of the component tolerance on the design.

   ____

   ____

7. What would you do to increase R_{id} and CMRR of the amplifier? Explain.

   ____

   ____

EXPERIMENTS

The students are strongly encouraged and recommended to build and test the amplifier circuit to validate the theoretical and computer simulation results.

1. Set up your final circuit.
2. Take dc biasing measurements to complete the experimental values in Table 14-1.
3. Apply a differential mode voltage: $v_{s1} = v_{id}/2 = 1$ mV and $v_{s2} = -v_{id}/2 = -1$ mV. Measure

   $v_{O1} =$ ________ mV; $v_{O2} =$ ________ mV; $v_{od} =$ ________ mV

   $A_d = \frac{v_{od}}{v_{id}} =$ ________ V/V; $R_{id} = \frac{v_{id}}{i_{id}} =$ ________ kΩ

4. Apply a common-mode voltage: $v_{s1} = v_{ic} = 10$ mV and $v_{s2} = v_{ic} = 10$ mV. Measure

   $v_{O1} =$ ________ mV; $v_{O2} =$ ________ mV; $v_{oc} =$ ________ mV

   $A_c = \frac{v_{oc}}{v_{ic}} =$ ________; $R_{ic} = \frac{v_{ic}}{i_{ic}} =$ ________ kΩ

5. Complete the experimental values in Table 14-1.

REPORT

1. Compare the results in Tables 14-1 and comment on any discrepancies.

   ____

   ____

2. Does the design meet the specifications? If not, explain the reasons.

   ____

   ____

3. What are the parameters that affect voltage gains? Explain.

4. What is the estimated cost of the amplifier?

5. Analyze and interpret the data due to any variations and practical limitations.

6. Describe the safety issues considered while conducting the experiment.

7. Describe the process to design and conduct experiments.

8. Conclusion and comment on achieving goals or objectives of this experiment.

ATTACH ALL PLOTS/GRAPHS TO YOUR REPORT

CHAPTER

15 Design of a BJT Operational Amplifier

Learning Objectives

To design a BJT operational amplifier to meet specified performance parameters. You will use computer simulation to verify the design and evaluate the performance of the amplifier.

After the end of this experiment, you should be able to

- Select the circuit topology, and describe the operation of a BJT operational amplifier and its small-signal equivalent circuit.
- Analyze and design a BJT differential amplifier to meet the given specifications.

PRE-LAB ASSIGNMENT

Read on *Operational Amplifiers* (e.g., Rashid's Section 16.5: BJT Op-Amps).

DESIGN SPECIFICATIONS

Design a BJT operational amplifier to meet the following specifications:

- Differential voltage gain, $|A_d| = v_{od}/v_d = 10^3 \pm 5\%$.
- Differential input resistance $R_{id} \geq 150\ k\Omega \pm 5\%$
- Output resistance $R_o \leq 200\ \Omega \pm 5\%$.
- Common-mode rejection ratio, CMRR $= 10^4 \pm 10\%$.
- Unity-gain bandwidth $f_u \geq 10^4 \pm 10\%$.
- dc supply voltages, $V_{CC} = V_{EE} = 15\ V$
- Use NPN transistors of type 2N2222, and PNP transistors of type 2N2907A. Assume $\beta_F = 255$ for 2N2222 and $\beta_F = 231$ for 2N2907A (if not available, use any other BJT that is available).

Hint: You can select any circuit topology using BJTs as long as you meet the specifications.

PAPER–PENCIL DESIGN

Note: Select the component values closest to the practical values.

1. Decide on the circuit topology, and attach it with the report.
2. Find the components values of your circuit.
3. Calculate the differential-mode parameters.

A_d = ________; R_{id} = ________ kΩ; R_o = ________ kΩ

4. Calculate the common-mode parameters.

A_c = ________; R_{ic} = ________ kΩ

5. Complete the calculated values in Table 15-1.

Table 15-1 Parameters of BJT op-amp

	A_d	R_{id} (kΩ)	A_c	R_{ic} (kΩ)	CMRR	R_o (Ω)	SR (V/μs)	f_u (kHz)
Calculated								
Simulated								
Experimental								

COMPUTER SIMULATION

Software Tools: PSpice, OrCAD, Multisim, LTSpice, or any electronic circuit simulator.

1. Simulate your circuit by using computer simulation to find the transfer function of differential-mode parameters. From the simulation output file, record and complete the simulated values in Table 15-1.

A_d = ________V/V; R_{id} = ________ kΩ; R_o = ________ Ω

2. Simulate your circuit by using computer simulation to find the common-mode parameters from the transfer function analysis. From the simulation output file, record and complete the simulated values in Table 15-1.

A_c = ________V/V; R_{ic} = ________ kΩ

3. Simulate your circuit by using computer simulation to find the frequency response of the output voltage. From the simulation plot of the voltage gain, find the unity-gain bandwidth. Record and complete the simulated values in Table 15-1.

f_u = ________ kHz

4. Assign ±5% tolerance to all circuit elements. Run the simulation for the worst-case maximum output voltage. Does your design meet the specifications under worst-case conditions? If not, change the component values so that the specifications are met. Record these values.

________ ________ ________ ________

5. Run the computer simulation with your suggested values in step 4 and complete the simulated values in Table 15-1.

A_d = ________ V/V; R_{id} = ________ kΩ; R_o = ________ Ω

A_c = ________ V/V; R_{ic} = ________ kΩ; CMRR = ________

f_u = ________ kHz

Comment on the effects of the component tolerance on the design.

____

____

____

EXPERIMENTS

The students are strongly encouraged and recommended to build and test the amplifier circuit to validate the theoretical and computer simulation results.

1. Set up your final circuit.
2. Apply a differential-mode voltage. Measure

A_d = ________ V/V; R_{id} = ________ kΩ; R_o = ________ Ω

3. Apply a common-mode voltage. Measure

A_c = ________ V/V; R_{ic} = ________ kΩ

4. Measure the frequency response with a differential-mode voltage. Record f_u = ________ kHz.
5. Complete the experimental values in Table 15-1.

REPORT

1. Compare the results in Tables 15-1 and comment on any discrepancies.

____

____

2. Does the design meet the specifications? If not, explain the reasons.

____

____

3. What are the parameters that affect voltage gains? Explain.

4. What is the estimated cost of the amplifier?

5. Analyze and interpret the data due to any variations and practical limitations.

6. Describe the safety issues considered while conducting the experiment.

7. Describe the process to design and conduct experiments.

8. Conclusion and comment on achieving goals or objectives of this experiment.

ATTACH ALL PLOTS/GRAPHS TO YOUR REPORT

CHAPTER 16

Design of BJT Feedback Amplifiers

Learning Objectives

To design feedback amplifiers to give a specified bandwidth, gain, or input resistance. We will use computer simulation to verify the design and evaluate the performance of feedback amplifiers.

After the end of this experiment, you should be able to

- List the types and characteristics of feedback amplifiers.
- Analyze and design feedback amplifiers.

PRE-LAB ASSIGNMENT

Read on *Feedback Amplifiers* (e.g., Rashid's Sections 9.8–9.12: Analysis of Feedback Amplifiers).

DESIGN SPECIFICATIONS

Part I: Shunt–Shunt Feedback Amplifier

Design the feedback network (R_F, C_F) for the amplifier shown in Fig. 16-1 to meet the following specification:

- The bandwidth with feedback must be increased by 10 times, i.e., BWf = 10 BW ± 5%, where BW is the bandwidth without feedback.

Part II: Series–Shunt Feedback Amplifier

Design the feedback network (R_F, C_F) for the amplifier shown in Fig. 16-2 to meet the following specification:

- The input resistance with feedback must be increased by 100 times. i.e., $R_{if} = 100\ R_i$, where R_i is the mid-band input resistance without feedback.

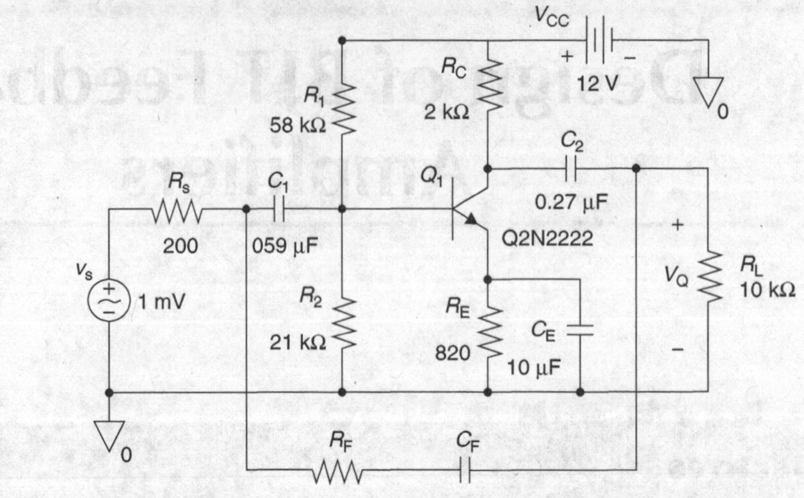

Figure 16-1 Shunt–shunt feedback amplifier

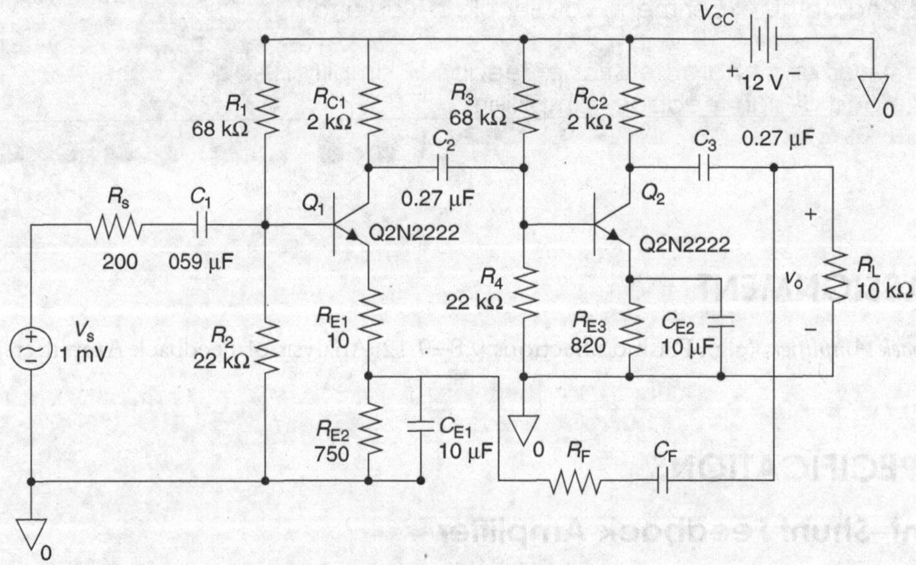

Figure 16-2 Series–shunt feedback amplifier

Part III: Shunt–Series Feedback Amplifier

Design the feedback network (R_F, C_F) for the amplifier shown in Fig. 16-3 to meet the following specification:

- The bandwidth with feedback must be increased by 10 times, i.e., BWf = 10 BW ± 5%, where BW is the bandwidth without feedback.

PAPER–PENCIL DESIGN

Note: Select the component values closest to the practical values.

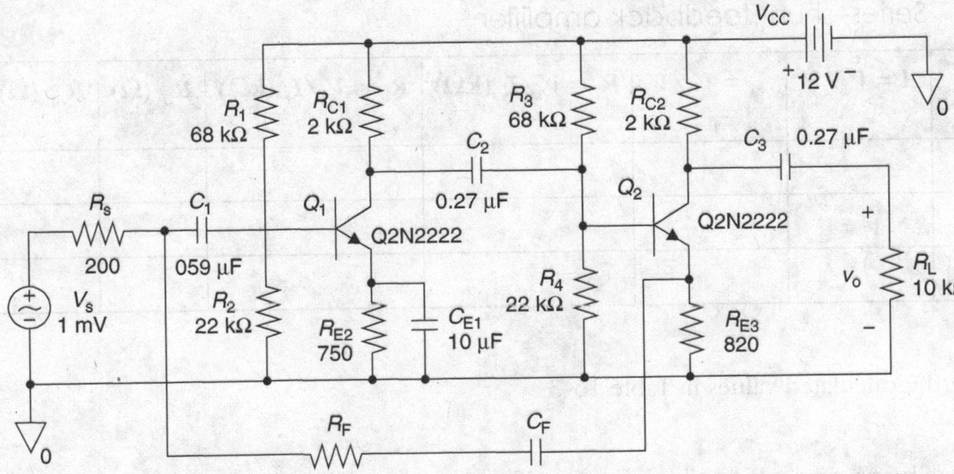

Figure 16-3 Shunt–series feedback amplifier

Part I: Shunt–Shunt Feedback Amplifier

1. After completing your design, write the circuit values.

   R_F = ________ kΩ; C_F = ________ µF

2. Complete the calculated values in Table 16-1.

Table 16-1 Shunt–shunt feedback amplifier

	$A = V_o/V_s$	$A_f = V_o/V_s$	$R_i = V_s/I_s$ (kΩ)	$R_{if} = V_s/I_s$ (kΩ)	R_o (Ω)	R_{of} (Ω)	BWf (kHz)
Calculated							
Simulated							
Experimental							

Part II: Series–Shunt Feedback Amplifier

1. After completing your design, write the circuit values.

   R_F = ________ kΩ; C_F = ________ µF

2. Complete the calculated values in Table 16-2.

Part III: Shunt–Series Feedback Amplifier

1. After completing your design, write the circuit values.

   R_F = ________ kΩ; C_F = ________ µF

Table 16-2 Series–shunt feedback amplifier

	$A = V_o/V_s$	$A_f = V_o/V_s$	$R_i = V_s/I_s$ (kΩ)	$R_{if} = V_s/I_s$ (kΩ)	R_o (Ω)	R_{of} (Ω)	BWf (kHz)
Calculated							
Simulated							
Experimental							

2. Complete the calculated values in Table 16-3.

Table 16-3 Shunt–series feedback amplifier

	$A = V_o/V_s$	$A_f = V_o/V_s$	$R_i = V_s/I_s$ (kΩ)	$R_{if} = V_s/I_s$ (kΩ)	R_o (Ω)	R_{of} (Ω)	BWf (kHz)
Calculated							
Simulated							
Experimental							

COMPUTER SIMULATION

Software tools: PSpice, OrCAD, Multisim, LTSpice, or any electronic circuit simulator.

Part I: Shunt–Shunt Feedback Amplifier

1. Simulate the amplifier circuit shown in Fig.16-1 by using computer simulation to find the frequency response (ac analysis).

BWf $= f_H - f_L =$ ________ kHz; $|A| = \frac{v_o}{v_s}$ ________; $A_f = \frac{v_o}{v_s} =$ ________ V/V

$R_{if} =$ ________ kΩ; $R_{of} =$ ________ kΩ

2. Assign ±5% tolerance to all capacitors and resistors. Run the simulation for the worst-case maximum gain and record the following values:

BWf $= f_H - f_L =$ ________ kHz; $|A| = \frac{v_o}{v_s}$ ________; $A_f = \frac{v_o}{v_s} =$ ________ V/V

$R_{if} =$ ________ kΩ; $R_{of} =$ ________ kΩ

3. Does your design meet the specifications under the worst-case conditions? If not, adjust the values of resistance R_F and capacitor C_F to get desired bandwidth. Note these values.

$R_F =$ ________ kΩ; $C_F =$ ________ μF

4. Run the computer simulation with your suggested values in step 3 and complete the simulated values in Table 16-1.

   Comment on the effects of the component tolerance on the design.

   ____

   ____

Part II: Series–Shunt Feedback Amplifier

1. Simulate the amplifier circuit shown in Fig.16-2 by using computer simulation to find the frequency response (ac analysis).

   $BWf = f_H - f_L =$ ________ kHz; $|A| = \frac{v_o}{v_s}$ ________; $A_f = \frac{v_o}{v_s} =$ ________ V/V

   $R_{if} =$ ________ kΩ; $R_{of} =$ ________ kΩ

2. Assign ±5% tolerance to all capacitors and resistors. Run the simulation for the worst-case maximum gain, and record the following values:

   $BWf = f_H - f_L =$ ________ kHz; $|A| = \frac{v_o}{v_s}$ ________; $A_f = \frac{v_o}{v_s} =$ ________ V/V

   $R_{if} =$ ________ kΩ; $R_{of} =$ ________ kΩ

3. Does your design meet the specifications under the worst-case conditions? If not, adjust the values of resistance R_F and capacitor C_F to get desired bandwidth. Note these values.

   $R_F =$ ________ kΩ; $C_F =$ ________ μF

4. Run the computer simulation with your suggested values in step 3 and complete the simulated values in Table 16-2.

   Comment on the effects of the component tolerance on the design.

   ____

   ____

Part III: Shunt–Series Feedback Amplifier

1. Simulate the amplifier circuit shown in Fig. 16-3 by using computer simulation to find the frequency response (ac analysis).

   $BWf = f_H - f_L =$ ________ kHz; $|A| = \frac{v_o}{v_s}$ ________; $A_f = \frac{v_o}{v_s} =$ ________ V/V

R_{if} = ________ kΩ; R_{of} = ________ kΩ

2. Assign ±5% tolerance to all capacitors and resistors. Run the simulation for the worst-case maximum gain and record.

$BWf = f_H - f_L$ = ________ kHz; $|A| = \frac{v_o}{v_s}$ ________; $A_f = \frac{v_o}{v_s}$ = ________ V/V

R_{if} = ________ kΩ; R_{of} = ________ kΩ

3. Does your design meet the specifications under the worst-case conditions? If not, adjust the values of resistance R_F and capacitor C_F to get desired bandwidth. Note these values.

R_F = ________ kΩ; C_F = ________ μF

4. Run the computer simulation with your suggested values in step 3 and complete the simulated values in Table 16-3.

Comment on the effects of the component tolerance on the design.

____

____

EXPERIMENTS

The students are strongly encouraged and recommended to build and test the amplifier circuit to validate the theoretical and computer simulation results.

Part I: Shunt–Shunt Feedback Amplifier

1. Set up your final amplifier circuit as in Fig. 16-1.
2. Measure: $BWf = f_H - f_L$ = ________ kHz; $|A| = \frac{v_o}{v_s}$ ________; $A_f = \frac{v_o}{v_s}$ = ________ V/V

   R_{if} = ________ kΩ; R_{of} = ________ kΩ
3. Complete the experimental values in Table 16-1.

Part II: Series–Shunt Feedback Amplifier

1. Set up your final amplifier circuit as in Fig. 16-2.
2. Measure: $BWf = f_H - f_L$ = ________ kHz; $|A| = \frac{v_o}{v_s}$ ________; $A_f = \frac{v_o}{v_s}$ = ________ V/V

   R_{if} = ________ kΩ; R_{of} = ________ kΩ

3. Complete the experimental values in Table 16-2.

Part III: Shunt–Series Feedback Amplifier

1. Set up your final amplifier circuit in Fig. 16-3.

2. Measure: $BWf = f_H - f_L =$ ________ kHz; $|A| = \frac{v_o}{v_s}$ ________; $A_f = \frac{v_o}{v_s} =$ ________ V/V

   $R_{if} =$ ________ kΩ; $R_{of} =$ ________ kΩ

3. Complete the experimental values in Table 16-3.

REPORT

1. Compare the results in Tables 16-1 and comment on any discrepancies.

2. Does the design meet the specifications? If not, explain the reasons.

3. What are the parameters that affect bandwidth of the feedback amplifier? Explain.

4. What is the estimated cost of the amplifier?

5. Analyze and interpret the data due to any variations and practical limitations.

6. Describe the safety issues considered while conducting the experiment.

7. Describe the process to design and conduct experiments.

8. Conclusion and comment on achieving goals or objectives of this experiment.

ATTACH ALL PLOTS/GRAPHS TO YOUR REPORT

CHAPTER 17

Design of a Class-AB BJT Amplifier

Learning Objectives

To design a class-AB BJT amplifier to operate at a specified constant current. You will use computer simulation to verify the design and evaluate the performance of the class-AB amplifier.

After the end of this experiment, you should be able to

- Describe the operation and characteristics of a class-AB BJT amplifier.
- Analyze and design class-AB amplifiers to meet the given specifications.

PRE-LAB ASSIGNMENT

Read on *Class-AB Push−Pull Amplifiers* (e.g., Rashid's Section 10.9: Class-AB Push−Pull Amplifiers).

DESIGN SPECIFICATIONS

Design a class-AB amplifier with an active current source biasing as shown in Fig. 17-1 to meet the following specifications:

- Quiescent biasing current, $I_Q = 5$ mA ± 5%
- Load resistance, $R_L = 1$ kΩ
- dc supply, $V_{CC} = V_{EE} = 12$ V
- Input signal, $v_i = 0$–4 V (peak sinusoidal), 1 kHz
- Use NPN transistor 2N2222, PNP transistor 2N3307A, and diodes 1N4148. Assume $\beta_F = 255$ for 2N2222 and $\beta_F = 231$ for 2N2907A (if not available, use any other BJT that is available).

PAPER–PENCIL DESIGN

Note: Select the passive component values closest to the practical values.

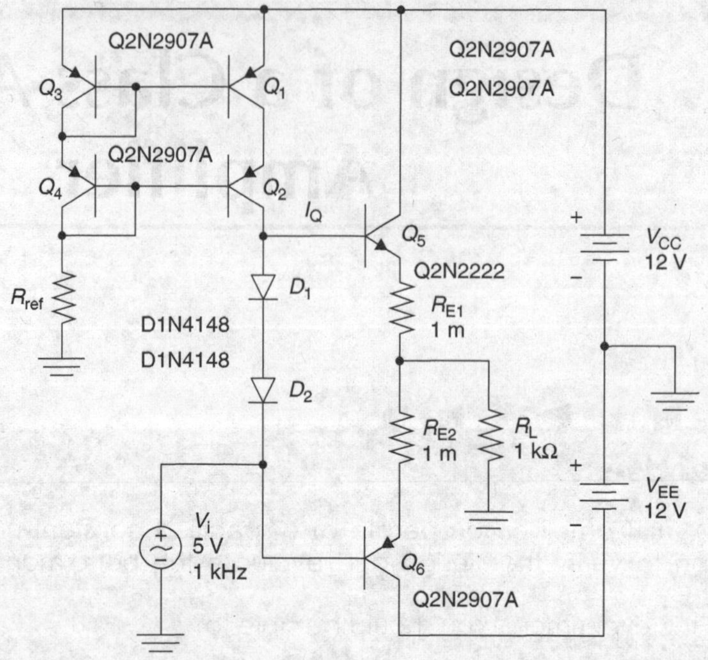

Figure 17-1 Class-AB amplifier with diodes and BJTs

1. After completing your paper–pencil design, write the circuit value.

   R_{ref} = ________ kΩ

2. Find the dc biasing currents.

   I_{C2} = ________ mA; I_{D1} = ________ μA; I_{B5} = ________ μA; I_{E5} = ________ mA

3. Calculate the maximum permissible load voltage $V_{p(max)}$, load current $I_{p(max)}$, output power $P_{L(max)}$, and efficiency η_{max}.

   $V_{p(max)}$ = ________ V; $I_{p(max)}$ = ________ mA; $P_{L(max)}$ = ________ W; η_{max} = ________ %.

Table 17-1 Class-AB amplifier with a Wilson current source

	I_{E5} (mA)	I_{B5} (μA)	I_{C2} (mA)	I_{D1} (mA)	$V_{p(max)}$ (V)	$I_{p(max)}$(mA)	$P_{L(max)}$ (W)	η_{max}
Calculated								
Simulated								
Experimental								

COMPUTER SIMULATION

Software tools: **PSpice, Or CAD, Multisim, LTSpice, or any electronic circuit simulator.**

1. Simulate the class-AB amplifier shown in Fig. 17-1 by using computer simulation to find the dc biasing information. From the simulation output file, complete the simulated values in Table 17-1.
2. Simulate the amplifier by using computer simulation to plot the output voltage $v_L(t)$ across the load resistance R_L. Since your input signal v_i is sinusoidal, the output voltage v_L should ideally be sinusoidal. Is the output voltage v_L sinusoidal?

   Compare the output voltage with the input voltage. Explain any differences or deviations.

   ____

   ____

3. From the plots of the input signal voltage $v_i(t)$ and the output voltage $v_L(t)$, find the voltage gain A_v and the input resistance R_i. Record.

   $v_{L(peak)} =$ ________ V; $v_{i(peak)} =$ ________ V; $A_v = \dfrac{v_{L\,(peak)}}{v_{i\,(peak)}} =$ ________ V/V

   $R_i = \dfrac{v_{i\,(peak)}}{i_{i\,(peak)}} =$ ________ kΩ

4. To find the output resistance R_o, run the simulation for $R_L = \infty$ (or say 10 MΩ), 10 kΩ. Calculate the output resistance R_o of the amplifier from the equation.

$$R_o = R_L \left[\frac{V_{L\,(no\text{-}load)} - V_{L\,(full\text{-}load)}}{V_{L\,(full\text{-}load)}} \right] = \_\_\_\_\_\_\_\_ \Omega \qquad (17.1)$$

5. Apply an input voltage at $v_i = 15 \sin (2000\,\pi t)$. Find the maximum limits of the output voltage and current.

   $V_{p(max)} =$ ________ V; $I_{p(max)} =$ ________ mA

6. Complete the simulated values in Table 17-1.
7. Plot the voltage transfer characteristic (v_L versus v_i). Record $v_L =$ ________ V at $v_i = 0$ V. Is $v_L = 0$ V at $v_i = 0$ V? If not, why? Explain.

   ____

   ____

   If you apply an input voltage at $v_i = 2 \sin (2000\,\pi t)$, what will be the output voltage?

   $v_L =$ ________

8. Replace the diodes in Fig. 17-1 with diode-connected BJTs as shown in Fig. 17-2. Find the dc biasing currents.

   $I_{C2} =$ ________ mA; $I_{E7} =$ ________ mA; $I_{B5} =$ ________ μA; $I_{E5} =$ ________ mA

   Compare these values and comment on the effect of replacing diodes by transistors.

   ____

   ____

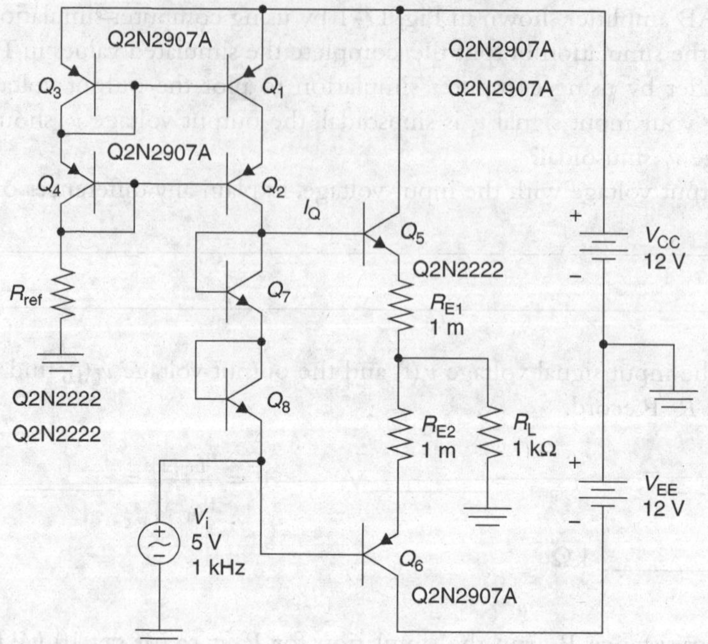

Figure 17-2 Class-AB amplifier with all BJTs

9. Apply an input voltage at $v_i = 15 \sin(2000 \eta t)$ in Fig. 17-2. Find the maximum limits of the output voltage and current.

   $V_{p(max)}$ = ________ V; $I_{p(max)}$ = ________ mA

   Compare these values and comment on the effect of replacing diodes by transistors.

   ____

   ____

   Plot the voltage transfer characteristic (v_L versus v_i) of the circuit in Fig. 17-2. Record v_L = ________ V at $v_i = 0$ V.

   Compare these values and comment on the effect of replacing diodes by transistors.

   ____

   ____

EXPERIMENTS

The students are strongly encouraged and recommended to build and test the amplifier circuit to validate the theoretical and computer simulation results.

1. Set up your final amplifier circuit as shown in Fig. 17-1. Observe the output voltage $v_L(t)$ and its peak value V_m.

2. Take dc biasing measurements to complete the experimental values in Table 17-1.

3. Measure: $v_{L(peak)}$ = ________ V; $v_{i(peak)}$ = ________ V

$$A_v = \frac{v_{L\,(peak)}}{v_{i\,(peak)}} \ \_\_\_\_\_\_\_\_ \text{ V/V}; \qquad R_i = \frac{v_{i\,(peak)}}{i_{i\,(peak)}} = \_\_\_\_\_\_\_\_ \text{ k}\Omega$$

4. Measure the output resistance R_o of the amplifier.

$V_{L(no\ load)}$ = ________ V; $V_{L(full\ load)}$ = ________ V; R_o= ________ Ω

5. Complete the experimental values in Table 17-1.

REPORT

1. Compare the results in Tables 17-1 and comment on any discrepancies.

____

____

2. Does the design meet the specifications? If not, explain the reasons.

____

____

3. What are the parameters that affect the voltage crossover and distortion? Explain.

____

____

4. What is the estimated cost of the amplifier?

____

____

5. Analyze and interpret the data due to any variations and practical limitations.

____

____

6. Describe the safety issues considered while conducting the experiment.

____

____

7. Describe the process to design and conduct experiments.

8. Conclusion and comment on achieving goals or objectives of this experiment.

ATTACH ALL PLOTS/GRAPHS TO YOUR REPORT

CHAPTER 18

Characteristics of BJT Inverters

Learning Objectives

To investigate the characteristics of BJT inverters. You will use computer simulation to plot the transfer characteristic and transient response of inverters.

After the end of this experiment, you should be able to

- Describe the voltage transfer characteristic of BJT inverters.
- Determine the performance parameters of inverters.

PRE-LAB ASSIGNMENT

Read on *BJT Inverters* (e.g., Rashid's Section 13.9: BJT Inverters).

COMPUTER SIMULATION

Software tools: PSpice, OrCAD, Multisim, LTSpice, or any electronic circuit simulator.

1. A BJT inverter is shown in Fig. 18-1. Run transient analysis using computer simulation to plot the input voltage v_s and output voltage v_o. The input is a pulse of 5 V at 100 kHz. R_L and C_L form the load.

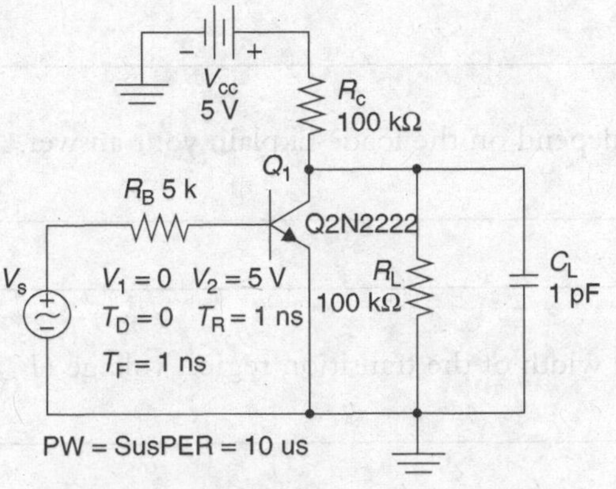

Figure 18-1 A BJT inverter

2. From the transient plots, find the delay time t_{pd1} (or t_{pHL}) for the logic high-to-low and t_{pd0} (or t_{pLH}) for low-to-high. The average of t_{pd1} and t_{pd0} is the average propagation time $t_{pd} = (t_{pd1} + t_{pd0})/2$. Complete the simulated values in Table 18-1.
3. Run the dc sweep of the input voltage v_s (from 0 to 5 V with an increment of 0.01 V).
4. Plot the voltage transfer characteristic (v_o versus v_s). From the transfer characteristic, find the V_{IL}, V_{IH}, V_{OL}, and V_{OH}. Complete the simulated values in Table 18-1.

Table 18-1 BJT inverter parameters

	t_{pd1} (ns)	t_{pd0} (ns)	t_{pd} (ns)	V_{IL} (V)	V_{IH} (V)	$V_{IW} = V_{IH} - V_{IL}$ (V)	V_{OL} (V)	V_{OH} (V)	$V_{LS} = V_{OH} - V_{OL}$ (V)
Simulated									
Experimental									

EXPERIMENTS

The students are strongly encouraged and recommended to build and test the diode circuit to validate the theoretical and computer simulation results (if not available, use any other BJT that is available).

1. Set up the BJT inverter as shown in Fig. 18-1 and apply a pulse input voltage. Measure t_{pd1}, t_{pd0}, and t_{pd}.

   t_{pd1} = ________ ns; t_{pd0} = ________ ns; t_{pd} = ________ ns

2. Apply dc input voltage in steps and plot the voltage transfer characteristic. Measure V_{IL}, V_{IH}, V_{OL}, and V_{OH}.

   V_{IL} = ________ V; V_{IH} = ________ V; V_{OL} = ________ V; V_{OH} = ________ V

3. Complete the experimental values in Table 18-1.

REPORT

1. Which factors influence the propagation delay time of an inverter? Explain.

   ____

   ____

2. Does the propagation time depend on the load? Explain your answer.

   ____

   ____

3. Which factors influence the width of the transition region voltage (V_{IW}) of an inverter? Explain.

   ____

   ____

4. How would you reduce the propagation delay of an inverter? Explain.

5. Analyze and interpret the data due to any variations and practical limitations.

6. Describe the safety issues considered while conducting the experiment.

7. Describe the process to design and conduct experiments.

8. Conclusion and comment on achieving goals or objectives of this experiment.

ATTACH ALL PLOTS/GRAPHS TO YOUR REPORT

PART III

FIELD-EFFECT TRANSISTORS (FETs) AND APPLICATIONS

CHAPTER

19

Characteristics and Biasing of Junction Field-Effect Transistors

Learning Objectives

To investigate the characteristics of junction field-effect transistors (JFETs) and to determine the JFET model parameters. You will use computer simulation to plot the JFET characteristics and to derive the small-signal parameters of a specific JFET.

After the end of this experiment, you should be able to

- Describe the voltage–current characteristics of JFETs.
- Derive the approximate model parameters of a JFET.

PRE-LAB ASSIGNMENT

Read on *Junction Field-Effect Transistors* (e.g., Rashid's Section 5.3: Field-Effect Transistors, *Microelectronics*, 1/e, 1900). Since JFETs are being replaced by MOSFETs, JFETs are not covered in the later edition of Rashid's textbook).

COMPUTER SIMULATION

Software tools: PSpice, OrCAD, Multisim, LTSpice, or any electronic circuit simulator.

Note: If these JFETs are not available, use any other JFET that is available.

1. Simulate the circuit shown in Fig. 19-1 by using computer simulation to plot the output characteristics of the JFET J2N3819. The dc drain voltage source V_{DD} has a nominal value of 5 V, and it is varied from 0 to 15 V with an increment of 0.1 V. The dc gate-source voltage source V_{GS} has a nominal value of 2 V, and it is varied from 0 to –3 V with an increment of –0.5 V.
2. Plot the output characteristics i_D versus v_{DS} for various values of the gate-source voltage V_{GS} as shown in Fig. 19-2. Add the line for V_{DD} = 12 V and R_D = 1 kΩ. This is also shown in Fig. 19-2.
3. For the Q-point for V_{GS} = –1.5 V, find

   I_D = ________ mA; V_{DS} = ________ V

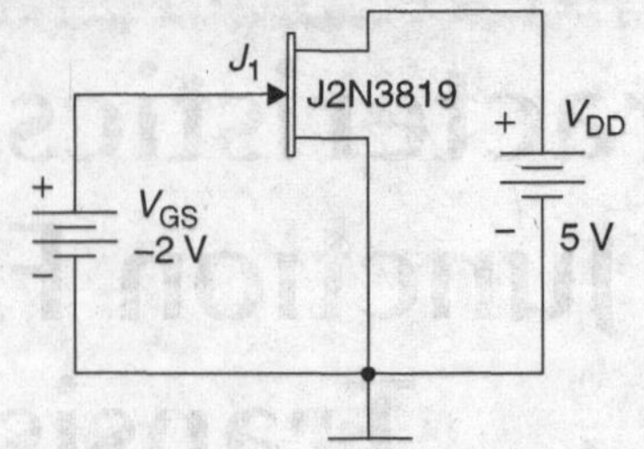

Figure 19-1 A JFET test circuit

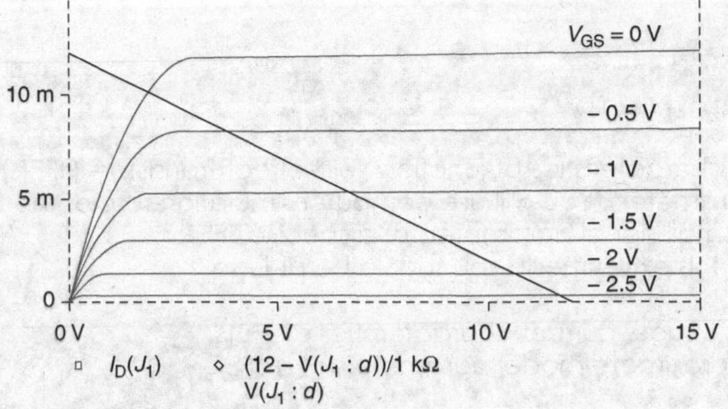

Figure 19-2 JFET characteristics

4. From the Q-point, find the small-signal model parameters.

$$g_m = \frac{2I_{DSS}}{|V_P|}\left(1 - \frac{V_{GS}}{V_p}\right) = \_\_\_\_\_\_\_\_ \text{mA/V}; \quad r_o = \frac{|V_m|}{I_D} = \_\_\_\_\_\_\_\_ \Omega$$

5. Simulate the self-biasing circuit in Fig. 19-3. From the simulation output file, find the small-signal JFET parameters and complete the simulated values in Table 19-1.

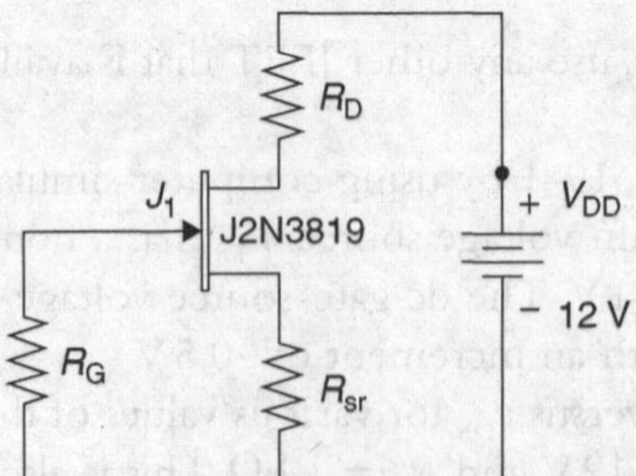

Figure 19-3 A self-biasing JFET circuit

Table 19-1 Self-biasing JFET circuit

	V_{GS} (V)	V_{DS} (V)	I_D (mA)	I_G (nA)	g_m (mA/V)	r_o (kΩ)
Calculated						
Simulated						
Experimental						

6. Run the sensitivity analysis of the circuit in Fig. 19-3 to find the sensitivity of the drain current I_D with respect to R_D and R_{sr}. Record the two sensitivity values.

   S_{RD} = ________; S_{Rsr} = ________

   I_D is most sensitive to which one of them, R_D or R_{sr}? Why?

   ____

   ____

7. If R_{sr} changes by ±10% and R_D changes by ±10%, what would be the percentage change in the drain current?

   ΔI_D = ________%

8. Find the resistor values of the self-biasing circuit in Fig. 19-4 so that I_D = 7 mA and V_{DS} = 5 V.

   R_D = ________ kΩ; R_{sr} = ________ kΩ; R_G = ________ kΩ

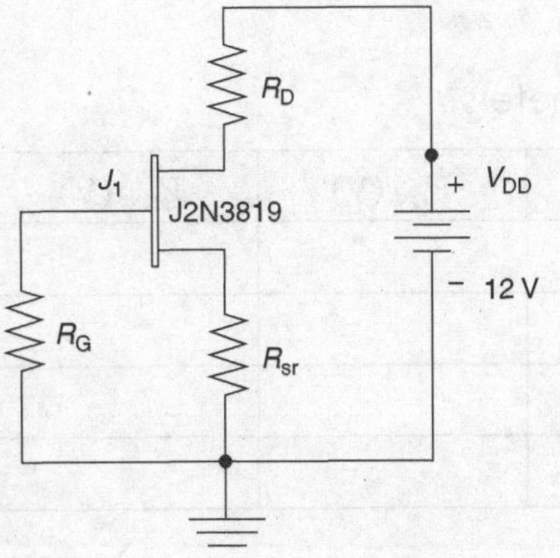

Figure 19-4 A self-biasing circuit

9. With those values in step 8, simulate the biasing circuit in Fig. 19-4. From the simulation output file, find the small-signal JFET parameters and complete the simulated values in Table 19-2.

Table 19-2 Design of self-biasing JFET circuit

	V_{GS} (V)	V_{DS} (V)	I_D (mA)	I_G (nA)	g_m (mA/V)	r_o (kΩ)
Calculated						
Simulated						
Experimental						

EXPERIMENTS

The students are strongly encouraged and recommended to build and test the JFET circuit to validate the theoretical and computer simulation results.

Procedure

Part 1

1. Use a curve tracer to plot the characteristics of your 2N3819 (or the one which is available). If a curve tracer is not available, skip Part 1.
2. Measure the small-signal transconductance g_m around the same operating point as in Fig. 19-3. Use the two nearest curves available.

   g_m = ________ mA/V

3. Use the cursors to measure the small-signal output resistance r_o at the same operating point. Note that r_o is the resistance proportional to the slope of the $i_D - v_{DS}$ curve, i.e., $1/r_o = \Delta i_D/\Delta v_{DS}$.

   r_o = ________ kΩ

4. Complete the curve-tracer values in Table 19-3.

Table 19-3 Transistor parameters

From	I_D (mA)	V_{GS} (V)	V_{DS} (V)	g_m (mA/V)	r_o (kΩ)
Curve tracer					
Simulated					
Data sheet					
Experimental					

Part 2

1. Set up the circuit shown in Fig. 19-3. Measure the biasing currents and voltages to complete Table 19-1.
2. Set up the circuit shown in Fig. 19-4. Measure the biasing currents and voltages to complete Table 19-2. Also, find the small-signal parameters to complete the practical values in Table 19-3.

REPORT

1. In designing the biasing point in Fig. 19-4, the values of I_D and V_{DS} were known. What would you do if these values are not given? Only V_{DS} and the peak value of the JFET, say, $I_{D(peak)} = I_{DSS} = 12$ mA are known. Explain.

2. As shown in Table 19-3, you can find the JFET parameters by different methods? Which one would you recommend? Why? Explain.

3. If you perform this experiment with a different transistor of the same type 2N3819, do you think you will get the same results? Explain your answer.

4. Analyze and interpret the data due to any variations and practical limitations.

5. Describe the safety issues considered while conducting the experiment.

6. Describe the process to design and conduct experiments.

7. Conclusion and comment on achieving goals or objectives of this experiment.

ATTACH ALL PLOTS/GRAPHS TO YOUR REPORT

CHAPTER

20

Design of a JFET Common-Source Amplifier

Learning Objectives

To design a JFET common-source amplifier to give a specified voltage gain. You will use computer simulation to verify the design and evaluate the performance of the amplifier.

After the end of this experiment, you will be able to

- Describe the operation of a JFET common-source amplifier and its small-signal equivalent circuit.
- Analyze and design a JFET common-source amplifier to meet the given specifications.

PRE-LAB ASSIGNMENT

Read on *Junction Field-Effect Transistors* (e.g., Rashid's Section 5.3: Field-Effect Transistors, Microelectronics, 1/e, 1999). Since JFETs are being replaced by MOSFETs, JFETs are not covered in the later edition of Rashid's Textbook).

DESIGN SPECIFICATIONS

Design the JFET common-source amplifier as shown in Fig. 20-1 to meet the following specifications:

- Voltage gain, $|A_v| = v_o/v_s = 5 \pm 5\%$
- Input resistance, $R_i = v_i/i_s \geq 500\ \text{k}\Omega$
- Load resistance, $R_L = 10\ \text{k}\Omega$
- Source resistance, $R_s = 200\ \Omega$
- DC supply, $V_{DD} = 12$ V
- Input signal, $v_s = 0-10$ mV (peak sinusoidal)
- Use JFET 2N3819 (if not available, use any other JFET)
- Quiescent drain current, $I_D = 5$ mA (assumed)

PAPER–PENCIL DESIGN

Note: Select the passive component values closest to the practical values.

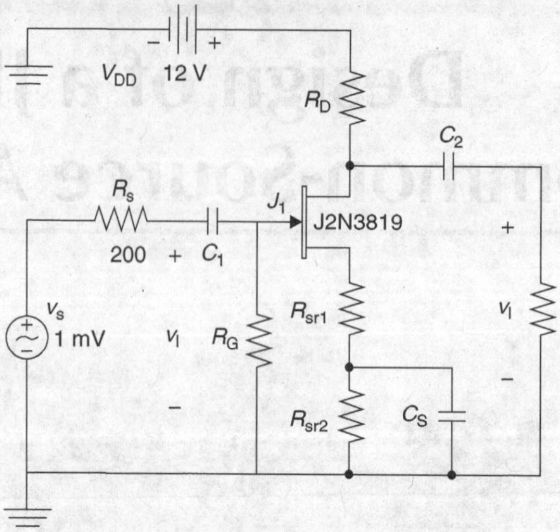

Figure 20-1 A JFET amplifier

1. After completing your paper–pencil design, write the circuit values.

R_D = ________ kΩ; R_G = ________ kΩ; R_{SR} (= R_{sr1} + R_{sr2}) = ________ kΩ

R_{sr1} = ________ Ω; R_{sr2} = ________ Ω

C_1 = ________ μF; C_2 = ________ μF; C_S = ________ μF

2. Complete the calculated values in Table 20-1.

Table 20-1 Biasing values and JFET parameters

	I_D (mA)	V_{GS} (V)	V_{DS} (V)	V_{SR}	V_G	r_o (kΩ)	g_m (mA/V)
Calculated							
Simulated							
Experimental							

COMPUTER SIMULATION

Software tools: PSpice, OrCAD, Multisim, LTSpice, or any electronic circuit simulator.

1. Simulate the amplifier circuit shown in Fig. 20-1 by using computer simulation to find the dc biasing information. From the simulation output file, complete the simulated values in Table 20-1.
2. Simulate the amplifier by using computer simulation to plot the output voltage $v_L(t)$ across the load resistance R_L.

Note: Since your input signal v_s is sinusoidal, the output voltage v_o should ideally be sinusoidal. If your output is distorted significantly, then your dc operating point is not set properly and you need to redesign your biasing circuit. A properly designed biasing circuit should allow the maximum swing of the drain current and the drain–source voltage without introducing any significant amount of signal distortion.

3. Plot the input signal voltage $v_s(t)$, output voltage $v_L(t)$, the voltage gain $A_v = v_L/v_s$, and the input resistance $R_i = v_i/i_s$. Record.

$v_{L(peak)}$ = ________ mV; $v_{s(peak)}$ = ________ mV; $A_v = \frac{v_{L\,(peak)}}{v_{s\,(peak)}}$ = ________

$R_i = \frac{v_{i\,(peak)}}{i_{s\,(peak)}}$ = ________ MΩ

4. Assign ±5% tolerance to all capacitors and resistors. Run the simulation for the worst-case maximum output voltage and record.

$v_{L(peak)}$ = ________ mV; $v_{s(peak)}$ = ________ mV; $A_v = \frac{v_{L\,(peak)}}{v_{s\,(peak)}}$ = ________

$R_i = \frac{v_{i\,(peak)}}{i_{s\,(peak)}}$ = ________ MΩ

5. Does your design meet the specifications under the worst-case conditions? If not, which resistance would you adjust to get the desired gain? Why? Explain.

____

____

Change the component values so that the specifications are met. Note these values.

____________ ____________ ____________

6. Reduce R_{sr1} to zero, and find the maximum voltage gain.

$A_{v\,(max)} = \frac{v_{L\,(peak)}}{v_{s\,(peak)}}$ = ________

7. If you find that the maximum voltage gain $A_{v(max)}$ is less than your desired value, what should you do? How would you meet the gain specifications? Explain.

____

____

8. Run the computer simulation with your suggested values in step 5 (try adjusting R_{sr1} and R_{sr2}) and complete the simulated values in Table 20-2.

Table 20-2 MOSFET amplifier parameters

	$R_i = v_{i(peak)}/i_{s(peak)}$ (kΩ)	$R_{in} = v_{s(peak)}/i_{s(peak)}$ (kΩ)	R_o (Ω)	$A_v = v_{L(peak)}/v_{s(peak)}$
Calculated				
Simulated				
Experimental				

9. To find the output resistance R_o, run the simulation for $R_L = \infty$ (or say 10 MΩ), 10 kΩ. Calculate the output resistance R_o of the amplifier from the equation.

$$R_o = R_L\left[\frac{V_{L\,(no\text{-}load)} - V_{L\,(full\text{-}load)}}{V_{L\,(full\text{-}load)}}\right] = \_\_\_\_\_\_\_\_ \Omega \tag{20.1}$$

10. Comment on the effects of the component tolerance on the design.

____

____

EXPERIMENTS

The students are strongly encouraged and recommended to build and test the amplifier circuit to validate the theoretical and computer simulation results.

1. Set up your final amplifier circuit. Observe the output voltage $v_L(t)$ and its peak value V_m.
2. Take dc biasing measurements to complete the experimental values in Table 20-1.
3. Measure: $v_{L(peak)}$ = ________ mV; $v_{s(peak)}$ = ________ mV; $A_v = \frac{v_{L\,(peak)}}{v_{s\,(peak)}}$ = ________ V/V

   $R_i = \frac{v_{i\,(peak)}}{i_{s\,(peak)}}$ = ________ kΩ; $R_{in} = \frac{v_{s\,(peak)}}{i_{s\,(peak)}}$ = ________ kΩ
4. Measure the output resistance R_o of the amplifier.

   $V_{L(no\ load)}$ = ________ mV; $V_{L(full\ load)}$ = ________ mV; R_o = ________ Ω
5. Complete the experimental values in Table 20-2.

REPORT

1. Compare the results in Table 20-2 and comment on any discrepancies.

____

____

2. Does the voltage gain remain within the specifications? If not, explain the reasons.

3. What are the parameters that influence the output resistance R_o of the amplifier? Explain.

4. What is the estimated cost of the amplifier?

5. Analyze and interpret the data due to any variations and practical limitations.

6. Describe the safety issues considered while conducting the experiment.

7. Describe the process to design and conduct experiments.

8. Conclusion and comment on achieving goals or objectives of this experiment.

ATTACH ALL PLOTS/GRAPHS TO YOUR REPORT

CHAPTER

21 Characteristics and Biasing of MOSFETs

Learning Objectives

To investigate the characteristics of metal-oxide semiconductor field-effect transistors (MOSFETs) and to determine the MOSFET model parameters. You will use computer simulation to plot the MOSFET characteristics and to derive the small-signal parameters of a specific MOSFET.

After the end of this experiment, you should be able to

- Describe the voltage–current characteristics of MOSFETs.
- Derive the approximate model parameters of a MOSFET.

PRE-LAB ASSIGNMENT

Read on *Field-Effect Transistors* (e.g., Rashid's Section 6.10: MOSFET Amplifiers).

COMPUTER SIMULATION

Software tools: PSpice, OrCAD, Multisim, LTSpice, or any electronic circuit simulator.

Note: If these MOSFETs are not available, use any other MOSFET that is available.

1. Simulate the circuit shown in Fig. 21-1 by using computer simulation to plot the output characteristics of the MOSFET IRF 150 (or any other MOSFET that is available in your lab). The dc drain voltage source V_{DD} has a nominal value of 5 V, and it is varied from 0 to 15 V with an increment of 0.1 V. The dc gate–source voltage V_{GS} has a nominal value of 3 V, and it is varied from 0 to 3.6 V with an increment of 0.2 V.
2. Plot the output characteristics i_D versus v_{DS} for various values of the gate–source voltage v_{GS} as shown in Fig. 21-2. Add the line for V_{DD} = 12 V and R_D = 12 Ω. This is also shown in Fig. 21-2.
3. For the Q-point for V_{GS} = 3.2 V, find

   I_D = ________ mA; V_{DS} = ________ V; I_G = ________ pA

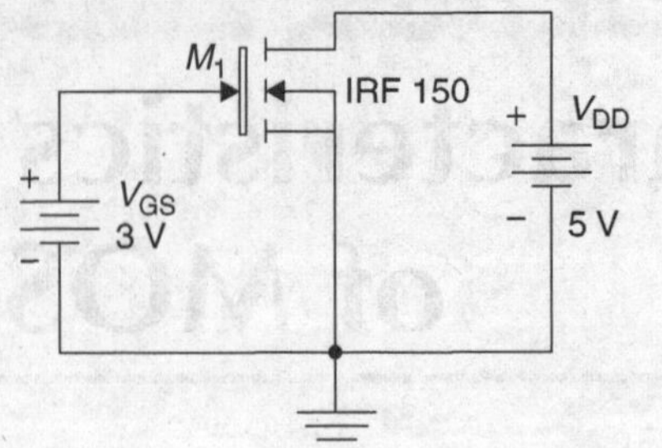

Figure 21-1 A MOSFET test circuit

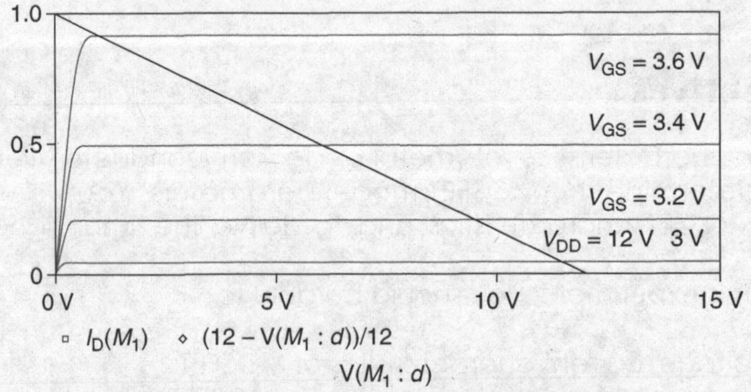

Figure 21-2 MOSFET characteristics

4. From the Q-point, find the small signal model parameters.

$g_m = 2K_p(V_{GS} - V_t) =$ ________ mA/V; $r_0 = \dfrac{|V_M|}{I_D} =$ ________ kΩ

5. Repeat steps 1–4 for the p-channel MOSFET IRF9140. Find the Q-point and the model parameters.

$V_{GS} = -4$V; $I_D =$ ________ mA; $I_G =$ ________ pA

$g_m = 2K_p(V_{GS} - V_t) =$ ________ mA/V; $r_0 = \dfrac{|V_M|}{I_D} =$ ________ kΩ

6. Find the resistor values of the MOSFET biasing circuit in Fig. 21-3 so that $I_D = 10$ mA and $V_{DS} = 3$V.

$R_D =$ ________ kΩ; $R_{sr} =$ ________ kΩ; $R_{G1} =$ ________ MΩ

7. Complete the calculated values in Table 21-1.
8. With those values in step 6, simulate the biasing circuit in Fig. 21-3. From the simulation output file, find the small-signal MOSFET parameters and complete the simulated values in Table 21-1.
9. Run the sensitivity analysis of the circuit in Fig. 21-3 to find the sensitivity of the drain current I_D with respect to R_D and R_{sr}. Record the two sensitivity values:

$s_{RD} =$ ________; $s_{Rsr} =$ ________

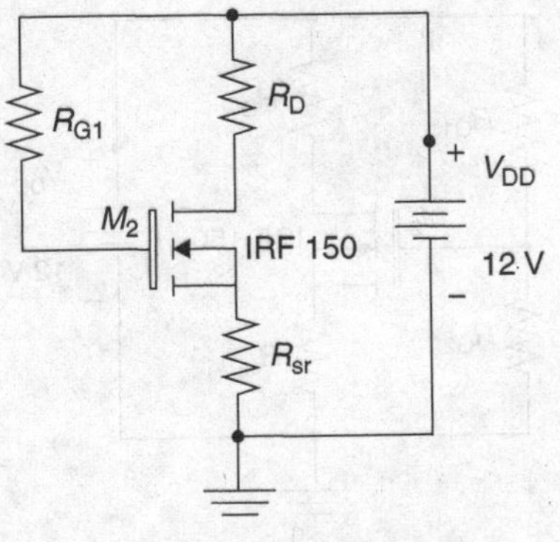

Figure 21-3 A MOSFET biasing circuit

Table 21-1 Design of MOSFET biasing circuit

	V_{GS} (V)	V_{DS} (V)	I_D (mA)	I_G (nA)	g_m (mA/V^2)
Calculated					
Simulated					
Practical					

I_D is more sensitive to which of the two, R_D or R_{sr}? Why? Explain.

____

____

If R_{sr} changes by ±10% and R_D changes by 10%, what would be percentage change in the drain current?

ΔI_D = __________%

10. Find the resistor values of the stabilized-biasing circuit in Fig. 21-4 so that I_D = 1 mA and V_{DS} = 3 V. Complete the calculated values in Table 21-2.

R_D = ________ kΩ; R_{sr} = ________ kΩ; R_{G1} = ________ MΩ; R_{G2} = ________ MΩ

11. With those values in step 10, simulate the biasing circuit in Fig. 21-4. From the simulation output file, find the small-signal MOSFET parameters and complete simulated values in Table 21-2.

Table 21-2 Design of MOSFET stabilized-biasing circuit

	V_{GS} (V)	V_{DS} (V)	I_D (mA)	I_G (nA)	g_m (mA/V^2)	r_o (kΩ)
Calculated						
Simulated						
Experimental						

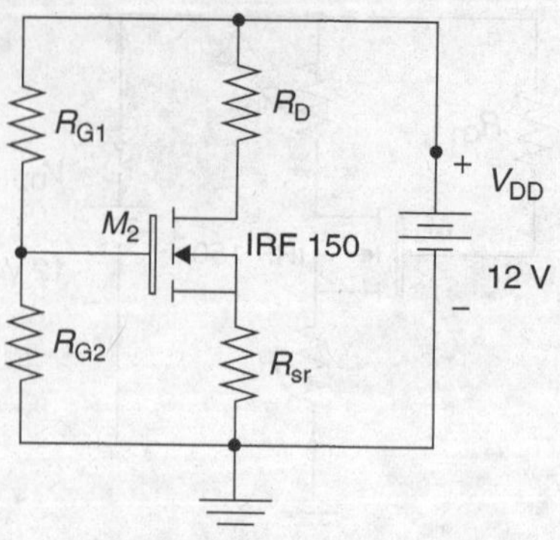

Figure 21-4 A MOSFET stabilized-biasing circuit

EXPERIMENTS

The students are strongly encouraged and recommended to build and test the diode circuit to validate the theoretical and computer simulation results.

Procedure

Part 1

1. Use a curve tracer to plot the characteristics of your IRF150 (or the one which is available). If a curve tracer I_s is not available, skip Part 1.
2. Measure the small-signal transconductance g_m around the same operating point as in Fig. 21-3. Use the two nearest curves available.

   g_m = ________ mA/V

3. Use the cursors to measure the small-signal output resistance r_o at the same operating point. Note that r_o is the resistance proportional to the slope of the $i_D - v_{DS}$ curve, i.e., $1/r_o = \Delta i_D/\Delta v_{DS}$.

   R_o = ________ kΩ

4. Complete the curve-tracer values in Table 21-3.

Table 21-3 MOSFET parameters

From	I_D (mA)	V_{GS} (V)	V_{DS} (V)	g_m (mA/V²)	r_o (kΩ)
Curve tracer					
Simulated					
Data sheet					
Practical					

Part 2

1. Set up the circuit shown in Fig. 21-3. Measure the biasing currents and voltages to complete the practical values in Table 21-1.
2. Set up the circuit shown in Fig. 21-4. Measure the biasing currents and voltages to complete the practical values in Table 21-2. Also, find the small-signal parameters to complete the practical values in Table 21-3.

REPORT

1. In designing the biasing point in Fig. 21-4 (or Fig. 10-3), the values of I_D and V_{DS} were known. What would you do if these values are not given? Only V_{DS} and the MOSFET type (say IRF150) are known. Explain.

____

____

2. As shown in Table 21-3, you can find the MOSFET parameters by different methods. Which one would you recommend? Why? Explain.

____

____

3. If you perform this experiment with a different transistor of the same type as IRF150, do you think you will get the same results? Explain your answer.

____

____

4. Analyze and interpret the data due to any variations and practical limitations.

____

____

5. Describe the safety issues considered while conducting the experiment.

____

____

6. Describe the process to design and conduct experiments.

____

____

7. Conclusion and comment on achieving goals or objectives of this experiment.

____

____

____

ATTACH ALL PLOTS/GRAPHS TO YOUR REPORT

CHAPTER 22

Design of a MOSFET Common-Source Amplifier

Learning Objectives

To design a MOSFET common-source amplifier to give a specified voltage gain. You will use computer simulation to verify the design and evaluate the performance of the amplifier.

After the end of this experiment, you will be able to

- Describe the operation of a MOSFET common-source amplifier and its small-signal equivalent circuit.
- Analyze and design a MOSFET common-source amplifier to meet the given specifications.

PRE-LAB ASSIGNMENT

Read on *MOSFET Common-Source Amplifiers* (e.g., Rashid's Section 6.15: Common-Source Amplifiers with a Resistive Load).

DESIGN SPECIFICATIONS

Design the MOSFET common-source amplifier (as shown in Fig. 22-1) to meet the following specifications:

- Voltage gain, $|A_v| = v_o/v_s = 5 \pm 5\%$
- Input resistance, $R_i = v_i/i_s \geq 1\ \text{M}\Omega$
- Load resistance, $R_L = 10\ \text{k}\Omega$
- Source resistance, $R_s = 1\ \text{k}\Omega$
- DC supply voltage, $V_{DD} = 12$ V
- Input signal, $v_s = 0$–1 mV (peak sinusoidal)
- Use MOSFET IRF150 (if not available, use any other MOSFET that is available)
- Quiescent drain current, $I_D = 5$ mA (assumed)

PAPER–PENCIL DESIGN

Note: Select the passive component values closest to the practical values.

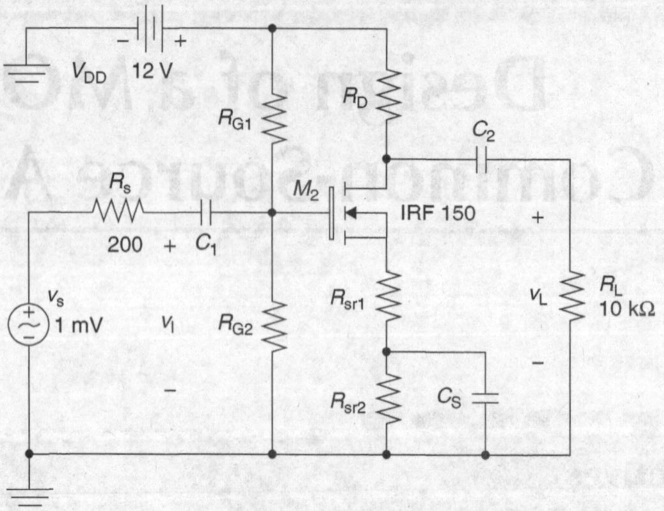

Figure 22-1 A MOSFET amplifier

1. After completing your paper–pencil design, write the circuit values.

R_D = ________ kΩ; R_{G1} = ________ MΩ; R_{G2} = ________ MΩ

R_{SR} (= $R_{sr1} + R_{sr2}$) = ________ kΩ; R_{sr1} = ________ Ω; R_{sr2} = ________ Ω

C_1 = ________ μF; C_2 = ________ μF; C_S = ________ μF

2. Complete the calculated values in Table 22-1.

Table 22-1 Biasing values and MOSFET parameters

	I_D (mA)	V_{GS} (V)	V_{DS} (V)	V_{SR}	V_G	r_o (kΩ)	g_m (mA/V²)
Calculated							
Simulated							
Experimental							

COMPUTER SIMULATION

Software tools: PSpice, OrCAD, Multisim, LTSpice, or any electronic circuit simulator.

1. Simulate the amplifier circuit shown in Fig. 22-1 by using computer simulation to find the dc biasing information. From the simulation output file, complete the simulated values in Table 22-1.
2. Simulate the amplifier by using computer simulation to plot the output voltage $v_L(t)$ across the load resistance R_L.

Note: Since your input signal v_s is sinusoidal, the output voltage v_o should ideally be sinusoidal. If your output is distorted significantly, then your dc operating point is not set properly and you need to redesign your biasing circuit. A properly designed biasing circuit should allow the maximum swing of the drain current and the drain–source voltage without introducing any significant amount of signal distortion.

3. Plot the input signal voltage $v_s(t)$, output voltage $v_L(t)$, voltage gain $A_v = v_L/v_s$, and input resistance $R_i = v_i/i_s$. Record.

$v_{L(peak)}$ = ________ mV; $v_{s(peak)}$ = ________ mV; $A_v = \frac{v_{L\,(peak)}}{v_{s\,(peak)}}$ = ________

$R_i = \frac{v_{i\,(peak)}}{i_{s\,(peak)}}$ = ________ MΩ

4. Assign ±5% tolerance to all capacitors and resistors. Run the simulation for the worst-case maximum output voltage and record.

$v_{L(peak)}$ = ________ mV; $v_{s(peak)}$ = ________ mV; $A_v = \frac{v_{L\,(peak)}}{v_{s\,(peak)}}$ = ________

$R_i = \frac{v_{i\,(peak)}}{i_{s\,(peak)}}$ = ________ MΩ

5. Does your design meet the specifications under the worst-case conditions? If not, which resistance would you adjust to get the desired gain? Why? Explain.

____

____

Change the component values so that the specifications are met. Note these values.

________________ ________________ ________________

6. Reduce R_{sr1} to zero, and find the maximum voltage gain.

$A_{v\,(max)} = \frac{v_{L\,(peak)}}{v_{s\,(peak)}}$ = ________

7. If you find that the maximum voltage gain $A_{v(max)}$ is less than your desired value, what should you do? How would you meet the gain specifications? Explain.

____

____

8. Run the computer simulation with your suggested values in step 5 (try adjusting R_{sr1} and R_{sr2}) and complete the simulated values in Table 22-2.

Table 22-2 MOSFET amplifier parameters

	$R_i = v_{i(peak)}/i_{s(peak)}$ (kΩ)	$R_{in} = v_{s(peak)}/i_{s(peak)}$ (kΩ)	R_o (Ω)	$A_v = v_{L(peak)}/v_{s(peak)}$
Calculated				
Simulated				
Experimental				

9. To find the output resistance R_o, run the simulation for $R_L = \infty$ (or say 10 MΩ), 10 kΩ. Calculate the output resistance R_o of the amplifier from the equation.

$$R_o = R_L \left[\frac{V_{L\,(no\text{-}load)} - V_{L\,(full\text{-}load)}}{V_{L\,(full\text{-}load)}} \right] = \_\_\_\_\_\_\_\_ \Omega \tag{22.1}$$

10. Comment on the effects of the component tolerance on the design.

____

____

EXPERIMENTS

The students are strongly encouraged and recommended to build and test the amplifier circuit to validate the theoretical and computer simulation results.

1. Set up your final amplifier circuit. Observe the output voltage $v_L(t)$ and its peak value V_m.
2. Take dc biasing measurements to complete the experimental values in Table 22-1.

3. Measure: $v_{L(peak)}$ = ________ mV; $v_{s(peak)}$ = ________ mV; $A_v = \dfrac{v_{L\,(peak)}}{v_{s\,(peak)}}$ = ________ V/V

$R_i = \dfrac{v_{i\,(peak)}}{i_{s\,(peak)}}$ = ________ kΩ; $R_{in} = \dfrac{v_{s\,(peak)}}{i_{s(peak)}}$ = ________ kΩ

4. Measure the output resistance R_o of the amplifier.

$V_{L(no\ load)}$ = ________ mV; $V_{L(full\ load)}$ = ________ mV; R_o = ________ Ω

5. Complete the experimental values in Table 22-2.

REPORT

1. Compare the results in Tables 20-2, and comment on any discrepancies.

____

____

2. Does the voltage gain remain within the specifications? If not, explain the reasons.

3. What are the parameters that influence the output resistance R_o of the amplifier? Explain.

4. What is the estimated cost of the amplifier?

5. Analyze and interpret the data due to any variations and practical limitations.

6. Describe the safety issues considered while conducting the experiment.

7. Describe the process to design and conduct experiments.

8. Conclusion and comment on achieving goals or objectives of this experiment.

ATTACH ALL PLOTS/GRAPHS TO YOUR REPORT

CHAPTER

23 Design of a MOSFET Common-Drain Amplifier

Learning Objectives

To design MOSFET common-drain amplifiers to give a unity voltage gain, a low output resistance, and a high input resistance. We will use computer simulation to verify the design and evaluate the performance of the amplifiers.

After the end of this experiment, you will be able to

- Describe the operation and characteristics of a common-drain amplifier.
- Analyze and design a common-drain amplifier to meet the given specifications.

PRE-LAB ASSIGNMENT

Read on *Common-Drain Amplifiers* (e.g., Rashid's Section 5.16: Common-Drain Amplifiers).

DESIGN SPECIFICATIONS

Design the common-drain amplifier (source follower) as shown in Fig. 23-1 to meet the following specifications:

- Voltage gain, $|A_v| = v_o/v_s \cong 1$
- Input resistance, $R_i = v_i/i_s \geq 500$ kΩ
- Output resistance, $R_o \leq 250$ Ω
- Load resistance, $R_L = 10$ kΩ
- Source resistance, $R_s = 200$ Ω
- DC supply voltage, $V_{DD} = 12$ V
- Input signal, $v_s = 0$–2 mV (peak sinusoidal), 1 kHz
- Use MOSFET IRF150 (if not available, use any other MOSFET that is available).
- Quiescent drain current, $I_D = 5$ mA (assumed)

PAPER–PENCIL DESIGN

Note: Select the passive component values closest to the practical values.

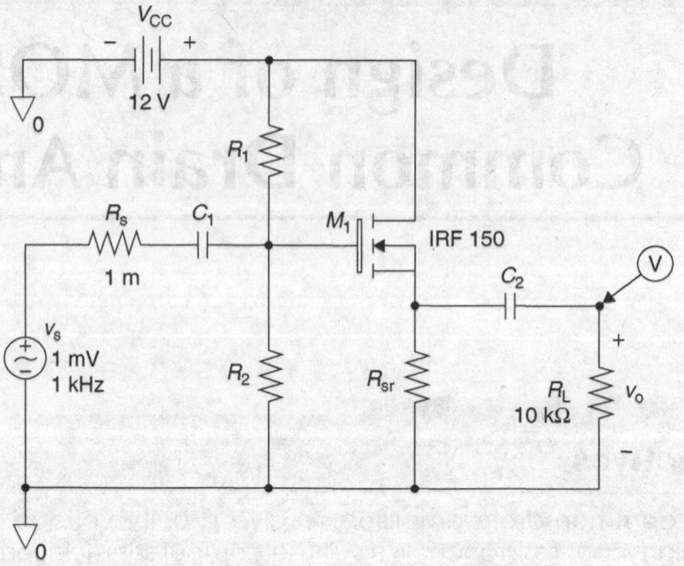

Figure 23-1 A MOSFET source follower

1. After completing your paper–pencil design, write the circuit values.

   R_1 = ________ kΩ; R_2 = ________ kΩ; R_{sr} = ________ kΩ

   C_1 = ________ μF; C_2 = ________ μF

2. Complete the calculated values in Table 23-1.

Table 23-1 Biasing values of MOSFET source follower

	I_D (mA)	V_{GS} (V)	V_{DS} (V)	V_{SR}	V_G	r_o (kΩ)	g_m (mA/V²)
Calculated							
Simulated							
Experimental							

COMPUTER SIMULATION

Software tools: PSpice, OrCAD, Multisim, LTSpice, or any electronic circuit simulator.

1. Simulate the source-follower circuit shown in Fig. 23-1 by using computer simulation to find the dc biasing information. From the simulation output file, complete simulated values in Table 23-1.
2. Simulate the amplifier by using computer simulation to plot the output voltage $v_L(t)$ across the load resistance R_L.
   Note: Since your input signal v_s is sinusoidal, the output voltage v_L should ideally be sinusoidal. If your output is distorted significantly, then your dc operating point is not set properly and you need to redesign your biasing circuit. A properly designed biasing circuit should allow the maximum swing of

the collector current and the collector–emitter voltage without introducing any significant amount of signal distortion.

3. Plot the input signal voltage $v_s(t)$, output voltage $v_L(t)$, voltage gain $A_v = v_L/v_s$, and the input resistance $R_i = v_i/i_s$. Record.

$v_{L(peak)}$ = ________ mV; $v_{s(peak)}$ = ________ mV; $A_v = \frac{v_{L(peak)}}{v_{s(peak)}}$ = ________ V/V

$R_i = \frac{v_{i(peak)}}{i_{s(peak)}}$ = ________ kΩ

4 Assign ±5% tolerance to all capacitors and resistors. Run the simulation for the worst-case maximum output voltage and record.

$v_{L(peak)}$ = ________ mV; $v_{s(peak)}$ = ________ mV; $A_v = \frac{v_{o(peak)}}{v_{s(peak)}}$ = ________

$R_i = \frac{v_{i(peak)}}{i_{s(peak)}}$ = ________ kΩ

5. To find the output resistance R_o, run the simulation for $R_L = \infty$ (or say 10 MΩ), 10 kΩ. Calculate the output resistance R_o of the amplifier from the following equation:

$$R_o = R_L \left[\frac{V_{L\,(no\text{-}load)} - V_{L\,(full\text{-}load)}}{V_{L\,(full\text{-}load)}} \right] = \underline{\qquad\qquad}\ \Omega \tag{23.1}$$

6. Does your design meet the specifications under the worst-case conditions? If not, which resistance would you adjust to get the desired gain? Why?

____

____

Change the component values so that the specifications are met. Note these values.

________________ ________________ ________________

7. Run the computer simulation with your suggested values in step 6 (try adjusting R_E) and complete the simulated values in Table 23-2.

Table 23-2 Source-follower parameters

	$R_i = v_{i(peak)}/i_{s(peak)}$ (kΩ)	$R_{in} = v_{s(peak)}/i_{s(peak)}$ (kΩ)	R_o (Ω)	$A_v = v_{L(peak)}/v_{s(peak)}$
Calculated				
Simulated				
Experimental				

8. Comment on the effects of the component tolerance on the design.

____

____

EXPERIMENTS

The students are strongly encouraged and recommended to build and test the amplifier circuit to validate the theoretical and computer simulation results.

1. Set up your final emitter-follower circuit in Fig. 23-1. Take dc biasing measurements to complete the experimental values in Table 23-1.
2. Observe the output voltage $v_L(t)$ and its peak value V_m.
3. Measure: $v_{L(peak)}$ = ________ mV; $v_{s(peak)}$ = ________ mV; $A_v = \frac{v_{L\,(peak)}}{v_{s\,(peak)}}$ = ________ V/V

   $R_i = \frac{v_{i\,(peak)}}{i_{s\,(peak)}}$ = ________ kΩ; $R_{in} = \frac{v_{s(peak)}}{i_{s(peak)}}$ = ________ kΩ

4. Measure the output resistance R_o of the amplifier.

   $V_{L(no\ load)}$ = ________ mV; $V_{L(full\ load)}$ = ________ mV; R_o = ________ Ω

5. Complete the experimental values in Table 23-2.

REPORT

1. Compare the results in Tables 23-2 and comment on any discrepancies.

____

____

____

2. Does the output resistance remain within the specifications? If not, explain the reasons.

____

____

____

3. What are the parameters that influence the output resistance R_o? Explain.

____

____

____

4. What is the estimated cost of the amplifier?

5. Analyze and interpret the data due to any variations and practical limitations.

6. Describe the safety issues considered while conducting the experiment.

7. Describe the process to design and conduct experiments.

8. Conclusion and comment on achieving goals or objectives of this experiment.

ATTACH ALL PLOTS/GRAPHS TO YOUR REPORT

CHAPTER

24 Design of a Multistage MOSFET Amplifier

Learning Objectives

To design a multistage MOSFET amplifier to give a specified voltage gain. You will use computer simulation to verify the design and evaluate the performance of the amplifier.

After the end of this experiment, you will be able to

- Describe the operation of a multi-stage amplifier.
- Analyze and design a multi-stage amplifier to meet given specifications.

PRE-LAB ASSIGNMENT

Read on *Multistage BJT Amplifiers* (e.g., Rashid's Section 5.20: Multistage Amplifiers).

DESIGN SPECIFICATIONS

Design the multistage MOSFET amplifier as shown in Fig. 24-1 to meet the following specifications. The values as shown in Fig. 24-1 are only for illustrations, not the correct values.

- Voltage gain, $|A_v| = v_L/v_s = 35 \pm 5\%$
- Input resistance, $R_i = v_i/i_s \geq 500\ \text{k}\Omega$
- Output resistance, $R_o \leq 250\ \Omega$
- Load resistance, $R_L = 10\ \text{k}\Omega$
- Source resistance, $R_s = 200\ \Omega$ (you will need to add resistance in series with the signal generator)
- dc supply voltage, $V_{DD} = 12\text{V}$
- Input signal, $v_s = 0\text{–}10$ mV (peak sinusoidal), 1 kHz
- Use MOSFET IRF150 (if not available, use any other MOSFET that is available).
- Quiescent drain current, $I_D = 5$ mA (assumed)

PAPER–PENCIL DESIGN

Note: Select the passive component values closest to the practical values. The component values in Fig. 24-1 are shown for illustrations only.

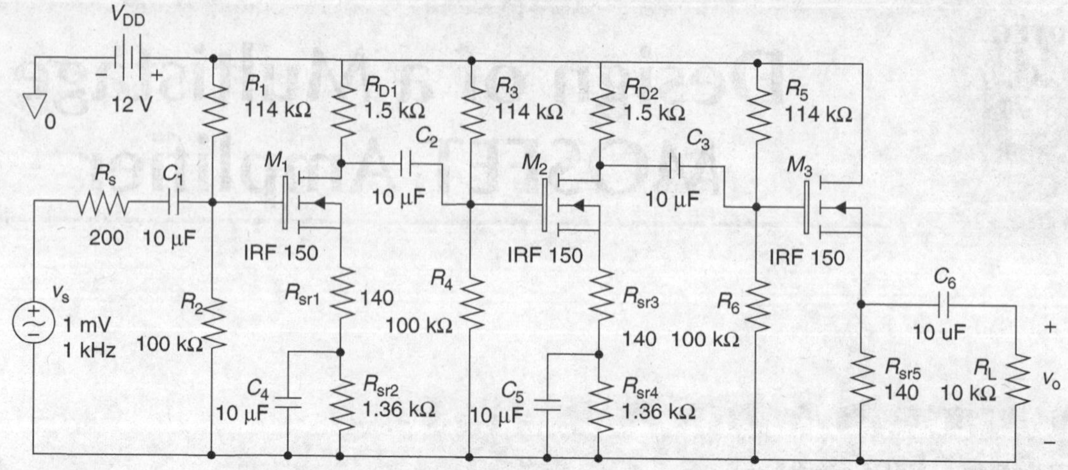

Figure 24-1 A multistage MOSFET amplifier

1. After completing your paper–pencil design, write the circuit values.

R_{D1} = ________ kΩ; R_{D2} = ________ kΩ

R_1 = ________ kΩ; R_2 = ________ kΩ; R_3 = ________ kΩ

R_4 = ________ kΩ; R_5 = ________ kΩ; R_6 = ________ kΩ

R_{srr1} = ________ Ω: R_{sr2} = ________ Ω; R_{sr3} = ________ Ω

R_{sr4} = ________ Ω; R_{er55} = ________ Ω

C_1 = ________ μF; C_2 = ________ μF; C_3 = ________ μF

C_4 = ________ μF; C_5 = ________ μF

COMPUTER SIMULATION

Software tools: PSpice, OrCAD, Multisim, LTSpice, or any electronic circuit simulator.

1. Simulate the amplifier by using computer simulation to plot the output voltage $v_L(t)$ across the load resistance R_L.
   Note: Since your input signal v_s is sinusoidal, the output voltage v_L should ideally be sinusoidal. If your output is distorted significantly, then your dc operating point is not set properly and you need to redesign your biasing circuit. A properly designed biasing circuit should allow the maximum swing of the collector currents and the collector–emitter voltages without introducing any significant amount of signal distortion.
2. Plot the input signal voltage $v_s(t)$, output voltage $v_L(t)$, voltage gain $A_v = v_L/v_s$, and input resistance $R_i = v_i/i_s$. Record.

$v_{L(peak)}$ = ________ mV; $v_{s(peak)}$ = ________ mV; $A_v = \frac{v_{L\,(peak)}}{v_{s\,(peak)}}$ = ________

$R_i = \frac{v_{i\,(peak)}}{i_{s\,(peak)}} =$ ________ kΩ

3. Assign ±5% tolerance to all capacitors and resistors. Run the simulation for the worst-case maximum output voltage and record.

$v_{L(peak)} =$ ________ mV; $v_{s(peak)} =$ ________ mV; $A_v = \frac{v_{o\,(peak)}}{v_{s\,(peak)}} =$ ________

$R_i = \frac{v_{i\,(peak)}}{i_{s\,(peak)}} =$ ________ kΩ

4. Does your design meet the specifications under the worst-case conditions? If not, which resistance would you adjust to get the desired gain? Why? Explain.

____

____

Change the component values so that the specifications are met. Note these values.

________ ________ ________ ________

5. Reduce R_{E1} and R_{E3} to zero (while increasing R_{E2} and R_{E4} by the same amount) and find the maximum voltage gain.

$A_{v\,(max)} = \frac{v_{L\,(peak)}}{v_{s\,(peak)}} =$ ________ V/V

6. If you find that the maximum voltage gain $A_{v(max)}$ is less than the desired value, what should you do? How would you meet the gain specifications? Explain.

____

____

7. Run the simulation with your suggested values in step 4 and complete the simulated values in Table 24-1.
8. To find the output resistance R_o, run the simulation for $R_L = \infty$ (or say 10 MΩ), 10 kΩ. Calculate the output resistance R_o of the amplifier from the equation.

$$R_o = R_L \left[\frac{V_{L\,(no\text{-}load)} - V_{L\,(full\text{-}load)}}{V_{L\,(full\text{-}load)}} \right] = \text{\_\_\_\_\_\_\_\_ } \Omega \qquad (24.1)$$

9. Comment on the effects of the component tolerance on the design.

____

____

Table 24-1 Multistage JFET amplifier parameters

	$R_i = v_{i(peak)}/i_{s(peak)}$ (kΩ)	$R_{in} = v_{s(peak)}/i_{s(peak)}$ (kΩ)	R_o (Ω)	$A_v = v_{L(peak)}/v_{s(peak)}$
Calculated				
Simulated				
Experimental				

EXPERIMENTS

The students are strongly encouraged and recommended to build and test the amplifier circuit to validate the theoretical and computer simulation results.

1. Set up your final amplifier circuit. Observe the output voltage $v_L(t)$ and its peak value V_m.

2. Measure: $v_{L(peak)}$ = ________ mV; $v_{s(peak)}$ = ________ mV; $A_v = \dfrac{v_{L(peak)}}{v_{s(peak)}}$ = ________ V/V

   $R_i = \dfrac{v_{i(peak)}}{i_{s(peak)}}$ = ________ kΩ; $R_{in} = \dfrac{v_{s(peak)}}{i_{s(peak)}}$ = ________ kΩ

3. Measure the output resistance R_o of the amplifier.

   $V_{L(no\ load)}$ = ________ mV; $V_{L(full\ load)}$ = ________ mV; R_o = ________ Ω

4. Complete the experimental values in Table 24-1.

REPORT

1. Compare the results in Tables 24-1 and comment on any discrepancies.

____

____

2. Does the voltage gain remain within the specifications? If not, explain the reasons.

____

____

3. What are the parameters that influence the voltage gain A_v of the amplifier? Explain.

____

____

4. What is the estimated cost of the amplifier?

5. Analyze and interpret the data due to any variations and practical limitations.

6. Describe the safety issues considered while conducting the experiment.

7. Describe the process to design and conduct experiments.

8. Conclusion and comment on achieving goals or objectives of this experiment.

ATTACH ALL PLOTS/GRAPHS TO YOUR REPORT

CHAPTER 25

Design of a CS-MOSFET Amplifier for Frequency Response

Learning Objectives

To design a multistage MOSFET amplifier to give a specified voltage gain. You will use computer simulation to verify the design and evaluate the performance of the amplifier.

After the end of this experiment, you should be able to

- Describe the frequency characteristics of common-source amplifiers and the circuit elements that contribute to the frequency response.
- Analyze and design common-source amplifiers to meet certain frequency specifications.

PRE-LAB ASSIGNMENT

Read on *Frequency Response of MOSFET Amplifiers* (e.g., Rashid's Section 8.13: Frequency Response of Common-Source Amplifiers).

DESIGN SPECIFICATIONS

Design the MOSFET common-source amplifier as shown in Fig. 25-1 to meet the following specifications. The values shown in Fig. 25-1 are only for illustrations, not the correct values.

- Voltage gain, $|A_v| = v_o/v_s = 25 \pm 5\%$
- Low cut-off frequency, $f_L = 1$ kHz ± 5%
- High cut-off frequency, $f_H = 250$ kHz ± 5%
- Input resistance, $R_i = v_i/i_s \geq 500$ kΩ
- Load resistance, $R_L = 25$ kΩ
- Source resistance, $R_s = 200$ Ω
- dc supply voltage, $V_{DD} = 12$ V
- Input signal, $v_s = 0-1$ mV (peak sinusoidal), 230 Hz to 300 kHz
- Use MOSFET IRF150 (if not available, use any other MOSFET that is available).
- Quiescent drain current, $I_D = 5$ mA (assumed)

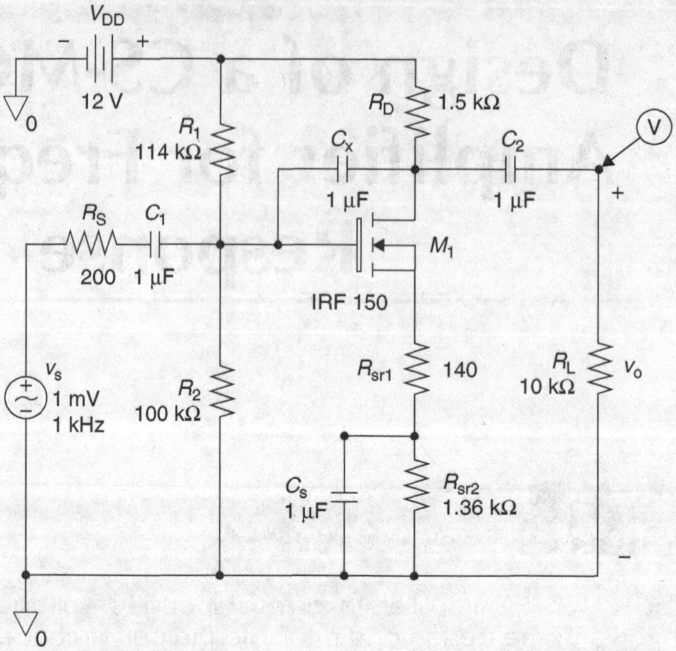

Figure 25-1 A MOSFET amplifier

PAPER–PENCIL DESIGN

Note: Select the passive component values closest to the practical values. The component values in Fig. 25-1 are shown for illustrations only.

1. After completing your design, write the circuit values.

R_D = ________ kΩ; R_1 = ________ kΩ; R_2 = ________ kΩ

R_{sr1} = ________ Ω; R_{sr2} = ________ Ω

C_1 = ________ μF; C_2 = ________ μF; C_S = ________ μF; C_x = ________ nF

2. Complete the calculated values in Table 25-1.

Table 25.1 Frequency response of JFET amplifiers

	Calculated	Simulated	Experimental
f_L (kHz)			
f_H (kHz)			
$A_{v(mid)}$			

COMPUTER SIMULATION

Software tools: **PSpice, OrCAD, Multisim, LTSpice, or any electronic circuit simulator.**

1. Simulate the amplifier circuit shown in Fig. 25-1 by using computer simulation to find the frequency response (ac analysis).

$$A_{v(mid)} = \frac{v_{o(peak)}}{v_{s(peak)}} = \_\_\_\_\_\_\_\_ \text{V/V}; \quad f_L = \_\_\_\_\_\_\_\_ \text{kHz}; \quad f_H = \_\_\_\_\_\_\_\_ \text{kHz}$$

2. Assign ±5% tolerance to all capacitors and resistors. Run the simulation for the worst-case maximum gain and record.

$$A_{v(mid)} = \frac{v_{o(peak)}}{v_{s(peak)}} = \_\_\_\_\_\_\_\_; \quad f_L = \_\_\_\_\_\_\_\_ \text{kHz}; \quad f_H = \_\_\_\_\_\_\_\_ \text{kHz}$$

3. Does your design meet the specifications under the worst-case conditions? If not, which resistance(s) would you adjust to get the desired gain? Which capacitor(s) would you adjust to get the desired cut-off frequencies? Why? Explain.

____

____

Change the component values so that the specifications are met. Note these values.

__________ __________ __________ __________

4. Run the computer simulation with your suggested values in step 3 and complete the simulated values in Table 25-1.
Comment on the effects of the component tolerance on the design.

____

____

EXPERIMENTS

The students are strongly encouraged and recommended to build and test the amplifier circuit to validate the theoretical and computer simulation results.

1. Set up your final amplifier circuit. Observe the output voltage $v_L(t)$ and its peak value V_m.

2. Measure: $v_{L(peak)} = \_\_\_\_\_\_\_\_$ mV; $v_{s(peak)} = \_\_\_\_\_\_\_\_$ mV; $A_v = \frac{v_{L(peak)}}{v_{s(peak)}} = \_\_\_\_\_\_\_\_$ V/V

$$R_i = \frac{v_{i(peak)}}{i_{s(peak)}} = \_\_\_\_\_\_\_\_ \text{k}\Omega; \quad R_{in} = \frac{v_{s(peak)}}{i_{s(peak)}} = \_\_\_\_\_\_\_\_ \text{k}\Omega$$

3. Measure the output resistance R_o of the amplifier.

$V_{L(\text{no load})}$ = ________ mV; $V_{L(\text{full load})}$ = ________ mV; R_o = ________ Ω

4. Complete the experimental values in Table 25-1.

REPORT

1. Compare the results in Tables 25-1 and comment on any discrepancies.

____

____

____

2. Does the frequency limits remain within the specifications? If not, explain the reasons.

____

____

____

3. What are the parameters that influence the high and low frequencies? Explain.

____

____

____

4. What is the estimated cost of the amplifier?

____

5. Analyze and interpret the data due to any variations and practical limitations.

____

____

6. Describe the safety issues considered while conducting the experiment.

____

____

____

7. Describe the process to design and conduct experiments.

8. Conclusion and comment on achieving goals or objectives of this experiment.

ATTACH ALL PLOTS/GRAPHS TO YOUR REPORT

CHAPTER 26

Actively Biased MOSFET Common-Source Amplifier

Learning Objectives

To investigate the characteristic of a common-source amplifier biased by a MOSFET current source. You will use computer simulation to evaluate the performance of the common-source amplifier.

After the end of this experiment, you should be able to

- Describe the operation of a MOSFET current source and its small-signal equivalent circuit.
- Describe the transfer characteristic of an actively biased common-source amplifier.
- Analyze an actively biased common-source amplifiers.

PRE-LAB ASSIGNMENT

Read on *Active-Biased MOSFET Amplifiers* (e.g. Rashid's Section 5.15: Active-Biased CS-Amplifiers).

PAPER–PENCIL ANALYSIS

A common-source amplifier as shown in Fig. 26-1 is biased by a MOSFET current source. Use all identical N-type MOSFETs of type IRF150 and P-type MOSFETs of type IRF9140 (if not available, use any other MOSFET that is available). Assume the following SPICE model parameters:

.MODEL IRF150 NMOS (KP = 20.53U VTO = 2.831 L = 2U W = 0.3 LAMBDA = 5M)

.MODEL IRF9140 PMOS (KP = 10.15U VTO= −3.67 L = 2U W = 1.9 LAMBDA = 5M)

1. Find the dc collector and base biasing currents.

   $I_{D1} = I_{D2} =$ ________ mA; $V_{GS1} = V_{GS2} =$ ________ V

2. Calculate the output resistances of the transistors: r_{o1} for M_1 and r_{o2} for M_2

   $r_{o1} =$ ________ kΩ; $r_{o2} =$ ________ kΩ

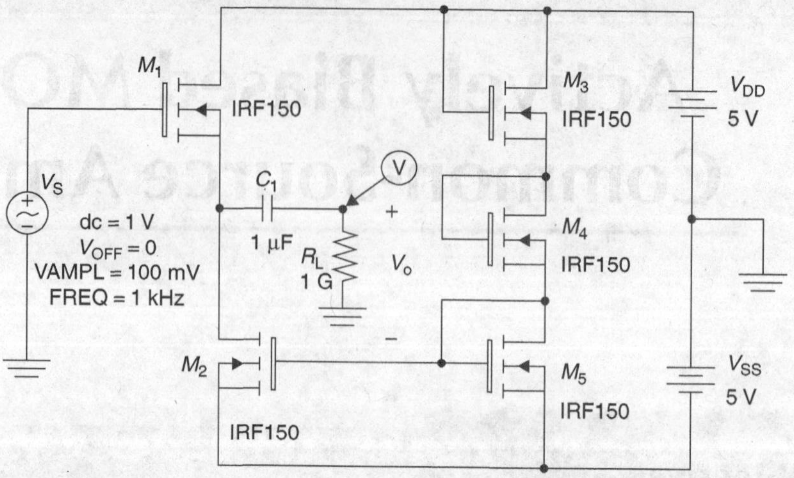

Figure 26-1 An active-biased common-source amplifier

3. Calculate the small-signal parameters of the common-source amplifier.

$A_v = \frac{v_{L\,(peak)}}{v_{i\,(peak)}} =$ ________ V/V; $R_i = \frac{v_{i\,(peak)}}{i_{s\,(peak)}} =$ ________ kΩ; $R_o =$ ________ Ω

4. Complete the calculated values in Table 26-1.

Table 26-1 Biasing values and amplifier parameters

	I_{C1} (mA)	I_{B1} (µA)	r_{01} (kΩ)	r_{02} (kΩ)	A_v	R_i (kΩ)	R_o (Ω)
Calculated							
Simulated							
Experimental							

COMPUTER SIMULATION

Software tools: PSpice, OrCAD, Multisim, LTSpice, or any electronic circuit simulator.

1. Simulate the source-follower circuit shown in Fig. 26-1 by using computer simulation to find the dc biasing information. From the simulation output file, complete the simulated values in Table 26-1.
2. Simulate the amplifier by using computer simulation to plot the output voltage $v_L(t)$ across the load resistance R_L. Since your input signal v_i is sinusoidal, the output voltage v_L should ideally be sinusoidal. Is the output voltage v_L sinusoidal?

____

____

Compare the output voltage with the input voltage. Explain any differences or deviations.

____

____

3. From the plots of the input signal voltage $v_i(t)$ and the output voltage $v_L(t)$, find the voltage gain A_v and the input resistance R_i. Record.

$v_{L(peak)}$ = ________ mV; $v_{i(peak)}$ = ________ mV; $A_v = \frac{v_{L\,(peak)}}{v_{s\,(peak)}}$ = ________

$R_i = \frac{v_{i\,(peak)}}{i_{s\,(peak)}}$ = ________ kΩ

4. To find the output resistance R_o, run the simulation for $R_L = \infty$ (or say 10 MΩ), 10 kΩ. Calculate the output resistance R_o of the amplifier from the following equation:

$$R_o = R_L\left[\frac{V_{L\,(no\text{-}load)} - V_{L\,(full\text{-}load)}}{V_{L\,(full\text{-}load)}}\right] = \_\_\_\_\_\_\_\_\ \Omega \qquad (26.1)$$

5. Complete the simulated values in Table 26-1.

EXPERIMENTS

The students are strongly encouraged and recommended to build and test the amplifier circuit to validate the theoretical and computer simulation results.

1. Set up your final amplifier circuit as shown in Fig. 26-1. Observe the output voltage $v_L(t)$ and its peak value V_m.
2. Take dc biasing measurements to complete the experimental values in Table 26-1.

3. Measure: $v_{L(peak)}$ = ________ mV; $v_{i(peak)}$ = ________ mV; $A_v = \frac{v_{L\,(peak)}}{v_{s\,(peak)}}$ = ________ V/V

$R_i = \frac{v_{i\,(peak)}}{i_{s\,(peak)}}$ = ________ kΩ

4. Measure the output resistance R_o of the amplifier.

$V_{L(no\ load)}$ = ________ V; $V_{L(full\ load)}$ = ________ V; R_o = ________ Ω

5. Complete the experimental values in Table 26-1.

REPORT

1. Compare the results in Table 26-1 and comment on any discrepancies.

2. You will notice that the output voltage is shifted up/down ward. What causes this shift? Explain.

   How would you reduce the dc biasing current I_{D1} of M_1? Explain.

   If you change the dc supply voltage ($V_{CC} = 10\,V$), what would you do to keep the dc biasing current I_{C1} the same as the values for $V_{CC} = 15\,V$. Explain.

3. What are the advantages of an active biasing?

4. What are the disadvantages of an active biasing?

5. What is the estimated cost of the amplifier?

6. Analyze and interpret the data due to any variations and practical limitations.

7. Describe the safety issues considered while conducting the experiment.

____

____

8. Describe the process to design and conduct experiments.

____

____

9. Conclusion and comment on achieving goals or objectives of this experiment.

____

____

____

ATTACH ALL PLOTS/GRAPHS TO YOUR REPORT

CHAPTER 27

Design of Active-Biased MOSFET Current Sources

Learning Objectives

To design active MOSFET current sources to give a specified constant current. You will use computer simulation to verify the design and evaluate the performance of current sources.

After the end of this experiment, you should be able to

- Describe the operation of constant MOSFET current sources and their small-signal equivalent circuit.
- Analyze and design MOSFET current sources to meet the given specifications.

PRE-LAB ASSIGNMENT

Read on *Active MOSFET Current Sources* (e.g., Rashid's Section 14.5: MOSFET Current Sources).

DESIGN SPECIFICATIONS

Design a MOSFET current-source to bias-source follower (as shown in Fig. 27-1) to meet the following specifications:

- Quiescent biasing current, $I_Q = I_{D1} = I_{D2} = 370$ mA ± 5%
- Voltage gain, $|A_v| = v_L/v_s \approx 1.0$
- Load resistance, $R_L = 27$ kΩ
- dc supply voltage, $V_{DD} = -V_{SS} = 5$ V
- Input signal, $v_i = 10-100$ mV (peak sinusoidal), 1 kHz
- Use all identical N-type MOSFETs of type IRF150 (if not available, use any other MOSFET that is available). Assume SPICE model parameters of

.MODEL IRF150 NMOS (KP = 20.53U VTO = 2.831 L = 2U W = 0.3 LAMBDA = 5M)

PAPER–PENCIL DESIGN

Note: Select the passive component values closest to the practical values. The component values in Fig. 27-1 are shown for illustrations only.

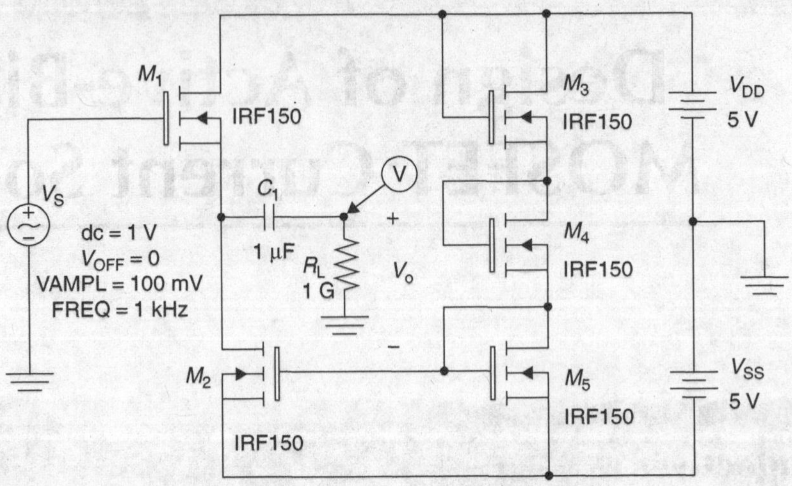

Figure 27-1 Source follower with a MOSFET current source

1. After completing your paper–pencil design, write the circuit value.

   V_{GS1} = ________ V; V_{GS2} = ________ V; V_{GS3} = ________ V

   g_{m1} = ________ A/V²; g_{m2} = ________ A/V²; g_{m3} = ________ A/V²

2. Find the dc biasing currents.

   I_{D1} = ________ mA; I_{D2} = ________ µA; I_{D3} = ________ µA

3. Calculate the output resistance r_{o1} for M_1, r_{o2} for M_2, and r_{o3} for M_3.

   r_{o1} = ________ kΩ; r_{o2} = ________ kΩ; r_{o3} = ________ kΩ

4. Calculate the small-signal parameters of the source follower.

   $A_v = \dfrac{v_{L(peak)}}{v_{i(peak)}}$ = ________ V/V; $R_i = \dfrac{v_{i(peak)}}{i_{i(peak)}}$ = ________ kΩ; R_o = ________ Ω

5. Complete the calculated values in Table 27-1.

Table 27-1 Source follower with a MOSFET current source

	I_Q (mA)	I_{D3} (µA)	r_{01} (kΩ)	r_{03} (kΩ)	A_v	R_i (kΩ)	R_o (Ω)
Calculated							
Simulated							
Experimental							

COMPUTER SIMULATION

Software tools: PSpice, OrCAD, Multisim, LTSpice, or any electronic circuit simulator.

1. Simulate the emitter-follower circuit shown in Fig. 27-1 by using computer simulation to find the dc biasing information. From the simulation output file, complete the simulated values in Table 27-1.
2. Simulate the amplifier by using computer simulation to plot the output voltage $v_L(t)$ across the load resistance R_L. Since your input signal v_i is sinusoidal, the output voltage v_L should ideally be sinusoidal. Is the output voltage v_L sinusoidal?

____

Compare the output voltage with the input voltage. Explain any differences or deviations.

____

____

3. From the plots of the input signal voltage $v_i(t)$ and the output voltage $v_L(t)$, find the voltage gain A_v and the input resistance R_i. Record.

$v_{L(peak)}$ = ________ mV; $v_{i(peak)}$ = ________ mV; $A_v = \frac{v_{L\,(peak)}}{v_{i\,(peak)}}$ = ________

$R_i = \frac{v_{i\,(peak)}}{i_{i\,(peak)}}$ = ________ kΩ

4. To find the output resistance R_o, run the simulation for $R_L = \infty$ (or say 10 MΩ), 10 kΩ. Calculate the output resistance R_o of the amplifier from the following equation:

$$R_o = R_L\left[\frac{V_{L\,(no\text{-}load)} - V_{L\,(full\text{-}load)}}{V_{L\,(full\text{-}load)}}\right] = \_\_\_\_\_\_\_\_\ \Omega \qquad (27.1)$$

5. Complete the simulated values in Table 27-1.
6. Plot the voltage transfer characteristic (v_L versus v_i). Record v_L = ________ V at v_i = 0 V. Is v_L = 0 V at v_i = 0 V? If not, why? Explain.

____

____

If you apply an input voltage of $v_i = 1\sin(2000\pi t)$, what will be the expression for the instantaneous output voltage?

v_o = ________

EXPERIMENTS

The students are strongly encouraged and recommended to build and test the amplifier circuit to validate the theoretical and computer simulation results.

1. Set up your final amplifier circuit shown in Fig. 27-1. Observe the output voltage $v_L(t)$ and its peak value V_m.
2. Take dc biasing measurements to complete the experimental values in Table 27-1.
3. Measure: $v_{L(peak)}$ = ______ V; $v_{i(peak)}$ = ______ mV

   $A_v = \frac{v_{L(peak)}}{v_{i(peak)}}$ = ______ V/V; $R_i = \frac{v_{i(peak)}}{i_{i(peak)}}$ = ______ kΩ

4. Measure the output resistance R_o of the amplifier.

   $V_{L(no\ load)}$ = ______ V; $V_{L(full\ load)}$ = ______ V; R_o = ______ Ω

5. Complete the experimental values in Table 27-1.

REPORT

1. Compare the results in Tables 27-1 and comment on any discrepancies.

   ____

   ____

2. Does the design meet the specifications? If not, explain the reasons.

   ____

   ____

3. What are the parameters that influence the input and output resistances? Explain.

   ____

   ____

4. What is the estimated cost of the amplifier?

   ____

   ____

5. Analyze and interpret the data due to any variations and practical limitations.

   ____

   ____

6. Describe the safety issues considered while conducting the experiment.

   ____

   ____

7. Describe the process to design and conduct experiments.

8. Conclusion and comment on achieving goals or objectives of this experiment.

ATTACH ALL PLOTS/GRAPHS TO YOUR REPORT

CHAPTER

28 Characteristics of MOSFET Differential Amplifiers

Learning Objectives

To investigate the characteristics of MOSFET differential amplifiers with a current-source biasing. You will use computer simulation to evaluate the performance of differential amplifiers.

After the end of this experiment, you should be able to

- Describe the operation and characteristics of MOSFET differential amplifiers and their small-signal equivalent circuit.
- Analyze differential pairs with a constant current-source biasing.

PRE-LAB ASSIGNMENT

Read on *Differential Amplifiers* (e.g., Rashid's Section 15.4: MOSFET Differential Amplifiers).

PAPER–PENCIL ANALYSIS

A MOSFET differential pair as shown in Fig. 28-1 is biased by a MOSFET current source. Use all identical N-type MOSFETs of type IRF150 and P-type MOSFETs of type IRF9140 (if not available, use any other MOSFET that is available). Assume SPICE model parameters of

.MODEL IRF150 NMOS (KP = 20.53U VTO = 2.831 L = 2U W = 0.3 LAMBDA = 5M)

.MODEL IRF9140 PMOS (KP = 10.15U VTO = −3.67 L = 2U W = 1.9 LAMBDA = 5M)

1. Find the dc biasing currents.

   I_{D2} = ________ mA; I_{D4} = ________ μA; I_{D5} = ________ A

2. Calculate the small-signal output resistance r_{o2} for M_2, r_{o4} for M_4, and r_{o5} for M_5.

   r_{o2} = ________ kΩ; r_{o4} = ________ kΩ; r_{o5} = ________ kΩ

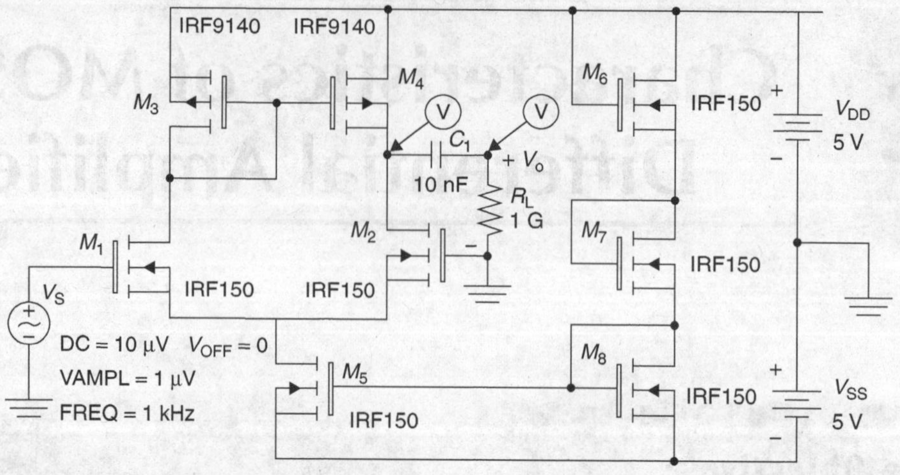

Figure 28-1 MOSFET differential amplifier with current-source biasing

3. Calculate the small-signal transconductance for g_{m2} for M_2, g_{m4} for M_4, and g_{m5} for M_5.
4. Calculate the differential-mode small-signal parameters of the amplifier, i.e., for $v_{s1} = v_{id}/2$ and $v_{s2} = -v_{id}/2$. Assume the output is taken as $v_{od} = v_{O1} - v_{O2}$.

$$A_d = \frac{v_{od}}{v_{id}} = \_\_\_\_\_\_\_\_\_\_ \text{ V/V}; \qquad R_{id} = \frac{v_{id}}{i_{id}} = \_\_\_\_\_\_\_\_\_\_ \text{ k}\Omega$$

5. Calculate the common-mode small-signal parameters of the amplifier, i.e., for $v_{s1} = v_{ic}$ and $v_{s2} = v_{ic}$.

$$A_c = \frac{v_{oc}}{v_{ic}} = \_\_\_\_\_\_\_\_\_\_ \text{ V/V}; \qquad R_{ic} = \frac{v_{ic}}{i_{ic}} = \_\_\_\_\_\_\_\_\_\_ \text{ k}\Omega$$

6. Complete the calculated values in Table 28-1.

Table 28-1 Parameters of MOSFET differential amplifier

	I_Q (mA)	I_{C1} (mA)	A_d	R_{id} (kΩ)	A_c	R_{ic} (kΩ)	CMRR
Calculated							
Simulated							
Experimental							

COMPUTER SIMULATION

Software tools: **PSpice, OrCAD, Multisim, LTSpice, or any electronic circuit simulator.**

1. Simulate the differential amplifier circuit shown in Fig. 28-1 by using computer simulation to find the dc biasing information. From the simulation output file, complete the simulated values in Table 28-1.

2. Apply a differential mode voltage: $v_{s1} = v_{id}/2 = 1$ mA and $v_{s2} = -v_{id}/2 = 1$ mV. Simulate and record.

v_{O1} = ________ mV; v_{O2} = ________ mV; v_{od} = ________ mV

$A_d = \frac{v_{od}}{v_{id}}$ = ________ V/V; $R_{id} = \frac{v_{id}}{i_{id}}$ = ________ kΩ

3. Apply a common-mode voltage: $v_{s1} = v_{ic} = 10$ mV and $v_{s2} = v_{ic} = 10$ mV. Simulate and record

v_{O1} = ________ mV; v_{O2} = ________ mV; v_{oc} = ________ mV

$A_c = \frac{v_{oc}}{v_{ic}}$ = ________; $R_{ic} = \frac{v_{ic}}{i_{ic}}$ = ________ kΩ

4. Complete the simulated values in Table 28-1.
5. Set $v_{s1} = v_{id}/2 = 1$ mV and $v_{s2} = 0$V. Use dc analysis and plot the voltage transfer characteristic (v_{o1} versus v_{s1}). Record the slope of the plot, i.e., the voltage gain, A_d = ________ V/V. Compare this gain with that in step 2. Explain any differences or deviations.

____

____

EXPERIMENTS

The students are strongly encouraged and recommended to build and test the amplifier circuit to validate the theoretical and computer simulation results.

1. Set up the circuit as shown in Fig. 28-1.
2. Take dc biasing measurements to complete the experimental values in Table 28-1.
3. Apply a differential mode voltage: $v_{s1} = v_{id}/2 = 1$ mV and $v_{s2} = -v_{id}/2 = 1$ mV. Measure

v_{O1} = ________ mV; v_{O2} = ________ mV; v_{od} = ________ mV

$A_d = \frac{v_{od}}{v_{id}}$ = ________ V/V; $R_{id} = \frac{v_{id}}{i_{id}}$ = ________ kΩ

4. Apply a common-mode voltage: $v_{s1} = v_{ic} = 10$ mV and $v_{s2} = v_{ic} = 10$ mV. Measure.

v_{O1} = ________ mV; v_{O2} = ________ mV; v_{oc} = ________ mV

$A_c = \frac{v_{oc}}{v_{ic}}$ = ________ V/V; $R_{ic} = \frac{v_{ic}}{i_{ic}}$ = ________ kΩ

5. Complete the experimental values in Table 28-1.

REPORT

1. Compare the results in Tables 28-1 and comment on any discrepancies.

2. If you increase v_{s1} by a small amount, v_{O1} will decrease and v_{O2} will increase. Why? Explain.

3. How would you increase the differential-mode gain? Explain.

4. How would you reduce the common-mode gain of the amplifier? Explain.

5. What should be the characteristics of an ideal differential amplifier? Explain.

6. What is the estimated cost of the amplifier?

7. Analyze and interpret the data due to any variations and practical limitations.

8. Describe the safety issues considered while conducting the experiment.

9. Describe the process to design and conduct experiments.

10. Conclusion and comment on achieving goals or objectives of this experiment.

____

____

ATTACH ALL PLOTS/GRAPHS TO YOUR REPORT

CHAPTER

29 Design of a MOSFET Operational Amplifier

Learning Objectives

To design a MOSFET operational amplifier to meet specified performance parameters. You will use computer simulation to verify the design and evaluate the performance of the amplifier.

After the end of this experiment, you should be able to

- Select the circuit topology and describe the operation of a MOSFET operational amplifier and its small-signal equivalent circuit.
- Analyze and design a MOSFET operation amplifier to meet the given specifications.

PRE-LAB ASSIGNMENT

Read on *Operational Amplifiers* (e.g., Rashid's Section 16.4: CMOS Op-Amps).

DESIGN SPECIFICATIONS

Design a MOSFET operational amplifier to meet the following specifications:

- Differential voltage gain, $|A_d| = v_{od}/v_d = 10^3 \pm 5\%$
- Differential input resistance, $R_{id} \geq 150$ kΩ 5%
- Output resistance, $R_o \leq 200\ \Omega \pm 5\%$
- Common-mode rejection ratio, CMRR = 104 ± 10%
- Unity-gain bandwidth $f_u \geq 10^4 \pm 10\%$
- dc supply voltages, $V_{DD} = -V_{SS} = 12$ V
- Use all identical N-type MOSFETs of type IRF150 and P-type MOSFETs of type IRF9140 (if not available, use any other MOSFET that is available). Assume SPICE model parameters of

.MODEL IRF150 NMOS (KP = 20.53U VTO = 2.831 L = 2U W = 0.3 LAMBDA = 5M)

.MODEL IRF9140 PMOS (KP = 10.15U VTO = −3.67 L = 2U W = 1.9 LAMBDA = 5M)

Hint: You can select any circuit topology using MOSFETs as long as you meet the specifications.

PAPER–PENCIL DESIGN

Note: Select the passive component values closest to the practical values.

1. Decide on the circuit topology, and attach it with the report.
2. Find the component values of your circuit.
3. Calculate the differential-mode parameters.

$A_d =$ ________; $R_{id} =$ ________ kΩ; $R_o =$ ________ kΩ

4. Calculate the common-mode parameters.

$A_c =$ ________; $R_{ic} =$ ________ kΩ

5. Complete the calculated values in Table 29-1.

Table 29-1 Parameters of MOSFET op-amp

	A_d	R_{id} (kΩ)	A_c	R_{ic} (kΩ)	CMRR	R_o (Ω)	SR (V/μs)	f_u (kHz)
Calculated								
Simulated								
Experimental								

COMPUTER SIMULATION

Software tools: PSpice, OrCAD, Multisim, LTSpice, or any electronic circuit simulator.

1. Simulate your circuit by using computer simulation to find the transfer function of differential-mode parameters. From the simulation output file, record and complete the simulated values in Table 29-1.

$A_d =$ ________V/V; $R_{id} =$ ________ kΩ; $R_o =$ ________ Ω

2. Simulate your circuit by using computer simulation to find the common-mode parameters from the transfer function analysis. From the simulation output file, record and complete the simulated values in Table 29-1.

$A_c =$ ________V/V; $R_{ic} =$ ________ kΩ

3. Simulate your circuit by using computer simulation to find the frequency response of the output voltage. From the simulation plot of the voltage gain, find the unity-gain bandwidth. Record and complete the simulated values in Table 29-1.

$f_u =$ ________ kHz

4. Assign ±5% tolerance to all circuit elements. Run the simulation for the worst-case maximum output voltage. Does your design meet the specifications under worst-case conditions? If not, change the component values so that the specifications are met. Record these values.

________ ________ ________ ________

5. Run the computer simulation with your suggested values in step 4 and complete the simulated values in Table 29-1.

A_d = ________ V/V; R_{id} = ________ kΩ; R_o = ________ Ω

A_c = ________ V/V; R_{ic} = ________ kΩ; CMRR = ________

f_u = ________ kHz

Comment on the effects of the component tolerance on the design.

____

____

____

EXPERIMENTS

The students are strongly encouraged and recommended to build and test the amplifier circuit to validate the theoretical and computer simulation results.

1. Set up your final circuit.
2. Apply a differential mode voltage. Measure

A_d = ________ V/V; R_{id} = ________ kΩ; R_o = ________ Ω

3. Apply a common-mode voltage. Measure.

A_c = ________ V/V; R_{ic} = ________ kΩ

4. Measure the frequency response with a differential mode voltage. Record

f_u = ________ kHz

5. Complete the experimental values in Table 29-1.

REPORT

1. Compare the results in Table 29-1 and comment on any discrepancies.

____

____

2. Does the design meet the specifications? If not, explain the reasons.

____

____

3. What are the parameters that voltage gains? Explain.

____

____

4. What is the estimated cost of the amplifier?

____

____

5. Analyze and interpret the data due to any variations and practical limitations.

____

____

6. Describe the safety issues considered while conducting the experiment.

____

7. Describe the process to design and conduct experiments.

____

____

8. Conclusion and comment on achieving goals or objectives of this experiment.

____

____

ATTACH ALL PLOTS/GRAPHS TO YOUR REPORT

CHAPTER 30

Characteristics of CMOS Inverters

Learning Objectives

To investigate the characteristics of CMOS inverters. You will use computer simulation to plot the transfer characteristic and transient response of inverters.

After the end of this experiment, you should be able to

- Describe the voltage transfer characteristic of CMOS inverters.
- Determine the performance parameters of CMOS inverters.

PRE-LAB ASSIGNMENT

Read on *Read on MOS Inverters* (e.g., Rashid's Section 13.8: CMOS Inverters).

COMPUTER SIMULATION

Software tools: PSpice, OrCAD, Multisim, LTSpice, or any electronic circuit simulator.
Use all identical N-type MOSFETs of type IRF150 and P-type MOSFETs of type IRF9140 (if not available, use any other MOSFET that is available). Assume SPICE model parameters of

.MODEL IRF150 NMOS (KP = 20.53U VTO = 2.831 L = 2U W = 0.3 LAMBDA = 5M)

.MODEL IRF9140 PMOS (KP = 10.15U VTO = −3.67 L = 2U W = 1.9 LAMBDA = 5M)

1. A CMOS inverter is shown in Fig. 30-1. Run transient analysis to plot the input voltage v_s and output voltage v_o. The input is a pulse of 5 V at 100 kHz. R_L and C_L form the load.
2. From the transient plots, find the delay time t_{pd1} (or t_{pHL}) for the logic high-to-low, and t_{pd0} (or t_{pLH}) for the low-to-high. The average of t_{pd1} and t_{pd0} is the average propagation time $t_{pd} = (t_{pd1} + t_{pd0})/2$. Complete the simulated values in Table 30-1.
3. Run the dc sweep of the input voltage v_s (from 0 to 5 V with an increment of 0.01 V).
4. Plot the voltage transfer characteristic (v_o versus v_s). From the transfer characteristic, find V_{IL}, V_{IH}, V_{OL}, and V_{OH}. Complete the simulated values in Table 30-1.

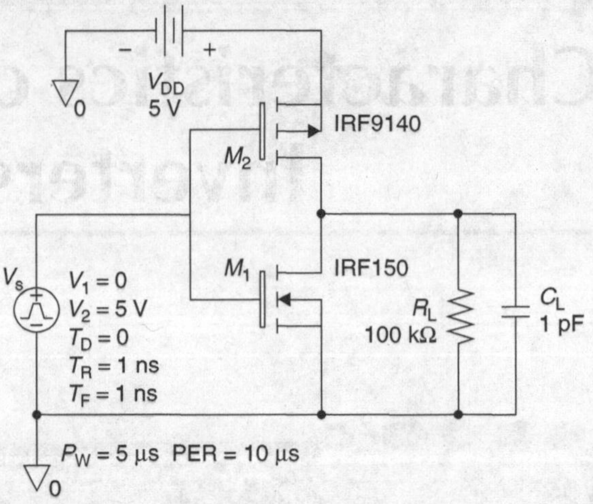

Figure 30-1 CMOS inverter

Table 30-1 CMOS inverter parameters

	t_{pd1} (ns)	t_{pd0} (ns)	t_{pd} (ns)	V_{IL} (V)	V_{IH} (V)	$V_{IW} = V_{IH} - V_{IL}$ (V)	V_{OL} (V)	V_{OH} (V)	$V_{LS} = V_{OH} - V_{OL}$ (V)
Simulated									
Experimental									

EXPERIMENTS

The students are strongly encouraged and recommended to build and test the diode circuit to validate the theoretical and computer simulation results.

1. Set up the CMOS inverter in Fig. 30-1 and apply a pulse input voltage. Measure t_{pd1}, t_{pd0}, and t_{pd}.

   t_{pd1} = ________ ns; t_{pd0} = ________ ns; t_{pd} = ________ ns

2. Apply dc input voltage in steps and plot the voltage transfer characteristic. Measure V_{IL}, V_{IH}, V_{OL}, and V_{OH}.

   V_{IL} = ________ V; V_{IH} = ________ V; V_{OL} = ________ V; V_{OH} = ________ V

3. Complete the experimental values in Table 30-1.

REPORT

1. Which factors influence the propagation delay time of an inverter? Explain.

   ____

   ____

2. Does the propagation time depend on the load? Explain your answer.

3. Which factors influence the width of the transition region (V_{IW}) of an inverter? Explain.

4. How would you reduce the propagation delay of an inverter? Explain.

5. Analyze and interpret the data due to any variations and practical limitations.

6. Describe the safety issues considered while conducting the experiment.

7. Describe the process to design and conduct experiments.

8. Conclusion and comment on achieving goals or objectives of this experiment.

ATTACH ALL PLOTS/GRAPHS TO YOUR REPORT

PART IV

OPERATIONAL AMPLIFIERS (OP-AMPS) AND APPLICATIONS

CHAPTER 31

Design of Op-Amp Non-Inverting, Inverting, and Difference Amplifiers

Learning Objectives

To design operational amplifier (op-amp) circuits to perform a specified function with a specified voltage gain. You will use computer simulation to verify the design and evaluate the performance of current sources.

After the end of this experiment, you should be able to

- Describe the characteristics and basic applications of op-amps to perform specified inverting and non-inverting functions.
- Analyze and design simple op-amp circuits to meet certain specifications.

PRE-LAB ASSIGNMENT

Read on *Op-Amp Circuits* (e.g., Rashid's Section 2.4: Non-Inverting Amplifiers; Section 2.5: Inverting Amplifiers).

DESIGN SPECIFICATIONS

Use op-amp μA741 whose $R_i = 2\ \text{M}\Omega$, $A_o = 10^5$, and $R_o = 75\ \Omega$. Assume dc supply voltages, $V_{CC} = -V_{EE} = 12\ \text{V}$.

Part I: Non-Inverting Amplifier

Design the non-inverting amplifier shown in Fig. 31-1 to meet the following specifications:

- Closed-loop voltage gain, $A_f = v_o/v_s = 100\ \text{V/V} \pm 5\%$.
- Input signal voltages, $v_s = 1\ \text{mV}$ (peak sinusoidal), 1 kHz.
- The input current from the signal source v_s must be less than 1 nA.

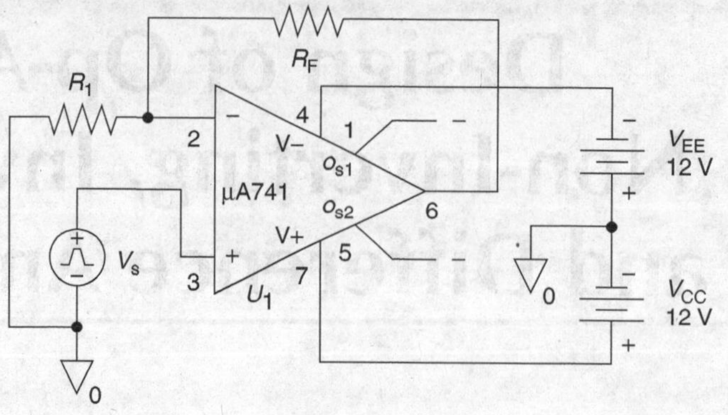

Figure 31-1 Non-inverting op-amp amplifier

Part II: Inverting Amplifier

Design the inverting amplifier shown in Fig. 31-2 to meet the following specifications:

- Closed-loop voltage gain, $A_f = v_o/v_s = -100$ V/V ± 5%.
- Input signal voltage, $v_s = 1$ mV (sinusoidal peak), 1 kHz.
- The input current from the signal source is ≤ 1 μA.

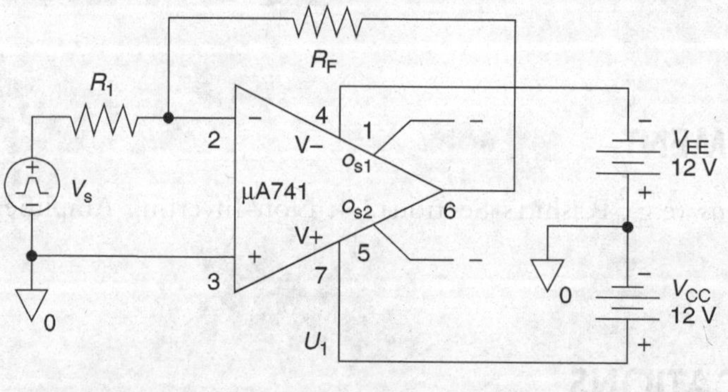

Figure 31-2 Inverting op-amp amplifier

Part III: Difference Amplifier

Design the difference amplifier shown in Fig. 31-3 to meet the following specifications:

- Input signal voltages, $v_a = 1$ mV (sinusoidal peak), 1 kHz; $v_b = 2$ mV (sinusoidal peak), 1 kHz
- Output voltage gain, $v_o = 100\,(v_a - v_b)$
- Input current from the signal source v_b must be less than 1 μA.

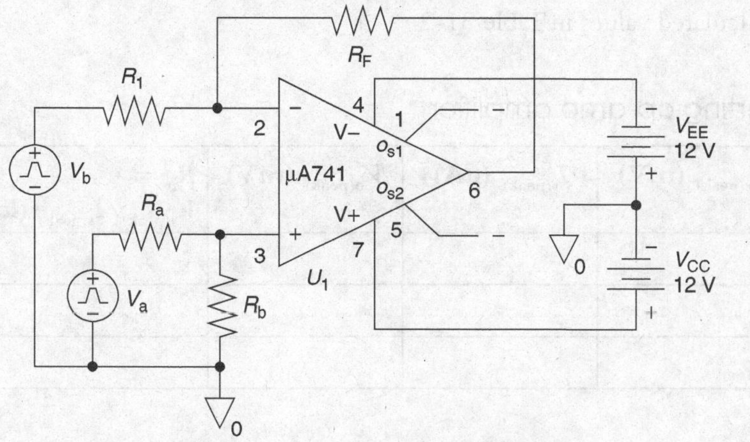

Figure 31-3 Difference op-amp amplifier

PAPER–PENCIL DESIGN

Note: Select the passive component values closest to the practical values.

Part I: Non-Inverting Amplifier

1. After completing your design, write the circuit values.

   R_1 = ________ kΩ; R_F = ________ kΩ

2. Complete the calculated values in Table 31-1.

Table 31-1 Non-inverting op-amp amplifier

	$V_{s(peak)}$ (mV)	$I_{s(peak)}$ (μA)	$V_{o(peak)}$ (mV)	$R_{in} = V_{s(peak)}/I_{s(peak)}$ (kΩ)	$A_v = V_{o(peak)}/V_{s(peak)}$
Calculated					
Simulated					
Experimental					

Part II: Inverting Amplifier

1. After completing your design, write the circuit values.

   R_1 = ________ kΩ; R_F = ________ kΩ

2. Complete the calculated values in Table 31-2.

Table 31-2 Inverting op-amp amplifier

	$V_{s(peak)}$ (mV)	$I_{s(peak)}$ (μA)	$V_{o(peak)}$ (mV)	$R_{in} = V_{s(peak)}/I_{s(peak)}$ (kΩ)	$A_v = V_{o(peak)}/V_{s(peak)}$
Calculated					
Simulated					
Experimental					

Part III: Difference Amplifier

1. After completing your design, write the circuit values.

R_1 = ________ kΩ; R_F = ________ kΩ; R_a = ________ kΩ; R_b = ________ kΩ

2. Complete the calculated values in Table 31-3.

Table 31-3 Difference op-amp amplifier

	$V_{s(peak)}$ (mV)	$I_{s(peak)}$ (μA)	$V_{o(peak)}$ (mV)	$R_{in} = V_{s(peak)}/I_{s(peak)}$ (kΩ)	$A_v = V_{o(peak)}/[V_{a(peak)} - V_{b(peak)}]$
Calculated					
Simulated					
Experimental					

COMPUTER SIMULATION

Software Tools: PSpice, Or CAD, Multisim, LTSpice, or any electronic circuit simulator.

Part I: Non-Inverting Amplifier

1. Simulate the amplifier shown in Fig. 31-1 by using computer simulation with an input signal voltage, v_s = 1 mV (sinusoidal peak), 1 kHz.
2. Assign ±5% tolerance to all resistors. Run the simulation for the worst-case maximum output voltage and record.

$v_{L(peak)}$ = ________ mV; $v_{s(peak)}$ = ________ mV; $A_v = \dfrac{v_{L(peak)}}{v_{s(peak)}}$ = ________

$R_i = \dfrac{v_{i(peak)}}{i_{s(peak)}}$ = ________ MΩ

3. Does your design meet the specifications under the worst-case conditions? If not, which resistance would you adjust to get the desired gain? Why? Explain.

____

____

Change the component values so that the specifications are met. Note these values.

______________ ______________ ______________

4. Run the computer simulation with your suggested values in step 3 and complete the simulated values in Table 31-1.

Part II: Inverting Amplifier

1. Simulate the amplifier shown in Fig. 31-2 by using computer simulation with an input signal voltage, $v_s = 1$ mV (sinusoidal peak), 1 kHz.
2 Assign ±5% tolerance to all resistors. Run the simulation for the worst-case maximum output voltage and record.

$v_{L\,(peak)} =$ ________ mV; $v_{s\,(peak)} =$ ________ mV, $A_v = \dfrac{v_{L(peak)}}{v_{s(peak)}} =$ ________

$R_i = \dfrac{v_{i(peak)}}{i_{s(peak)}} =$ ________ MΩ

3. Does your design meet the specifications under the worst-case conditions? If not, which resistance would you adjust to get the desired gain? Why? Explain.

____

____

Change the component values so that the specifications are met. Note these values.

______________ ______________ ______________

4. Run the computer simulation with your suggested values in step 3 and complete the simulated values in Table 31-2.

Part III: Difference Amplifier

1. Simulate the amplifier shown in Fig. 31-3 by using computer simulation with input signal voltages $v_a = 2$ mV and $v_b = 1$ mV (sinusoidal peak), 1 kHz. Make sure that these voltages are in phase.
2. Assign ±5% tolerance to all resistors. Run the simulation for the worst-case maximum output voltage and record.

$v_{o\,(peak)} =$ ________ mV; $v_{a\,(peak)} =$ ________ mV; $v_{b\,(peak)} =$ ________ mV

$A_v = \dfrac{v_{L\,(peak)}}{[v_{a(peak)} - v_{b(peak)}]} =$ ________

3. Does your design meet the specifications under the worst-case conditions? If not, which resistance would you adjust to get the desired gain? Why? Explain.

____

____

Change the component values so that the specifications are met. Note these values.

______________ ______________ ______________

4. Run the computer simulation with your suggested values in step 3 and complete the simulated values in Table 31-3.

EXPERIMENTS

The students are strongly encouraged and recommended to build and test the amplifier circuit to validate the theoretical and computer simulation results.

Part I: Non-Inverting Amplifier

1. Set up your final circuit of the amplifier as in Fig. 31-1. Observe the output voltage $v_L(t)$ and its peak value V_m.
2. Complete the experimental values in Table 31-1.

Part II: Inverting Amplifier

1. Set up your final circuit of the amplifier in Fig. 31-2. Observe the output voltage $v_L(t)$ and its peak value V_m.
2. Complete the experimental values in Table 31-2.

Part III: Difference Amplifier

1. Set up your final circuit of the amplifier in Fig. 31-3. Observe the output voltage $v_L(t)$ and its peak value V_m.
2. Complete the experimental values in Table 31-3.

REPORT

1. Compare the results in Tables 31-1, 31-2, and 31-3. Comment on any discrepancies.

____

____

2. Does the design meet the specifications? If not, explain the reasons.

____

____

3. What are the parameters that influence the input and output resistances? Explain.

4. What is the estimated cost of the amplifier?

5. Analyze and interpret the data due to any variations and practical limitations.

6. Describe the safety issues considered while conducting the experiment.

7. Describe the process to design and conduct experiments.

8. Conclusion and comment on achieving goals or objectives of this experiment.

ATTACH ALL PLOTS/GRAPHS TO YOUR REPORT

CHAPTER 32

Design of Op-Amp Inverting Integrator and Differentiator

Learning Objectives

To design operational amplifier (op-amp) circuits to perform a specified function with a specified voltage gain. You will use computer simulation to verify the design and evaluate the performance of current sources.

After the end of this experiment, you should be able to

- Describe the characteristics and basic applications of op-amps to perform specified differentiating and integrating functions.
- Analyze and design simple op-amp circuits to meet certain specifications.

PRE-LAB ASSIGNMENT

Read on *Op-Amp Circuits* (e.g., Rashid's Section 2.8: Integrators; Section 2.9: Integrators).

DESIGN SPECIFICATIONS

Use op-amp μA741 whose $R_i = 2\ \text{M}\Omega$, $A_o = 10^5$, and $R_o = 75\ \Omega$. Assume dc supply voltages, $V_{CC} = -V_{EE} = 12\text{V}$.

Part I: Inverting Integrator

Design the inverting integrator shown in Fig. 32-1 to meet the following specifications:

- Input signal voltage, $v_s = 10$ mV, 50 Hz (square wave).
- Output voltage, $v_o = -10 \int v_s\, dt$ (with zero initial conditions).
- The dc input current from the signal source must be less than 10 mA.

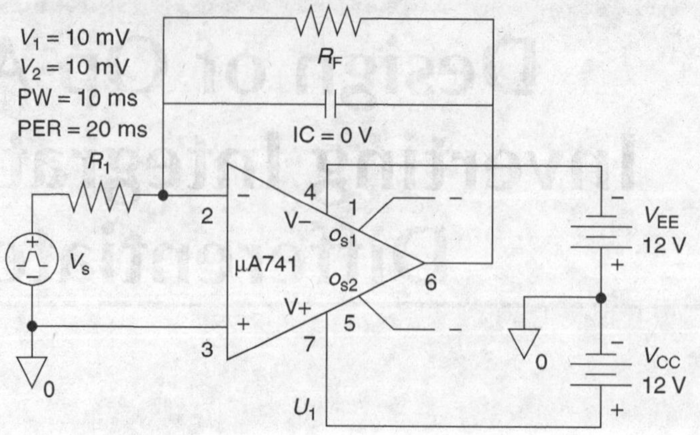

Figure 32-1 Inverting integrator

Part II: Inverting Differentiator

Design the inverting differentiator shown in Fig. 32-2 to meet the following specifications:

- Input signal voltage, v_s = 10 mV, 1 kHz (speak sine wave or triangular wave).
- Output voltage, $v_o = -10\ dvs/dt$.
- Frequency for the differentiation to be ineffective, f_b = 5 kHz.

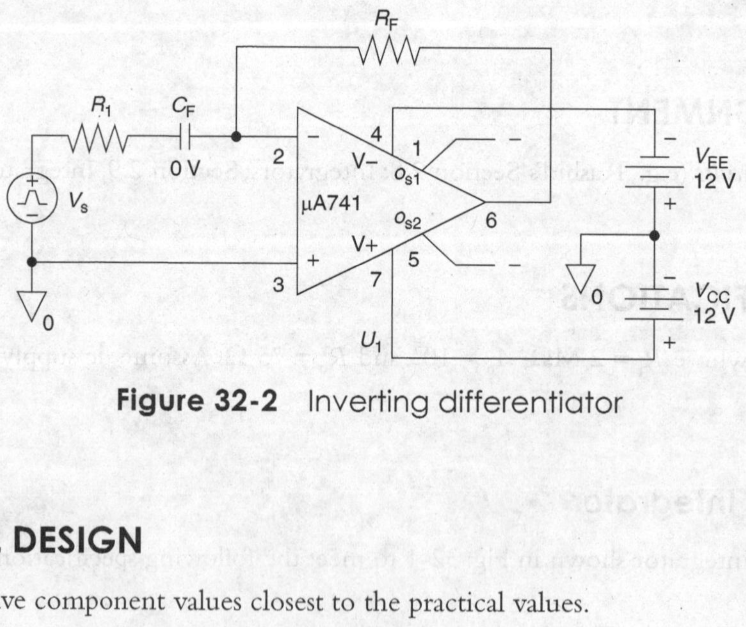

Figure 32-2 Inverting differentiator

PAPER–PENCIL DESIGN

Note: Select the passive component values closest to the practical values.

Part I: Inverting Integrator

1. After completing your design, write the circuit values.

R_1 = ________ kΩ; R_F = ________ kΩ; C_F = ________ nF

2. Complete the calculated values in Table 32-1.

Table 32-1 Inverting integrator

	Instantaneous v_s (mV)	Instantaneous v_o (mV)	$A_v = V_o\text{(peak)}/V_s\text{(peak)}$
Calculated			
Simulated			
Experimental			

Part II: Inverting Differentiator

After completing your design, write the circuit values. Complete the calculated values in Table 32-1.

R_1 = ________ kΩ; R_F = ________ kΩ; C_F = ________ nF

Table 32-2 Inverting Differentiator

	Instantaneous v_s (mV)	Instantaneous v_o (mV)	$A_v = V_o\text{(peak)}/V_s\text{(peak)}$
Calculated	1 sin 2000πt		
Simulated			
Experimental			

COMPUTER SIMULATION

Software Tools: PSpice, OrCAD, Multisim, LTSpice, or any electronic circuit simulator.

Part I: Inverting Integrator

1. Simulate the amplifier shown in Fig. 32-1 by using computer simulation with an input signal voltage, v_s = 10 mV (square wave), 50 Hz.
2. Assign ±5% tolerance to all resistors and capacitors. Run the simulation for the worst-case maximum output voltage and record.

$v_{o(peak)}$ = ________ mV; $v_{a(peak)}$ = ________ mV; $v_{b(peak)}$ = ________ mV

$A_v = \dfrac{v_{L(peak)}}{v_{s(peak)}}$ = ________

3. Does your design meet the specifications under the worst-case conditions? If not, which resistance or capacitor would you adjust to get the desired gain? Why? Explain.

____

____

Change the component values so that the specifications are met. Note these values.

____________ ____________ ____________

4. Run the computer simulation with your suggested values in step 3 and complete the simulated values in Table 32-1.

Part II: Inverting Differentiator

1. Simulate the amplifier shown in Fig. 32-2 by using computer simulation with an input signal voltage, v_s = 10 mV (square wave), 50 Hz.
2. Assign ±5% tolerance to all resistors and capacitors. Run the simulation for the worst-case maximum output voltage and record.

$v_{o(peak)}$ = ________ mV; $v_{a(peak)}$ = ________ mV; $v_{b(peak)}$ = ________ mV

$$A_v = \frac{v_{L(peak)}}{v_{s(peak)}} = \_\_\_\_\_\_\_\_$$

3. Does your design meet the specifications under the worst-case conditions? If not, which resistance or capacitor would you adjust to get the desired gain? Why? Explain.

____

____

Change the component values so that the specifications are met. Note these values.

____________ ____________ ____________

4. Run the computer simulation with your suggested values in step 3 and complete the simulated values in Table 32-2.

EXPERIMENTS

The students are strongly encouraged and recommended to build and test the amplifier circuit to validate the theoretical and computer simulation results.

Part I: Inverting Integrator

1. Set up your final circuit of the amplifier in Fig. 32-1. Observe the output voltage $v_L(t)$ and its peak value V_m.
2. Complete the experimental values in Table 32-1.

Part II: Inverting Differentiator

1. Set up your final circuit of the amplifier as in Fig. 32-2. Observe the output voltage $v_L(t)$ and its peak value V_m.
2. Complete the experimental values in Table 32-2.

REPORT

1. Compare the results in Tables 32-1 and 32-2. Comment on any discrepancies.

2. Does the design meet the specifications? If not, explain the reasons.

3. What are the parameters that influence the input and output resistances? Explain.

4. What is the estimated cost of the amplifier?

5. Analyze and interpret the data due to any variations and practical limitations.

6. Describe the safety issues considered while conducting the experiment.

7. Describe the process to design and conduct experiments.

8. Conclusion and comment on achieving goals or objectives of this experiment.

ATTACH ALL PLOTS/GRAPHS TO YOUR REPORT

CHAPTER

33 Design of an Op-Amp Instrumentation Amplifier

Learning Objectives

To design an instrument amplifier to give a specified difference voltage gain. You will use computer simulation to verify the design and evaluate the performance of the instrumentation amplifier.

After the end of this experiment, you should be able to

- Describe the operation and characteristics of instrumentation amplifiers.
- Analyze and design instrumentation amplifiers.

PRE-LAB ASSIGNMENT

Read on *Op-Amp Circuits* (e.g., Rashid's Section 2.7: Instrumentation Amplifiers).

DESIGN SPECIFICATIONS

Design an instrument amplifier that has two inputs v_a and v_b. The specifications are

- Output voltage, $v_o = \left[100(v_a - v_b) + 10\dfrac{d(v_a - v_b)}{dt}\, dt\right] \pm 5\%$
- Input signals: $v_a = 10$ mV $\sin(20\pi t)$ and $v_b = 8$ mV $\sin(20\pi t + 30°)$
- Input current drawn from either of the signal source must be less than 10 nA.
- dc supply, $V_{CC} = -V_{EE} = 15\,\text{V}$
- Use op-amps μA741 or LF411

PAPER–PENCIL DESIGN

Note: Select the passive component values closest to the practical values.

1. Decide on the circuit topology.

2. Find the components values of your circuit. List the values.

__________ __________ __________ __________

__________ __________ __________ __________

COMPUTER SIMULATION

Software Tools: PSpice, OrCAD, Multisim, LTSpice, or any electronic circuit simulator.

1. Simulate your circuit by using computer simulation to plot the transient response. Plot the input voltage and the output voltage of your circuit. From plots of the input and output voltages, note the multiplying factors.

$$v_o = \underline{\hspace{2cm}} (v_a - v_b) + \underline{\hspace{2cm}} \frac{d(v_a - v_b)}{dt} dt$$

2. Assign ±5% tolerance to all circuit elements. Run the simulation for the worst-case maximum output voltage. Does your design meet the specifications under worst-case conditions? If not, change the component values so that the specifications are met. Note these values.

__________ __________ __________ __________

3. Run the computer simulation with your suggested values in step 2. From plots of the input and output voltages, note the final multiplying factors.

$$v_o = \underline{\hspace{2cm}} (v_a - v_b) + \underline{\hspace{2cm}} \frac{d(v_a - v_b)}{dt} dt$$

Comment on the effects of the component tolerance on the design.

____

____

EXPERIMENTS

The students are strongly encouraged and recommended to build and test the amplifier circuit to validate the theoretical and computer simulation results.

1. Set up your final circuit.
2. Apply appropriate input signals to your circuit. Measure final multiplying factors.

$$v_o = \underline{\hspace{2cm}} (v_a - v_b) + \underline{\hspace{2cm}} \frac{d(v_a - v_b)}{dt} dt$$

REPORT

1. Compare the results from the computer simulation and experiment. Comment on any discrepancies.

2. Does the design meet the specifications? If not, explain the reasons.

3. What are the parameters that influence the input and output resistances? Explain.

4. What is the estimated cost of the amplifier?

5. Analyze and interpret the data due to any variations and practical limitations.

6. Describe the safety issues considered while conducting the experiment.

7. Describe the process to design and conduct experiments.

8. Conclusion and comment on achieving goals or objectives of this experiment.

ATTACH ALL PLOTS/GRAPHS TO YOUR REPORT

CHAPTER

34

Frequency Response of Op-Amp Non-Inverting, Inverting, and Difference Amplifiers

Learning Objectives

To investigate the frequency characteristics of op-amp inverting and non-inverting amplifiers. You will use computer simulation to evaluate the frequency characteristics of an op-amp circuits.

After the end of this experiment, you should be able to

- Describe the frequency response of op-amp inverting and non-inverting amplifiers.
- Determine the effects of op-amp frequency limit on the circuit performance.
- Analyze an op-amp circuit to find its gain and frequency limits.

PRE-LAB ASSIGNMENT

Read on *Op-Amp Circuits* (e.g., Rashid's Section 2.4: Non-Inverting Amplifiers; Section 2.5: Inverting Amplifiers).

PAPER–PENCIL CALCULATIONS

Use op-amp μA741 whose $R_i = 2\ M\Omega$, $A_o = 10^5$, $R_o = 75\ \Omega$, break frequency $f_b = 10$ Hz, and unity-gain bandwidth $f_u = 1$ MHz.

Part I: Inverting Amplifier

An inverting amplifier is shown in Fig. 34-1. Find the low-frequency gain A_{low}, the high break frequency f_H, and the gain-bandwidth product GBW = $A_{low} \times f_H$. Complete the calculated values in Table 34-1.

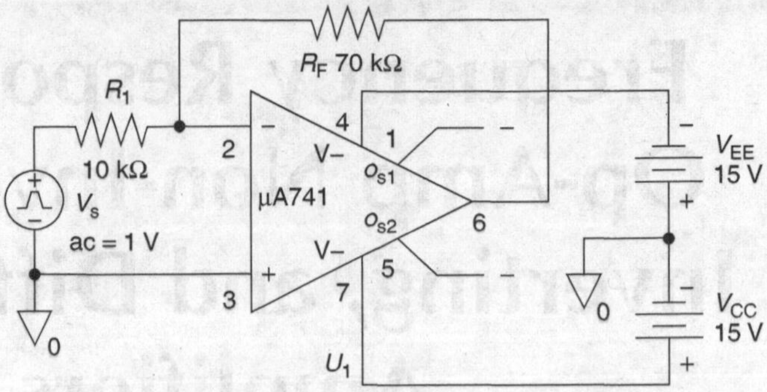

Figure 34-1 Inverting amplifier

Table 34-1 Inverting op-amp circuit

	$V_{s(peak)}$ (V)	$V_{o(peak)}$ (V)	$A_{low} = V_{o(peak)}/V_{s(peak)}$	f_H (kHz)	GBW (kHz)	f_u (kHz)
Calculated						
Simulated						
Experimental						

Part II: Non-Inverting Amplifier

A non-inverting amplifier is shown in Fig. 34-2. Find the low-frequency gain A_{low}, the high break frequency f_H, and the gain-bandwidth product GBW = $A_{low} \times f_H$. Complete the calculated values in Table 34.2.

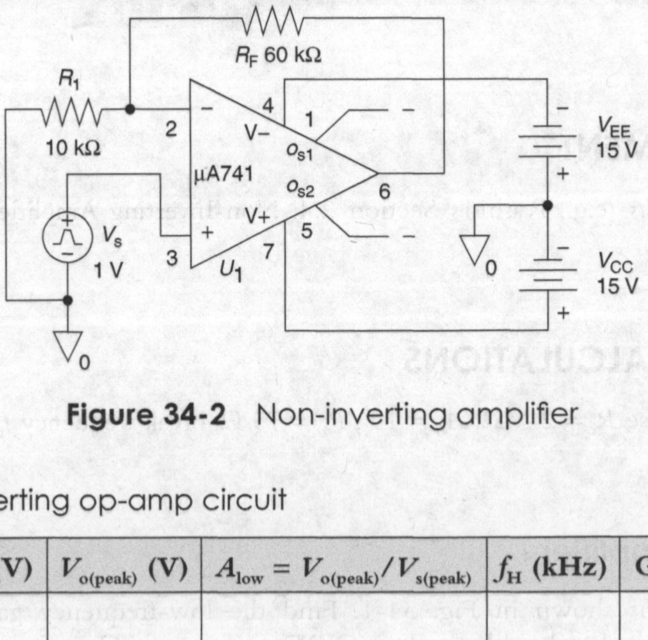

Figure 34-2 Non-inverting amplifier

Table 34-2 Non-inverting op-amp circuit

	$V_{s(peak)}$ (V)	$V_{o(peak)}$ (V)	$A_{low} = V_{o(peak)}/V_{s(peak)}$	f_H (kHz)	GBW (kHz)	f_u (kHz)
Calculated						
Simulated						
Experimental						

Part III: Unity-Gain Amplifier

A unity-gain amplifier is shown in Fig. 34-3. Find the low-frequency gain A_{low}, the high break frequency f_H, and the gain-bandwidth product GBW = $A_{low} \times f_H$. Complete the calculated values in Table 34.3.

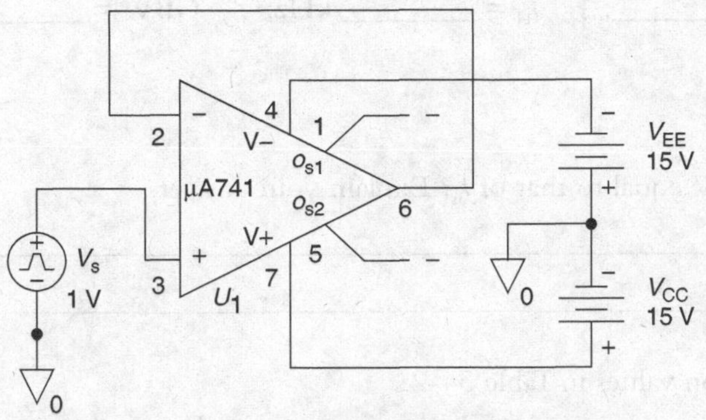

Figure 34-3 Unity-gain amplifier

Table 34-3 Non-inverting unity-gain inverter

	$V_{s(peak)}$ (V)	$V_{o(peak)}$ (V)	$A_{low} = V_{o(peak)}/V_{s(peak)}$	f_H (kHz)	GBW (kHz)	f_u (kHz)
Calculated						
Simulated						
Experimental						

COMPUTER SIMULATION

Software tools: PSpice, OrCAD, Multisim, LTSpice, or any electronic circuit simulator.

Part I: Inverting Amplifier

1. Simulate the amplifier circuit shown in Fig. 34-1 by using computer simulation to find the frequency response (ac analysis). Plot the voltage gain decibels (dB).

$A_{low} = \dfrac{v_{o(peak)}}{v_{s(peak)}} =$ ________; $f_H =$ ________ kHz; GBW = ________ kHz

$f_u =$ ________ kHz

Does the value of GBW equal to that of f_u? Explain your answer.

____

____

2. Complete the simulation values in Table 34-1.

Part II: Non-Inverting Amplifier

1. Simulate the amplifier circuit shown in Fig. 34-2 by using computer simulation to find the frequency response (ac analysis). Plot the voltage gain decibels (dB).

$A_{low} = \frac{v_{o(peak)}}{v_{s(peak)}} =$ ________; $f_H =$ ________ kHz; GBW = ________ kHz

$f_u =$ ________ kHz

Does the value of GBW equal to that of f_u? Explain your answer.

____

____

2. Complete the simulation values in Table 34-2.

Part III: Unity-Gain Amplifier

1. Simulate the amplifier circuit shown in Fig. 34-3 by using computer simulation to find the frequency response (ac analysis). Plot the voltage gain decibels (dB).

$A_{low} = \frac{v_{o(peak)}}{v_{s(peak)}} =$ ________; $f_H =$ ________ kHz; GBW = ________ kHz

$f_u =$ ________ kHz

Does the value of GBW equal to that of f_u? Explain your answer.

____

____

2. Complete the simulation values in Table 34-3.

EXPERIMENTS

The students are strongly encouraged and recommended to build and test the amplifier circuit to validate the theoretical and computer simulation results.

Part I: Inverting Amplifier

1. Set up your amplifier circuit in Fig. 34-1.
2. Measure

$A_{low} = \frac{v_{o(peak)}}{v_{s(peak)}} =$ ________; $f_H =$ ________ kHz; GBW = ________ kHz

$f_u =$ ________ kHz

3. Complete the experimental values in Table 34-1.

Part II: Non-Inverting Amplifier

1. Set up your amplifier circuit in Fig. 34-2.
2. Measure

$$A_{low} = \frac{v_{o(peak)}}{v_{s(peak)}} = \_\_\_\_\_\_\_\_; \quad f_H = \_\_\_\_\_\_\_\_ \text{ kHz}; \quad GBW = \_\_\_\_\_\_\_\_ \text{ kHz}$$

$$f_u = \_\_\_\_\_\_\_\_ \text{ kHz}$$

3. Complete the experimental values in Table 34-2.

Part III: Unity-Gain Amplifier

1. Set up your amplifier circuit as in Fig. 34-3.
2. Measure

$$A_{low} = \frac{v_{o(peak)}}{v_{s(peak)}} = \_\_\_\_\_\_\_\_; \quad f_H = \_\_\_\_\_\_\_\_ \text{ kHz}; \quad GBW = \_\_\_\_\_\_\_\_ \text{ kHz}$$

$$f_u = \_\_\_\_\_\_\_\_ \text{ kHz}$$

3. Complete the experimental values in Table 34-3.

REPORT

1. Compare the results in Tables 34-1, 34-2, and 34-3. Comment on any discrepancies.

____

____

2. Does the unity-gain bandwidth depend on the circuit configurations? Explain.

____

____

3. Why the unity-gain amplifier has the highest value of f_H? Why? Explain.

____

____

4. Is f_u of the amplifiers differ from that of the op-amp? If yes, why? Explain.

____

____

5. What is the estimated cost of the amplifier?

6. Analyze and interpret the data due to any variations and practical limitations.

7. Describe the safety issues considered while conducting the experiment.

8. Describe the process to design and conduct experiments.

9. Conclusion and comment on achieving goals or objectives of this experiment.

ATTACH ALL PLOTS/GRAPHS TO YOUR REPORT

CHAPTER 35

Frequency Response of Op-Amp Integrators and Differentiators

Learning Objectives

To investigate the frequency characteristics of op-amp integrators and differentiators. You will use computer simulation to evaluate the frequency characteristics of an op-amp circuits.

After the end of this experiment, you should be able to

- Describe the frequency response of op-amp integrators and differentiators.
- Determine the effects of op-amp frequency limit on the circuit performance.
- Analyze an op-amp circuit to find its gain and frequency limits.

PRE-LAB ASSIGNMENT

Read on *Op-Amp Circuits* (e.g., Rashid's Section 2.8: Integrators; Section 2.9: Differentiators).

PAPER–PENCIL CALCULATIONS

Use op-amp μA741 whose $R_i = 2$ MΩ, $A_o = 10^5$, $R_o = 75$ Ω, break frequency $f_b = 10$ Hz, and unity-gain bandwidth $f_u = 1$ MHz.

Part I: Op-Amp Integrator

An op-amp integrator is shown in Fig. 35-1. Find the low-frequency gain A_{low}, the high break frequency f_H, and the gain bandwidth product GBW = $A_{low} \times f_H$. Complete the calculated values in Table 35-1.

Part II: Op-Amp Differentiator

A differentiator is shown in Fig. 35-2. Find the low-frequency gain A_{low}, the high break frequency f_H, and the gain-bandwidth product GBW = $A_{low} \times f_H$. Complete the calculated values in Table 35-2.

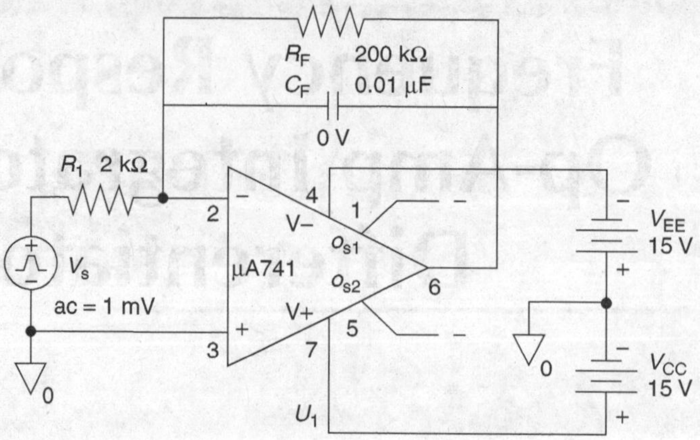

Figure 35-1 Op-amp integrator

Table 35-1 Op-Amp Integrator

	$V_{s(peak)}$ (V)	$V_{o(peak)}$ (V)	$A_{low} = V_{o(peak)}/V_{s(peak)}$	f_H (kHz)	BW (kHz)	GBW (kHz)	f_u (KHz)
Calculated							
Simulated							
Experimental							

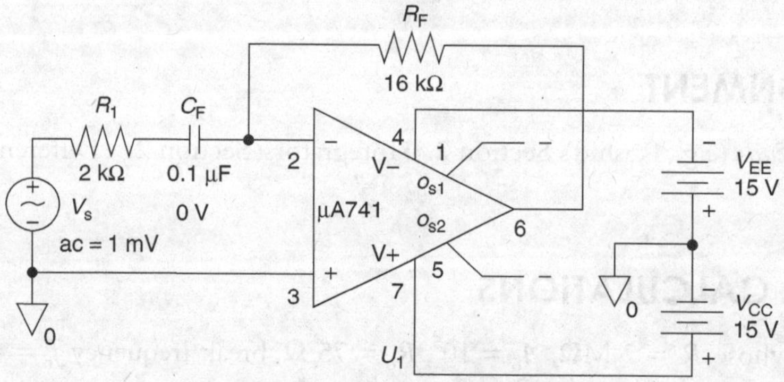

Figure 35-2 Differentiator

Table 35-2 Op-amp differentiator

	$V_{s(peak)}$ (V)	$V_{o(peak)}$ (V)	$A_{low} = V_{o(peak)}/V_{s(peak)}$	f_H (kHz)	BW (kHz)	GBW (kHz)	f_u (KHz)
Calculated							
Simulated							
Experimental							

COMPUTER SIMULATION

Software tools: PSpice, OrCAD, Multisim, LTSpice, or any electronic circuit simulator.

Part I: Op-Amp Integrator

1. Simulate the integrator circuit shown in Fig. 35-1 by using computer simulation to find the frequency response (ac analysis). Plot the voltage gain decibels (dB).

$A_{low} = \frac{v_{o(peak)}}{v_{s(peak)}} =$ ________; $f_L =$ ________ kHz; GBW = ________ kHz

$f_u =$ ________ kHz

Does the value of GBW equal to that of f_u? Explain your answer.

____

____

2. Complete the simulated values in Table 35-1.

Part II: Op-Amp Differentiator

1. Simulate the differentiator circuit shown in Fig. 35-2 by using computer simulation to find the frequency response (ac analysis). Plot the voltage gain decibels (dB).

$A_{low} = \frac{v_{o(peak)}}{v_{s(peak)}} =$ ________; $f_H =$ ________ kHz; $f_L =$ ________ kHz

BW = ________ kHz; GBW = ________ kHz

2. Complete the simulated values in Table 35-2.
3. Change $R_1 = 1\ k\Omega$. Simulate and record.

$A_{low} = \frac{v_{o(peak)}}{v_{s(peak)}} =$ ________; $f_H =$ ________ kHz; $f_L =$ ________ kHz

BW = ________ kHz; GBW = ________ kHz

Does this value differ from that in step 1? Explain your answer.

____

____

EXPERIMENTS

The students are strongly encouraged and recommended to build and test the amplifier circuit to validate the theoretical and computer simulation results.

Part I: Op-Amp Integrator

1. Set up your final amplifier circuit in Fig. 35-1.
2. Measure

$A_{low} = \frac{v_{o(peak)}}{v_{s(peak)}} =$ ________; $f_L =$ ________ kHz; GBW = ________ kHz

$f_u =$ ________ kHz

3. Complete the experimental values in Table 35-1.

Part II: Op-Amp Differentiator

1. Set up your final amplifier circuit in Fig. 35-2.
2. Measure

$A_{low} = \frac{v_{o(peak)}}{v_{s(peak)}} =$ ________; $f_H =$ ________ kHz; $f_L =$ ________ kHz

BW = ________ kHz; GBW = ________ kHz

3. Complete the experimental values in Table 35-2.

REPORT

1. Compare the results in Tables 35-1 and 35-2. Comment on any discrepancies.

____

____

2. Does the unity gain bandwidth depend on the circuit configurations? Explain.

____

____

3. Why the unity-gain amplifier has the highest value of f_H? Explain.

____

____

4. What is the slope of the gain (versus frequency) characteristic of the circuit in Fig. 17-1?

Slope = ________ dB/decade

5. Why does the differentiator exhibit a mid-band characteristic? Explain.

6. What is the estimated cost of the amplifier?

7. Analyze and interpret the data due to any variations and practical limitations.

8. Describe the safety issues considered while conducting the experiment.

9. Describe the process to design and conduct experiments.

10. Conclusion and comment on achieving goals or objectives of this experiment.

ATTACH ALL PLOTS/GRAPHS TO YOUR REPORT

CHAPTER

36 Feedback Op-Amp Circuits

Learning Objectives

To investigate the effects of feedback on op-amp circuits. You will use computer simulation to evaluate the performance of feedback op-amp circuits.

After the end of this experiment, you should be able to

- Describe the types and characteristics of feedback amplifiers.
- Analyze feedback amplifiers.

PRE-LAB ASSIGNMENT

Read on *Feedback Amplifiers* (e.g., Rashid's Sections 9.8–9.12: Analysis of Feedback Amplifiers).

PAPER–PENCIL ANALYSIS

Use op-amp μA741 whose $R_i = 2\ \text{M}\Omega$, $A_o = 10^5$, and $R_o = 75\ \Omega$. Assume dc supply voltages, $V_{CC} = -V_{EE} = 12\text{V}$.

Part I: Series–Shunt Feedback

Use feedback techniques to find the input resistance R_{if} $(= v_s/i_s)$, the output resistance R_{of}, and the closed-loop voltage gain A_f $(= v_o/v_s)$ for the feedback op-amp circuit shown in Fig. 36-1. Complete the calculated values in Table 36-1.

Table 36-1 Series–shunt feedback op-amp circuit

	$R_{if} = v_{s(rms)}/i_{s(rms)}$ (kΩ)	R_{of} (kΩ)	$A_f = v_o/v_s$
Calculated			
Simulated			
Practical			

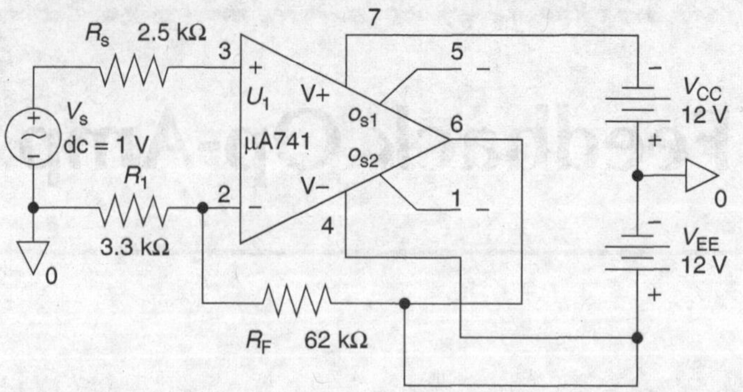

Figure 36-1 Series–shunt feedback op-amp circuit

Part II: Series–Series Feedback

Use feedback techniques to find the input resistance R_{if} $(= v_{s(rms)}/i_{s(rms)})$, the output resistance R_{of}, and the closed-loop voltage gain A_f $(=v_o/v_s)$ for the feedback op-amp circuit shown in Fig. 36-2. Complete the calculated values in Table 36-2.

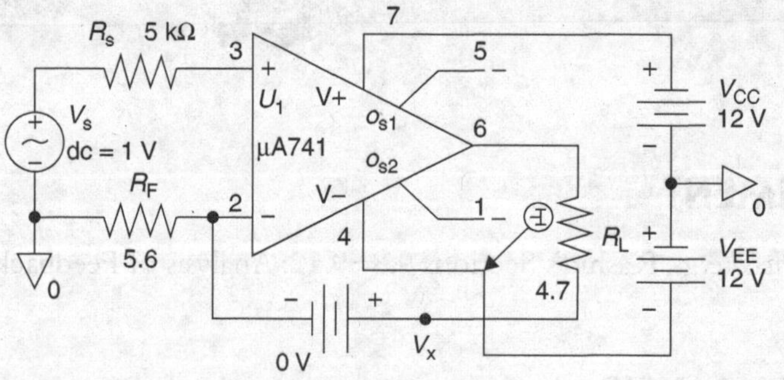

Figure 36-2 Series–series feedback op-amp circuit

Table 36-2 Series–series feedback op-amp circuit

	$R_{if} = v_{s(rms)}/i_{s(rms)}$ (kΩ)	R_{of} (kΩ)	$A_f = v_o/v_s$
Calculated			
Simulated			
Experimental			

Part III: Shunt–Shunt Feedback

Use feedback techniques to find the input resistance R_{if} $(= v_{s(rms)}/i_{s(rms)})$, the output resistance R_{of}, and the closed-loop voltage gain A_f $(= v_o/v_s)$ for the feedback op-amp circuit shown in Fig. 36-3. Complete the calculated values in Table 36-3.

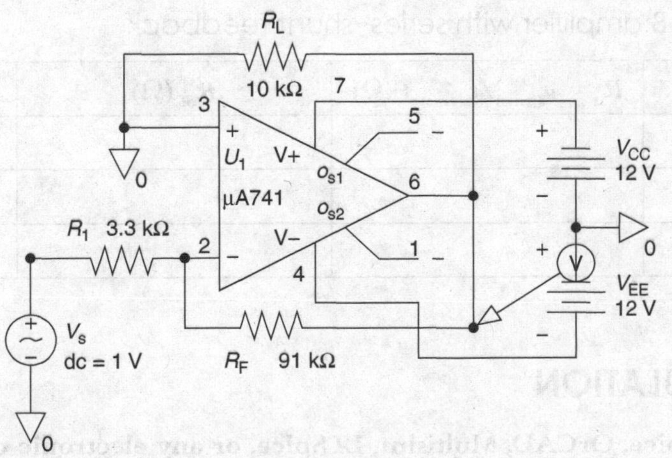

Figure 36-3 Shunt–shunt feedback op-amp circuit

Table 36-3 Shunt–shunt feedback op-amp circuit

	$R_{if} = v_{s(rms)}/i_{s(rms)}$ (kΩ)	R_{of} (Ω)	$A_f = v_o/v_s$
Calculated			
Simulated			
Experimental			

Part IV: Elimination of Distortion

A series–shunt feedback is applied to a class B amplifier as shown in Fig. 36-4. Use feedback techniques to find the input resistance R_{if} ($= v_{s(rms)}/i_{s(rms)}$), the output resistance R_{of}, and the closed-loop voltage gain A_f ($= v_o/v_s$). Complete the calculated values in Table 36-4.

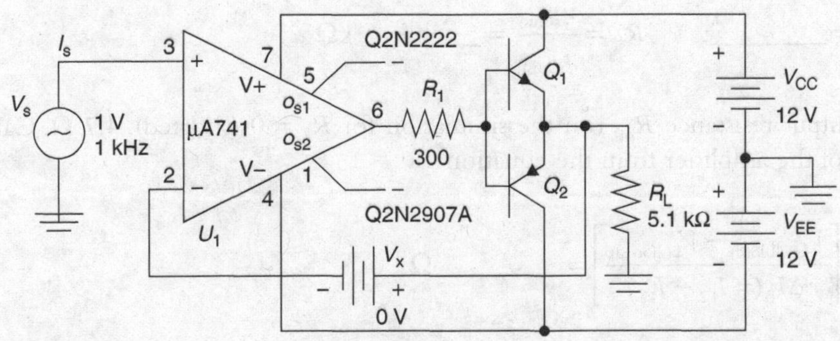

Figure 36-4 Eliminating distortion by feedback

Table 36-4 A class B amplifier with series–shunt feedback

	$R_{if} = v_{s(rms)}/i_{s(rms)}$ (kΩ)	R_{of} (Ω)	$A_f = v_o/v_s$
Calculated			
Simulated			
Experimental			

COMPUTER SIMULATION

Software Tools: PSpice, OrCAD, Multisim, LTSpice, or any electronic circuit simulator.

Part I: Series–Shunt Feedback

1. Simulate the amplifier shown in Fig. 36-1 by using computer simulation with an input signal voltage, $v_s = 10$ mV (sinusoidal peak), 1 kHz. Find the values of

$$A_f = \frac{v_o}{v_s} = \_\_\_\_\_\_\_\_ \text{V/V}; \qquad R_{if} = \frac{v_{s(rms)}}{i_{s(rms)}} = \_\_\_\_\_\_\_\_ \text{k}\Omega$$

2. To find the output resistance R_{of}, run the simulation for $R_L = \infty$ (or say10 MΩ), 10 k. Calculate the output resistance R_o of the amplifier from the equation.

$$R_{of} = R_L\left[\frac{V_{L(\text{no-load})} - V_{L(\text{full-load})}}{V_{L(\text{full-load})}}\right] = \_\_\_\_\_\_\_\_ \Omega \tag{36.1}$$

Complete the simulated values in Table 36-1.

Part II: Series–Series Feedback

1. Simulate the amplifier shown in Fig. 36-2 by using computer simulation with an input signal voltage, $v_s = 10$ mV (sinusoidal peak), 1 kHz. Find the values of

$$A_f = \frac{v_o}{v_s} = \_\_\_\_\_\_\_\_; \qquad R_{if} = \frac{v_{s(rms)}}{i_{s(rms)}} = \_\_\_\_\_\_\_\_ \text{k}\Omega$$

2. To find the output resistance R_{of}, run the simulation for $R_L = 0$ (shorted), 4.7 Ω. Calculate the output resistance R_{of} of the amplifier from the equation

$$R_{of} = R_L\left[\frac{V_{L(\text{full-load})} - V_{L(\text{shorted})}}{\Delta I_L (= I_{L2} - I_{L1})}\right] = \_\_\_\_\_\_\_\_ \Omega \tag{36.2}$$

Complete the simulated values in Table 36-2.

Part III: Shunt–Shunt Feedback

1. Simulate the amplifier shown in Fig. 36-3 by using computer simulation with an input signal voltage, $v_s = 10$ mV (sinusoidal peak), 1 kHz. Find the values of

$$A_f = \frac{v_o}{v_s} = \_\_\_\_\_\_\_\_\text{ V/V}; \qquad R_{if} = \frac{v_{s(rms)}}{i_{s(rms)}} = \_\_\_\_\_\_\_\_\text{ k}\Omega$$

2. To find the output resistance R_{of}, run the simulation for $R_L = \infty$ (or say10 MΩ), 10 kΩ. Calculate the output resistance R_o of the amplifier from the equation.

$$R_{of} = R_L\left[\frac{V_{L(\text{no-load})} - V_{L(\text{full-load})}}{V_{L(\text{full-load})}}\right] = \_\_\_\_\_\_\_\_\ \Omega \tag{36.3}$$

Complete the simulated values in Table 36-3.

Part IV: Elimination of Distortion

1. Run the transient analysis of the class B amplifier shown in Fig. 36-5. Plot and observe the input and output voltages. Is the output voltage sinusoidal? Explain any difference(s) between them.

____

____

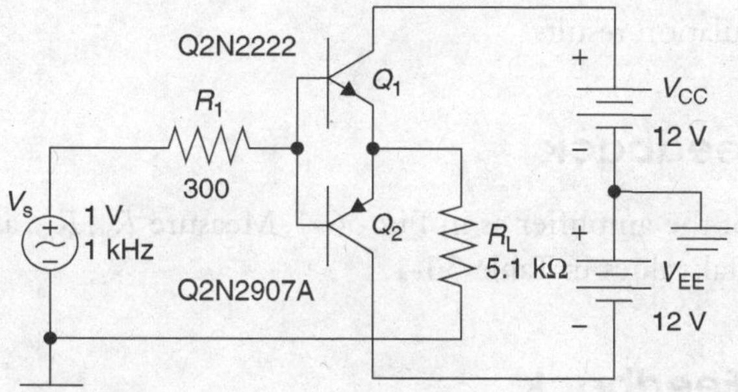

Figure 36-5 Class B amplifier

Plot the transfer characteristic by changing the x-variable to the input voltage v_s. Is the relationship linear (i.e., $v_o = v_s$)? Explain the transfer relationship.

____

____

Record: v_o (at $v_s = 0$) $= V_{o(\text{threshold})} = \_\_\_\_\_\_\_\_$ V

v_s (at $v_o = 0$) $= V_{s(\text{threshold})} = \_\_\_\_\_\_\_\_$ V

2. Run the transient analysis of the feedback amplifier shown in Fig. 36-5. Plot and observe the input and output voltages. Is the output voltages sinusoidal? Explain any difference(s) between them.

____

____

Plot the transfer characteristics by changing the *x*-variable to the input voltage v_s. Is the relationship linear (i.e., $v_o = v_s$)? Explain the transfer relationship.

____

____

Record: v_o (at $v_s = 0$) $= V_{o(threshold)} =$ __________ V

v_s (at $v_o = 0$) $= V_{s(threshold)} =$ __________ V

3. Compare the results in steps 1 and 2. Explain the effects of feedback on the performance of the class Bamplifier.

____

____

____

EXPERIMENTS

The students are strongly encouraged and recommended to build and test the amplifier circuit to validate the theoretical and computer simulation results.

Part I: Series–Shunt Feedback

1. Set up your final circuit of the amplifier as in Fig. 36-1. Measure R_{if}, R_{of}, and A_f.
2. Complete the experimental values in Table 36-1.

Part II: Series–Series Feedback

1. Set up your final circuit of the amplifier as in Fig. 36-2. Measure R_{if}, R_{of}, and A_f.
2. Complete the experimental values in Table 36-2.

Part III: Shunt–Shunt Feedback

1. Set up your final circuit of the amplifier in Fig. 36-3. Measure R_{if}, R_{of}, and A_f.
2. Complete the experimental values in Table 36-3.

Part IV: Elimination of Distortion

1. Set up your final circuit of the amplifier as in Fig. 36-4. Measure R_{if}, R_{of}, and A_f.
2. Complete the experimental values in Table 36-4.

Record: v_o (at $v_s = 0$) = $V_{o(threshold)}$ = ________V

v_s (at $v_o = 0$) = $V_{s(threshold)}$ = ________V

REPORT

1. What are the effects of series–shunt feedback on the input resistance, output resistance, and gain of an amplifier? Explain.

2. What are the effects of series–series feedback on the input resistance, output resistance, and the gain of an amplifier? Explain.

3. What are the effects of shunt–shunt feedback on the input resistance, output resistance, and gain of an amplifier? Explain.

4. Analyze and interpret the data due to any variations and practical limitations.

5. Describe the safety issues considered while conducting the experiment.

6. Describe the process to design and conduct experiments.

7. Conclusion and comment on achieving goals or objectives of this experiment.

ATTACH ALL PLOTS/GRAPHS TO YOUR REPORT

CHAPTER 37

Design of a Sallen – Key Band-Pass Active Filter

Learning Objectives

To design active filters to give a specified frequency response. You will use computer simulation to verify the design and evaluate the performance of active filters.

After the end of this experiment, you should be able to

- Describe the types and frequency characteristics of active filters.
- Analyze and design active filters.

PRE-LAB ASSIGNMENT

Read on *Op-Amp Active Filters* (e.g., Rashid's Section 11.10: Low-Pass Filters).

DESIGN SPECIFICATIONS

A low-pass filter can be cascaded with a high-pass filter to get the band-pass characteristics. Design the second-order active filter as shown in Fig. 37-1 to meet the following specifications:

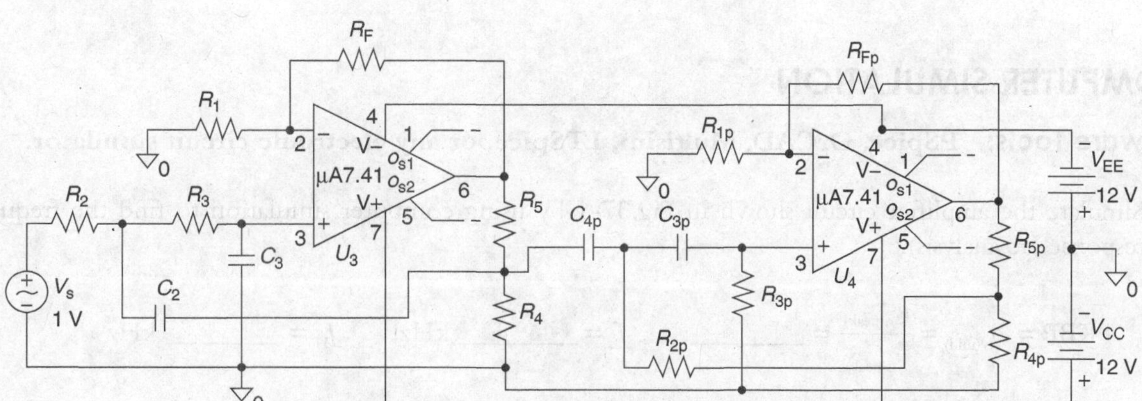

Figure 37-1 Sallen–Key active filter

- Pass-band voltage gain, $K_{BP} = K_H K_L = v_o/v_s = 240 \pm 5\%$
- Low cut-off (or 3-dB) frequency, $f_L = 10$ kHz $\pm$ 5%
- High cut-off (or 3-dB) frequency, $f_H = 100$ kHz
- Use op-amps μA741 or LF411
- dc supply voltages, $VCC = V_{EE} = 12$ V
- Input signal, $v_s = 10$ mV (peak sinusoidal)

PAPER–PENCIL DESIGN

Note: Select the passive component values closest to the practical values.

1. After completing your design, write the circuit values.

R_1 = ________ kΩ; R_2 = ________ kΩ; R_3 = ________ kΩ; R_4 = ________ kΩ

R_5 = ________ kΩ; R_F = ________ kΩ

R_{1p} = ________ kΩ; R_{2p} = ________ kΩ; R_{3p} = ________ kΩ; R_{4p} = ________ kΩ

R_{5p} = ________ kΩ R_{Fp} = ________ kΩ

C_2 = ________ nF; C_3 = ________ nF; C_{3p} = ________ nF; C_{4p} = ________ nF

2. Complete the calculated values in Table 37-1.

Table 37-1 Frequency response of Sallen–Key active filter

	Calculated	Simulated	Experimental
f_L (kHz)			
f_L (kHz)			
KBP			

COMPUTER SIMULATION

Software Tools: PSpice, OrCAD, Multisim, LTSpice, or any electronic circuit simulator.

1. Simulate the amplifier circuit shown in Fig.37-1 by using computer simulation to find the frequency response (ac analysis).

$$\text{KBP} = A_{v(\text{mid})} = \frac{v_{o(\text{peak})}}{v_{s(\text{peak})}} = \underline{\qquad\qquad};\quad f_L = \underline{\qquad\qquad}\ \text{kHz};\quad f_H = \underline{\qquad\qquad}\ \text{kHz}$$

2. Assign ±5% tolerance to all capacitors and resistors. Run the simulation for the worst-case maximum gain and record.

$$KBP = A_{v(mid)} = \frac{v_{o(peak)}}{v_{s(peak)}} = \_\_\_\_\_\_\_\_;\quad f_L = \_\_\_\_\_\_\_\_ \text{ kHz};\quad f_H = \_\_\_\_\_\_\_\_ \text{ kHz}$$

3. Does your design meet the specifications under the worst-case conditions? If not, which resistance(s) would you adjust to get the desired gain? Which capacitor(s) would you adjust to get the desired cut-off frequencies? Why? Explain.

____

____

Change the component values so that the specifications are met. Note these values.

__________ __________ __________ __________

4. Run the computer simulation with your suggested values in step 3 and complete the simulated values in Table 37-1.
Comment on the effects of the component tolerance on the design.

____

____

EXPERIMENTS

The students are strongly encouraged and recommended to build and test the amplifier circuit to validate the theoretical and computer simulation results.

1. Set up your final amplifier circuit as in Fig. 37-1.
2. Measure:

$$KBP = A_{v(mid)} = \frac{v_{o(peak)}}{v_{s(peak)}} = \_\_\_\_\_\_\_\_;\quad f_L = \_\_\_\_\_\_\_\_ \text{ kHz};\quad f_H = \_\_\_\_\_\_\_\_ \text{ kHz}$$

3. Complete the experimental values in Table 37-1.

REPORT

1. Compare the results from the computer simulation and experiment. Comment on any discrepancies.

____

____

2. Does the design meet the specifications? If not, explain the reasons.

____

____

3. What are the parameters that influence the low and high cut-off frequencies? Explain.

4. What is the estimated cost of the amplifier?

5. Analyze and interpret the data due to any variations and practical limitations.

6. Describe the safety issues considered while conducting the experiment.

7. Describe the process to design and conduct experiments.

8. Conclusion and comment on achieving goals or objectives of this experiment.

ATTACH ALL PLOTS/GRAPHS TO YOUR REPORT

CHAPTER

38 Design of a Butterworth Band-Pass Active Filter

Learning Objectives

To design Butterworth-active filters to give a specified frequency response. You will use computer simulation to verify the design and evaluate the performance of Butterworth active filters.

After the end of this experiment, you should be able to

- Describe frequency characteristics of Butterworth-active filters.
- Analyze and design Butterworth-active filters

PRE-LAB ASSIGNMENT

Read on *Op-Amp Active Filters* (e.g., Rashid's Section 11.10: Low Pass Filters; Section 11.11: High-Pass Filters).

DESIGN SPECIFICATIONS

A low-pass Butterworth filter can be cascaded with a high-pass Butterworth filter to get the band-pass characteristic. Design the second-order Butterworth active filter as shown in Fig. 38-1 to meet the following specifications:

- Pass-band voltage gain, $K_{BP} = K_H K_L = v_o/v_s = 1$ at $\omega = \omega_o$ (cut-off frequencies)
- Low cut-off (or 3-dB) frequency, $f_L = 10$ kHz ± 5%
- High cut-off (or 3-dB) frequency, $f_H = 100$ kHz ± 5%
- Use op-amps: µA741 or LF411
- dc supply voltages, $VCC = -V_{EE} = 12$ V
- Input signal, $v_s = 10$ mV (peak sinusoidal)

PAPER–PENCIL DESIGN

Note: Select the passive component values closest to the practical values.

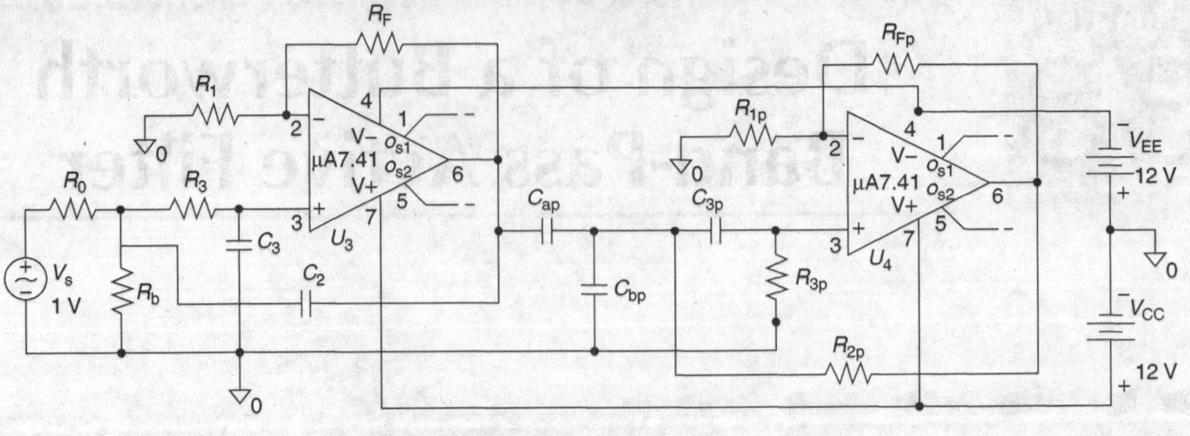

Figure 38-1 Butterworth active filter

1. After completing your design, write the circuit values.

R_a = ________ kΩ; R_b = ________ kΩ; R_1 = ________ kΩ; R_3 = ________ kΩ

R_F = ________ kΩ

R_{1p} = ________ kΩ; R_{2p} = ________ kΩ; R_{3p} = ________ kΩ; R_{Fp} = ________ kΩ

C_2 = ________ nF; C_3 = ________ nF; C_{3p} = ________ nF; C_{ap} = ________ pF

C_{bp} = ________ pF

2. Complete the calculated values in Table 38-1.

Table 38-1 Frequency response of Butterworth active filter

	Calculated	Simulated	Experimental
f_L (kHz)			
f_L (kHz)			
KBP			

COMPUTER SIMULATION

Software Tools: PSpice, OrCAD, Multisim, LTSpice, or any electronic circuit simulator.

1. Simulate the amplifier circuit shown in Fig. 38-1 by using computer simulation to find the frequency response (ac analysis).

$$K_{BP} = A_{v(mid)} = \frac{v_{o(peak)}}{v_{s(peak)}} = \_\_\_\_\_\_\_\_;\quad f_L = \_\_\_\_\_\_\_\_ \text{ kHz};\quad f_H = \_\_\_\_\_\_\_\_ \text{ kHz}$$

2. Assign ±5% tolerance to all capacitors and resistors. Run the simulation for the worst-case maximum gain and record.

$$K_{BP} = A_{v(mid)} = \frac{v_{o(peak)}}{v_{s(peak)}} = \_\_\_\_\_\_\_\_; \quad f_L = \_\_\_\_\_\_\_\_ \text{kHz}; \quad f_H = \_\_\_\_\_\_\_\_ \text{kHz}$$

3. Does your design meet the specifications under the worst-case conditions? If not, which resistance(s) would you adjust to get the desired gain? Which capacitor(s) would you adjust to get the desired cut-off frequencies? Why? Explain.

____

____

Change the component values so that the specifications are met. Note these values.

__________ __________ __________ __________

4. Run the computer simulation with your suggested values in step 3 and complete the simulated values in Table 38-1.

   Comment on the effects of the component tolerance on the design.

____

____

EXPERIMENTS

The students are strongly encouraged and recommended to build and test the amplifier circuit to validate the theoretical and computer simulation results.

1. Set up your final amplifier circuit in Fig. 38-1.
2. Measure

$$K_{BP} = A_{v(mid)} = \frac{v_{o(peak)}}{v_{s(peak)}} = \_\_\_\_\_\_\_\_; \quad f_L = \_\_\_\_\_\_\_\_ \text{kHz}; \quad f_H = \_\_\_\_\_\_\_\_ \text{kHz}$$

3. Complete the experimental values in Table 38-1.

REPORT

1. Compare the results from the computer simulation and experiment. Comment on any discrepancies.

____

____

2. Does the design meet the specifications? If not, explain the reasons.

3. What are the parameters that influence the low and high cut-off frequencies? Explain.

4. What is the estimated cost of the amplifier?

5. Analyze and interpret the data due to any variations and practical limitations.

6. Describe the safety issues considered while conducting the experiment.

7. Describe the process to design and conduct experiments.

8. Conclusion and comment on achieving goals or objectives of this experiment.

ATTACH ALL PLOTS/GRAPHS TO YOUR REPORT

CHAPTER 39

Op-Amp Phase-Shift Oscillators

Learning Objectives

To study the characteristics of oscillators and their conditions for sustained oscillations. We will use computer simulation to evaluate the performance of op-amp oscillators.

After the end of this experiment, you should be able to

- Describe the characteristics of phase-shift oscillators and the conditions for sustained oscillations.
- Analyze sinusoidal oscillators.

PRE-LAB ASSIGNMENT

Read on *Op-Oscillators* (e.g. Rashid's Sections 12.5.1: Phase-Shift Oscillator).

PAPER–PENCIL ANALYSIS

Use op-amp μA741 whose $R_i = 2\ M\Omega$, $A_o = 10^5$, and $R_o = 75\ \Omega$. Assume dc supply voltages, $V_{CC} = -V_{EE} = 12V$.

Part I: Phase-Shift Oscillator

A phase-shift oscillator is shown in Fig. 39-1. Find the output frequency f_o and the peak output voltage $V_{o(peak)}$. Complete the calculated values in Table 39-1.

Note: The component values in Fig. 39-1 are shown for illustrations only.

Table 39-1 Phase-shift op-amp oscillator

	f_o (kHz)	$V_{o(peak)}$ (V)	$K_f = R_F/R_1$	Sustained oscillation
Calculated				______Y; ______N
Simulated				______Y; ______N
Experimental				______Y; ______N

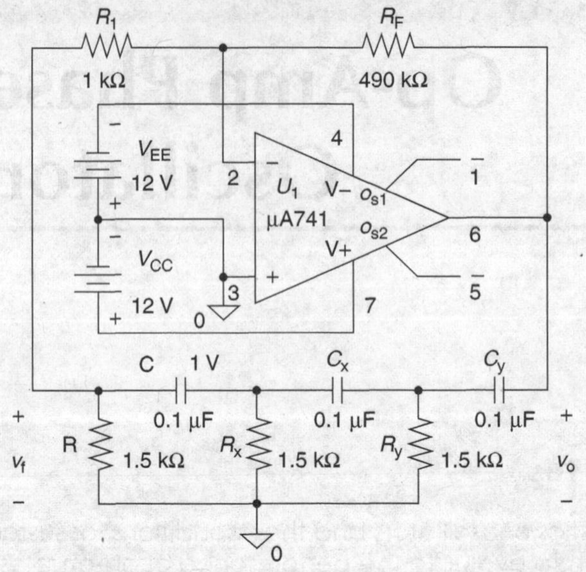

Figure 39-1 Phase-shift oscillator

Part II: Stabilized Phase-Shift Oscillator

A stabilization network consisting of two Zener diodes and a resistor R_b is connected across R_F as shown in Fig. 39-1. This is shown in Fig. 39-2. Find the output frequency f_o. and the peak output voltage $V_{o(peak)}$. Complete the calculated values in Table 39-2.

Note: The component values in Fig. 39-2 are shown for illustrations only.

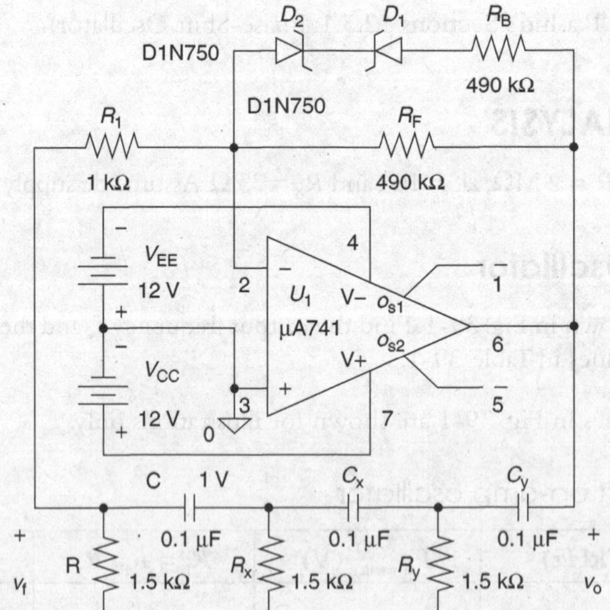

Figure 39-2 Stabilized phase-shift oscillator

Table 39-2 Stabilized phase-shift op-amp oscillator

	f_o (kHz)	$V_{o(peak)}$ (V)	$K_f = R_F/R_1$	Sustained oscillation
Calculated				_______Y; _______N
Simulated				_______Y; _______N
Experimental				_______Y; _______N

COMPUTER SIMULATION

Software tools: PSpice, OrCAD, Multisim, LTSpice, or any electronic circuit simulator.

Part I: Phase-Shift Oscillator

1. Simulate the oscillator shown in Fig. 39-1 by using computer simulation. Is the oscillation sustaining? If not, adjust the value of R_F (by increasing) until the oscillation builds up and sustains. Find the following values for sustained oscillation.

f_o = ________ kHz; $V_{o(peak)}$ = ________V; $K_f = \frac{R_F}{R_1}$ = ________

Complete the simulated values in Table 39-1.

Part II: Stabilized Phase-Shift Oscillator

1. Simulate the oscillator shown in Fig. 39-2 by using computer simulation. Is the oscillation sustaining? If not, adjust the value of R_F (by increasing) until the oscillation builds up and sustains. Find and record the values of

f_o = ________ kHz; $V_{o(peak)}$ = ________V; $K_f = \frac{R_F}{R_1}$ = ________

Complete the simulated values in Table 39-2.
Compare the results with those in part I. Comment on the effect of the stabilizing network on the output.

____

____

2. Adjust the value of $R_b = R_F$. Does the oscillation sustain? If not, why? Explain.

____

____

____

Adjust the value of R_1 (by reducing) until the oscillation builds up and sustains. Find and record the values of

$f_o =$ ________ kHz; $V_{o(peak)} =$ ________ V; $K_f = \frac{R_F}{R_1} =$ ________

EXPERIMENTS

The students are strongly encouraged and recommended to build and test the amplifier circuit to validate the theoretical and computer simulation results.

Part I: Phase-Shift Oscillator

1. Set up your final circuit of the oscillator in Fig. 39-1. Measure f_o, $V_{o(peak)}$, and K_f.
2. Complete the experimental values in Table 39-1.

Part II: Stabilized Phase-Shift Oscillator

1. Set up your final circuit of the oscillator in Fig. 39-2. Measure f_o, $V_{o(peak)}$, and K_f.
2. Complete the experimental values in Table 39-2.

REPORT

1. What is the effect of a stabilizing network on the operation of an oscillator? Explain.

2. What is the effect of the ratio K_f (= R_F/R_1) on the operation of an oscillator? Explain.

3. What is the purpose of assigning an initial voltage to a capacitor (e.g., 1 V for C_F) while simulating an oscillator circuit? Explain.

4. To adjust the oscillation frequency which element (capacitor or resistor) would you adjust? Explain.

5. If you find an oscillator is not building up, what would you do (or which elements would you adjust) to make it oscillate? Explain.

____

____

____

6. If you find an oscillator is building up the oscillation, but not sustaining the oscillation, what would you do to make it sustain oscillate? Explain.

____

____

7. Analyze and interpret the data due to any variations and practical limitations.

____

____

8. Describe the safety issues considered while conducting the experiment.

____

____

9. Describe the process to design and conduct experiments.

____

____

10. Conclusion and comment on achieving goals or objectives of this experiment.

____

____

ATTACH ALL PLOTS/GRAPHS TO YOUR REPORT

CHAPTER

40

Op-Amp Quadrature Oscillators

Learning Objectives

To study the characteristics of oscillators and their conditions for sustained oscillations. We will use computer to evaluate the performance of op-amp oscillators.

After the end of this experiment, you should be able to

- Describe the characteristics of quadrature oscillators and the conditions for sustained oscillations.
- Analyze sinusoidal oscillators.

PRE-LAB ASSIGNMENT

Read on *Op-Oscillators* (e.g., Rashid's Sections 12.5.2: Quadrature Oscillator).

PAPER–PENCIL ANALYSIS

Use op-amp μA741 whose $R_i = 2\ \text{M}\Omega$, $A_o = 10^5$, and $R_o = 75\ \Omega$. Assume dc supply voltages, $V_{CC} = -V_{EE} = 12$ V.

Part I: Quadrature Oscillator

A quadrature oscillator is shown in Fig. 40-1. Find the output frequency f_o and the peak output voltage $V_{o(peak)}$. Complete the calculated values in Table 40-1. Complete the calculated values in Table 40-1.

Note: The component values in Fig. 40-1 are shown for illustrations only.

Table 40-1 Quadrature op-amp oscillator

	f_o (kHz)	$V_{o(peak)}$ (V)	$K_f = R_F/R_1$	Sustained oscillation
Calculated				______Y; ______N
Simulated				______Y; ______N
Experimental				______Y; ______N

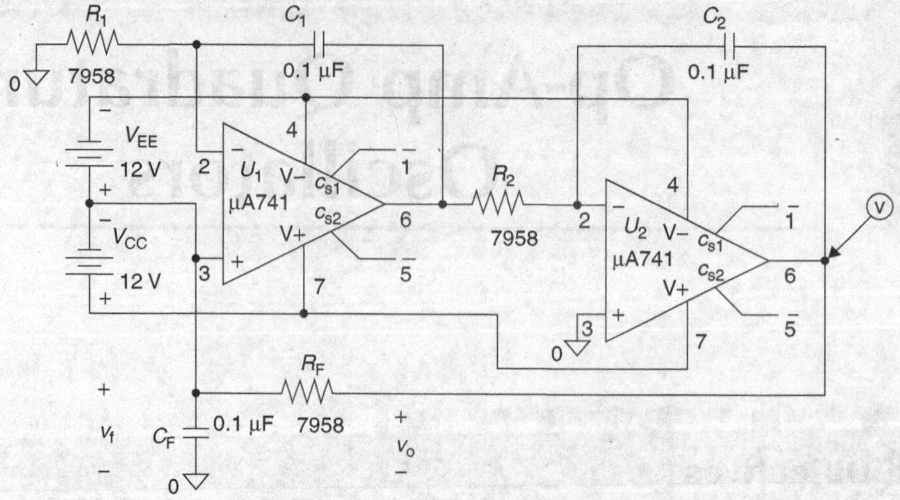

Figure 40-1 Quadrature oscillator

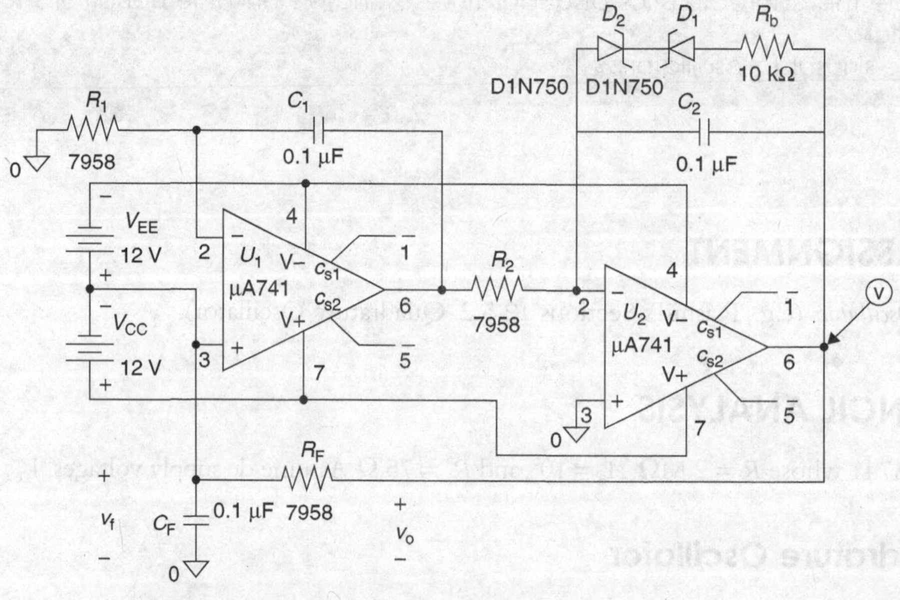

Figure 40-2 Stabilized quadrature oscillator

Table 40-2 Stabilized quadrature op-amp oscillator

	f_o (kHz)	$V_{o(peak)}$ (V)	$K_f = R_F/R_1$	Sustained oscillation
Calculated				______Y; ______N
Simulated				______Y; ______N
Experimental				______Y; ______N

Part II: Stabilized Quadrature Oscillator

A stabilization network consisting of two Zener diodes and a resistor R_b is connected across C_2 as shown in Fig. 40-2. Find the output frequency f_o and the peak output voltage $V_{o(peak)}$. Complete the calculated values in Table 40-2.

Note: The component values in Fig. 40-2 are shown for illustrations only.

COMPUTER SIMULATION

Software Tools: PSpice, OrCAD, Multisim, LTSpice, or any electronic circuit simulator.

Part I: Quadrature Oscillator

1. Simulate the oscillator shown in Fig. 40-1 by using computer simulation. Is the oscillation sustaining? If not, why?

____

____

Find and record the values:

$f_o =$ ________ kHz; $V_{o(peak)} =$ ________ V; $K_f = \dfrac{R_F}{R_1} =$ ________

Complete the simulated values in Table 40-1.

Part II: Stabilized Quadrature Oscillator

1. Simulate the oscillator shown in Fig. 40-2 by using computer simulation. Is the oscillation sustaining? If yes, why? Explain.

____

____

Find and record the values:

$f_o =$ ________ kHz; $V_{o(peak)} =$ ________ V; $K_f = \dfrac{R_F}{R_1} =$ ________

Complete the simulated values in Table 40-2.
Compare the results with those in part I. Comment on the effect of the stabilizing network on the output.

____

____

2. Adjust the value of $R_b = R_F$. Does the oscillation sustain? If not, why? Explain.

____

____

Adjust the value of R_1 (by reducing) until the oscillation builds up and sustains. Find and record the values of

$f_o =$ ________ kHz; $V_{o(peak)} =$ ________ V; $K_f = \dfrac{R_F}{R_1} =$ ________

3. If you need to change the oscillation frequency, which element will you change? Why? Explain.

____

____

EXPERIMENTS

The students are strongly encouraged and recommended to build and test the amplifier circuit to validate the theoretical and computer simulation results.

Part I: Quadrature Oscillator

1. Set up your final circuit of the oscillator in Fig. 40-1. Measure f_o, $V_{o(peak)}$; and K_f.
2. Complete the experimental values in Table 40-1.

Part II: Stabilized Quadrature Oscillator

1. Set up your final circuit of the oscillator in Fig. 40-2. Measure f_o, $V_{o(peak)}$, and K_f.
2. Complete the experimental values in Table 40-2.

REPORT

1. What is the effect of a stabilizing network on the operation of an oscillator? Explain.

____

____

2. What is the effect of the ratio K_f ($= R_F/R_1$) on the operation of an oscillator? Explain.

____

____

3. What is the purpose of assigning an initial voltage to a capacitor (e.g., 1 V for C_F) while simulating an oscillator circuit? Explain.

4. To adjust the oscillation frequency, which element (capacitor or resistor) would you adjust? Explain.

5. If you find an oscillator is not building up, what would you do (or which elements would you adjust) to make it oscillate? Explain.

6. If you find an oscillator is building up the oscillation, but not sustaining the oscillation, what would you do to make it sustain oscillation? Explain.

7. Analyze and interpret the data due to any variations and practical limitations.

8. Describe the safety issues considered while conducting the experiment.

9. Describe the process to design and conduct experiments.

10. Conclusion and comment on achieving goals or objectives of this experiment.

ATTACH ALL PLOTS/GRAPHS TO YOUR REPORT

CHAPTER

41

Design of an Op-Amp Phase-Shift Oscillator

Learning Objectives

To design op-amp oscillators to give a sinusoidal output voltage of specified frequency. You will use computer simulation to verify the design and evaluate the performance of oscillators.

After the end of this experiment, you should be able to

- Describe the characteristics of oscillators and their conditions for sustained oscillations.
- Analyze and design sinusoidal oscillators.

PRE-LAB ASSIGNMENT

Read on *Op-Oscillators* (e.g., Rashid's Sections 12.5.1: Phase-Shift Oscillator).

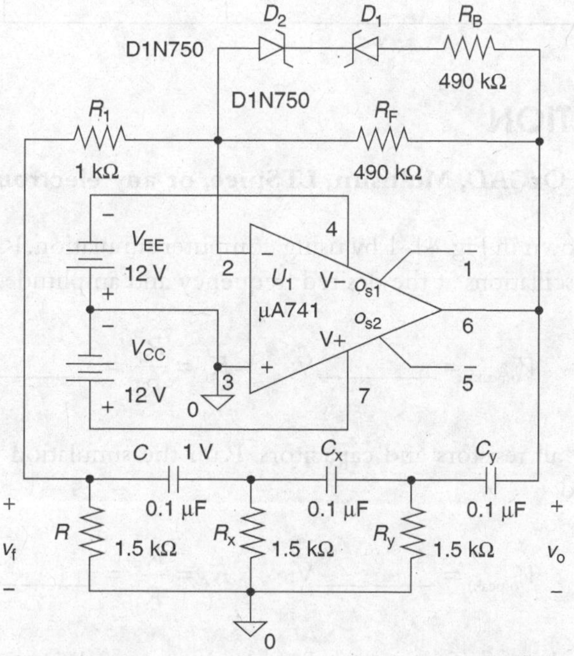

Figure 41-1 Quadrature oscillator

DESIGN SPECIFICATIONS

Use op-amp μA741 whose $R_i = 2\ \text{M}\Omega$, $A_o = 10^5$, and $R_o = 75\ \Omega$. Assume dc supply voltages, $V_{CC} = -V_{EE} = 12$ V. Design the quadrature oscillator shown in Fig. 41-1 to meet the following specifications:

- Oscillation frequency, $f_o = 450$ Hz ± 5%
- Peak output voltage, $V_{o(peak)} = 5$ V ± 5%

PAPER-PENCIL DESIGN

Note: Select the passive component values closest to the practical values. The component values in Fig. 41-1 are shown for illustrations only.

1. After completing your design, write the circuit values.

$R_1 =$ ________ kΩ; $R_F =$ ________ kΩ; $R = R_x = R_y =$ ________ kΩ

$R_b =$ ________ kΩ; $C = C_x = C_y =$ ________ μF

2. Complete the calculated values in Table 41-1.

Table 41-1 Quadrature oscillator

	f_o (kHz)	$V_{o(peak)}$ (V)	$K_f = R_F / R_1$	Sustained oscillation
Calculated				________Y; ________N
Simulated				________Y; ________N
Experimental				________Y; ________N

COMPUTER SIMULATION

Software Tools: PSpice, OrCAD, Multisim, LTSpice, or any electronic circuit simulator.

1. Simulate the amplifier shown in Fig. 41-1 by using computer simulation. Run transient analysis to ensure that the circuit sustains oscillations at the desired frequency and amplitude.

$f_o =$ ________ Hz; $V_{o(peak)} =$ ________ V; $K_f = \dfrac{R_F}{R_1} =$ ________

2. Assign ±5% tolerance to all resistors and capacitors. Run the simulation for the worst-case maximum output voltage and record.

$f_o =$ ________ Hz; $V_{o(peak)} =$ ________ V; $K_f = \dfrac{R_F}{R_1} =$ ________

3. Does your design meet the specifications under worst-case conditions? If not, which resistor(s) and capacitor(s) would you adjust to get the desired amplitude and frequency? Why?

Change the component values so that the specifications are met. Note these values.

4. Run the computer simulation with your suggested values in step 3 and complete the simulated values in Table 41-1.

EXPERIMENTS

The students are strongly encouraged and recommended to build and test the amplifier circuit to validate the theoretical and computer simulation results.

1. Set up your final circuit of the amplifier in Fig. 41-1. Observe the output voltage $v_L(t)$, its peak value $V_{o(peak)}$, and frequency f_o. If the circuit does not oscillate, adjust the circuit value(s) until it oscillates? Note these values.

2. Complete the experimental values in Table 41-1.

REPORT

1. Compare the results from the computer simulation and experiment. Comment on any discrepancies.

2. Does the design meet the specifications? If not, explain the reasons.

3. What are the parameters that influence the low and high cut-off frequencies? Explain.

4. What is the estimated cost of the oscillator?

5. Analyze and interpret the data due to any variations and practical limitations.

6. Describe the safety issues considered while conducting the experiment.

7. Describe the process to design and conduct experiments.

8. Conclusion and comment on achieving goals or objectives of this experiment.

ATTACH ALL PLOTS/GRAPHS TO YOUR REPORT

CHAPTER 42

Design of an Op-Amp Wein Bridge Oscillator

Learning Objectives

To design op-amp oscillators to give a sinusoidal output voltage of specified frequency. You will use computer simulation to verify the design and evaluate the performance of oscillators.

After the end of this experiment, you should be able to

- **Describe the characteristics of oscillators and their conditions for sustained oscillations.**
- **Analyze and design sinusoidal oscillators.**

PRE-LAB ASSIGNMENT

Read on *Op-Oscillators* (e.g., Rashid's Sections 12.5.4: Wein Bridge Oscillator).

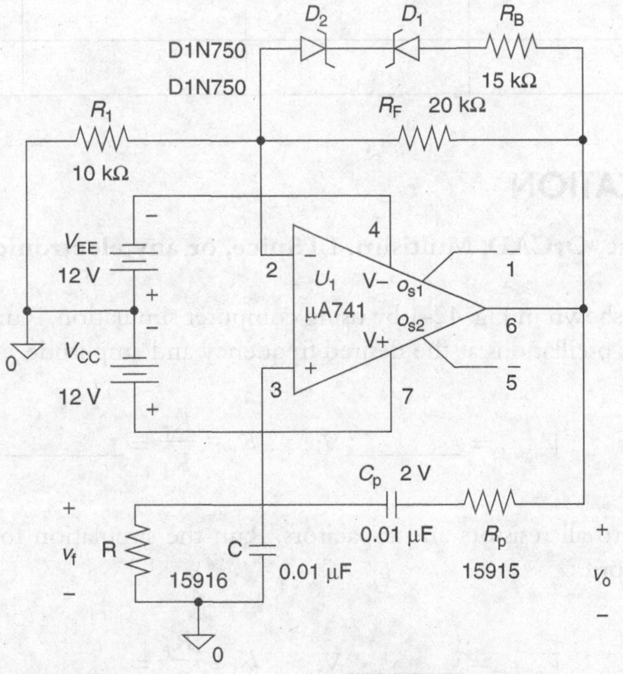

Figure 42-1 Wein bridge oscillator

DESIGN SPECIFICATIONS

Use op-amp μA741 whose $R_i = 2\ M\Omega$, $A_o = 10^5$, and $R_o = 75\ \Omega$. Assume dc supply voltages, $V_{CC} = -V_{EE} = 12V$. Design the Wein bridge oscillator shown in Fig. 42-1 to meet the following specifications:

- Oscillation frequency, $f_o = 8.5$ kHz ± 5%
- Peak output voltage, $V_{o(peak)} = 5$ V ± 5%
- dc supply voltages, $V_{CC} = -V_{EE} = 12$ V

PAPER–PENCIL DESIGN

Note: Select the pasive component values closest to the practical values. Note the component values in Fig. 42-1 are shown for illustrations only.

1. After completing your design, write the circuit values.

   $R_1 =$ ________ kΩ; $R_F =$ ________ kΩ; $R_b =$ ________ kΩ

   $R = R_D =$ ________ kΩ; $C = C_p =$ ____ μF

2. Complete the calculated values in Table 42-1.

Table 42-1 Wein bridge oscillator

	f_o (kHz)	$V_{o(peak)}$ (V)	$K_f = R_F/R_1$	Sustained oscillation
Calculated				________Y; ________N
Simulated				________Y; ________N
Experimental				________Y; ________N

COMPUTER SIMULATION

Software Tools: PSpice, OrCAD, Multisim, LTSpice, or any electronic circuit simulator.

1. Simulate the amplifier shown in Fig. 42-1 by using computer simulation. Run transient analysis to ensure that the circuit sustains oscillations at the desired frequency and amplitude.

   $f_o =$ ________ Hz; $V_{o(peak)} =$ ________ V; $K_f = \dfrac{R_F}{R_1} =$ ________

2. Assign ±5% tolerance to all resistors and capacitors. Run the simulation for the worst-case maximum output voltage and record.

   $f_o =$ ________ Hz; $V_{o(peak)} =$ ________ V; $K_f = \dfrac{R_F}{R_1} =$ ________

3. Does your design meet the specifications under worst-case conditions? If not, which resistor(s) and capacitor(s) would you adjust to get the desired amplitude and frequency? Why?

____

____

Change the component values so that the specifications are met. Note these values.

__________ __________ __________ __________

4. Run the computer simulation with your suggested values in step 3 and complete the simulated values in Table 42-1.

EXPERIMENTS

The students are strongly encouraged and recommended to build and test the amplifier circuit to validate the theoretical and computer simulation results.

1. Set up your final circuit of the amplifier in Fig. 42-1. Observe the output voltage $v_L(t)$, its peak value $V_{o(peak)}$, and frequency f_o. If the circuit does not oscillate, adjust the circuit value(s) until it oscillates? Note these values.

__________ __________ __________ __________

2. Complete the experimental values in Table 42-1.

REPORT

1. Compare the results from the computer simulation and experiment. Comment on any discrepancies.

____

____

2. Does the design meet the specifications? If not, explain the reasons.

____

____

3. What are the parameters that influence the low and high cut-off frequencies? Explain.

____

____

4. What is the estimated cost of the oscillator?

____

____

5. Analyze and interpret the data due to any variations and practical limitations.

6. Describe the safety issues considered while conducting the experiment.

7. Describe the process to design and conduct experiments.

8. Conclusion and comment on achieving goals or objectives of this experiment.

ATTACH ALL PLOTS/GRAPHS TO YOUR REPORT

CHAPTER

43

Design of a Precision Rectifier

Learning Objectives

To design a full-wave precision rectifier. You will use computer simulation to verify the design and evaluate the performance of the rectifier.

After the end of this experiment, you should be able to

- Describe the operation and characteristics of a full-wave precision rectifier.
- Analyze and design precision rectifiers.

PRE-LAB ASSIGNMENT

Read on *Precision Rectifiers* (e.g., Rashid's Section 17.3.4: Precision Full-Wave Rectifiers).

DESIGN SPECIFICATIONS

Design the precision rectifier shown in Fig. 43-1 to meet the following specifications:

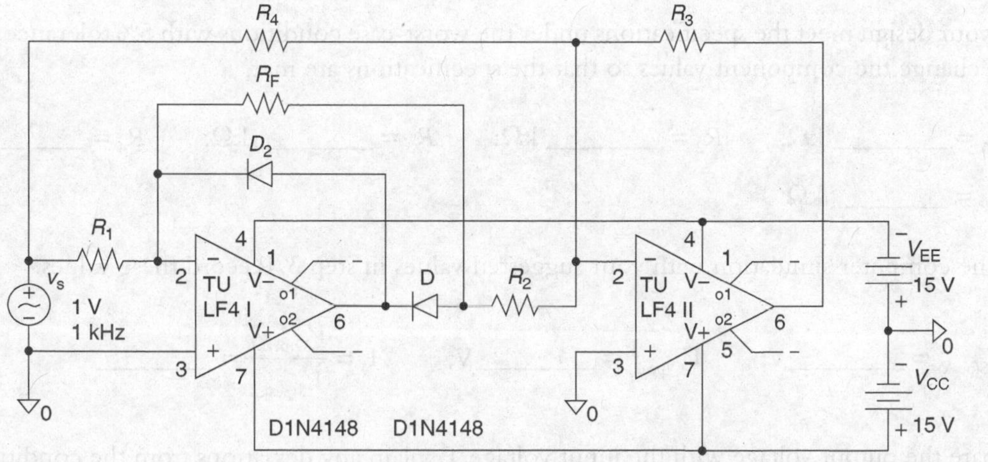

Figure 43-1 Precision full-wave rectifier

- Input voltage, $v_s = 1 \sin 2000\pi t$
- Output voltage, $v_o = |v_s|$
- Assume dc supply voltages, $V_{CC} = -V_{EE} = 15\text{ V}$
- Use op-amps μA741 or LF411

PAPER–PENCIL DESIGN

Note: Select the passive component values closest to the practical values.

1. After completing your design, write the circuit values.

$R_1 =$ ________ kΩ; $R_2 =$ ________ kΩ; $R_3 =$ ________ kΩ; $R_4 =$ ________ kΩ

$R_F =$ ________ kΩ

COMPUTER SIMULATION

Software Tools: PSpice, OrCAD, Multisim, LTSpice, or any electronic circuit simulator.

1. Simulate the rectifier circuit shown in Fig. 43-1 by using computer simulation. Run transient analysis to plot the output voltage $v_O(t)$ and the input voltage $v_s(t)$. Record their peak values.

$V_{S(peak)} =$ ________ V; $V_{O(peak)} =$ ________ V; $A_v = \frac{V_{O(peak)}}{V_{S(peak)}} =$ ________

2. Assign ±5% tolerance to all resistors. Run the simulation for the worst-case maximum output voltage. Plot both $v_S(t)$ and $v_O(t)$. Record.

$V_{S(peak)} =$ ________ V; $V_{O(peak)} =$ ________ V; $A_v = \frac{V_{O(peak)}}{V_{S(peak)}} =$ ________

3. Does your design meet the specifications under the worst-case conditions with 5% tolerance for resistors? If not, change the component values so that the specifications are met.

$R_1 =$ ________ kΩ; $R_2 =$ ________ kΩ; $R_3 =$ ________ kΩ; $R_4 =$ ________ kΩ

$R_F =$ ________ kΩ

4. Run the computer simulation with your suggested values in step 3. Record these values.

$V_{S(peak)} =$ ________ V; $V_{O(peak)} =$ ________ V; $A_v = \frac{V_{O(peak)}}{V_{S(peak)}} =$ ________

5. Compare the output voltage with the input voltage. Explain any deviations from the condition $v_o = |v_s|$.

____

6. Plot the transfer function $v_O(t)$ versus $v_S(t)$. Record the gain A_v = ________.
7. Reduce the input voltage to 20 mV. Simulate and plot the output. Comment on any deviations.

8. Replace the op-amp LF411 by µA741. Simulate and plot the output. Comment on any deviations.

EXPERIMENTS

The students are strongly encouraged and recommended to build and test the amplifier circuit to validate the theoretical and computer simulation results.

1. Set up your final circuit as shown in Fig. 43-1.
2. Observe the input voltage $v_s(t)$ and the output voltage $v_O(t)$.

REPORT

1. Compare the results from the computer simulation and experiment. Comment on any discrepancies.

2. Does the design meet the specifications? If not, explain the reasons.

3. What are the parameters that influence the limiting parameters? Explain.

4. What is the estimated cost of the rectifier?

5. Analyze and interpret the data due to any variations and practical limitations.

6. Describe the safety issues considered while conducting the experiment.

7. Describe the process to design and conduct experiments.

8. Conclusion and comment on achieving goals or objectives of this experiment.

ATTACH ALL PLOTS/GRAPHS TO YOUR REPORT

CHAPTER 44

Design of an Op-Amp Limiting Circuit

Learning Objectives

To design an adjustable limiting circuit to limit the output to specified levels. You will use computer simulation to verify the design and evaluate the performance of the limiter.

After the end of this experiment, you should be able to

- Describe the operation and characteristics of limiting circuits.
- Analyze and design limiting circuits to meet certain specifications.

PRE-LAB ASSIGNMENT

Read on *Op-Amp Limiting Circuits* (e.g., Rashid's Sections 17.3: Circuits with Op-Amps and Diodes).

DESIGN SPECIFICATIONS

Use op-amp μA741 whose $R_i = 2\ \text{M}\Omega$, $A_o = 10^5$, and $R_o = 75\ \Omega$. Assume dc supply voltages, $V_{CC} = -V_{EE} = 12\text{V}$. Design an adjustable voltage limiting circuit as shown in Fig. 44-1 to meet the following specifications:

- Voltage gain, $A_f = -10$
- Output voltage at the negative break, $v_{o(min)} = -5\ \text{V} \pm 5\%$
- Output voltage at the positive break, $v_{o(max)} = 6\ \text{V} \pm 5\%$
- Voltage gain between the breaks, $A_f = -10 \pm 5\%$
- Slope after break with a positive input (for $v_s > 0$) is $S_1 = -1/25$
- Slope after break with a negative input (for $v_s < 0$) is $S_2 = 1/44$
- Assume dc supply voltages, $V_{CC} = -V_{EE} = 15\ \text{V}$

PAPER–PENCIL DESIGN

Note: Select the passive component values closest to the practical values.

1. After completing your design, write the circuit values.

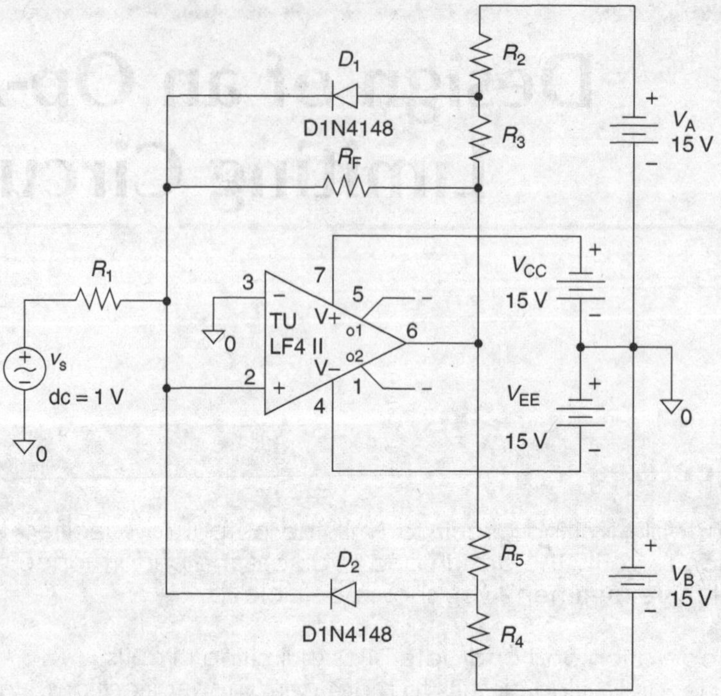

Figure 44-1 Adjustable voltage limiter

$R_1 =$ ________ kΩ; $R_2 =$ ________ kΩ; $R_3 =$ ________ kΩ; $R_4 =$ ________ kΩ

$R_5 =$ ________ kΩ; $R_F =$ ________ kΩ

2. Find the limiting voltages and slopes of the transfer characteristic v_O versus v_S.
3. Complete the calculated values in Table 44-1.

Table 44-1 Adjustable voltage limiter

	$V_{O(min)}$ (V)	$V_{s(min)}$ (V)	$V_{O(max)}$ (V)	$V_{S(max)}$ (V)	A_f	Slope S_1	Slope S_2
Calculated							
Simulated							
Experimental							

COMPUTER SIMULATION

Software tools: PSpice, OrCAD, Multisim, LTSpice, or any electronic circuit simulator.

1. Simulate the voltage limiting circuit shown in Fig. 44-1 by using computer simulation. Run dc sweep analysis to plot the transfer characteristic (the output voltage v_O versus the input voltage v_S). Record the values.

$V_{O(min)}$ = ________V; $V_{S(min)}$ = ________V; $V_{O(max)}$ = ________V; $V_{S(max)}$ = ________V

A_f = ________; Slope S_1 = ________; Slope S_1 = ________

2. Assign ±5% tolerance to all resistors. Run the simulation for the worst-case maximum transfer characteristic. Record.

$V_{O(min)}$ = ________V; $V_{S(min)}$ = ________V; $V_{O(max)}$ = ________V; $V_{S(max)}$ = ________V

A_f = ________; Slope S_1 = ________; Slope S_2 = ________

3. Does your design meet the specifications under the worst-case conditions with 5% tolerance for resistors? If not, change the component values so that the specifications are met. Note these values.

R_1 = ________ kΩ; R_2 = ________ kΩ; R_3 = ________ kΩ; R_4 = ________ kΩ

R_5 = ________ kΩ; R_F = ________ kΩ

4. Run the computer simulation with your suggested values in step 3. Record these values.

$V_{O(min)}$ = ________V; $V_{s(min)}$ = ________V; $V_{O(max)}$ = ________V; $V_{s(max)}$ = ________V

A_f = ________; Slope S_1 = ________; Slope S_2 = ________

5. Complete the simulated values in Table 44-1.

EXPERIMENTS

The students are strongly encouraged and recommended to build and test the amplifier circuit to validate the theoretical and computer simulation results.

1. Set up your final circuit as shown in Fig. 44-1.
2. Plot the transfer characteristic of v_O versus v_S.
3. Complete the experimental values in Table 44-1.

REPORT

1. Compare the results from the computer simulation and experiment. Comment on any discrepancies.

____

____

2. Does the design meet the specifications? If not, explain the reasons.

____

____

3. What are the parameters that influence the limiting parameters? Explain.

____

____

4. What is the estimated cost of the limiter?

____

____

5. Analyze and interpret the data due to any variations and practical limitations.

____

____

6. Describe the safety issues considered while conducting the experiment.

____

____

7. Describe the process to design and conduct experiments.

____

____

8. Conclusion and comment on achieving goals or objectives of this experiment.

____

____

ATTACH ALL PLOTS/GRAPHS TO YOUR REPORT

CHAPTER

45

Design of an Op-Amp Schmitt Trigger

Learning Objectives

To design a Schmitt trigger with a specified hysteresis band. We will use computer simulation to verify the design and evaluate the performance of a Schmitt trigger.

After the end of this experiment, you should be able to

- Describe the characteristics and operation of a Schmitt trigger, which will exhibit a specified hysteresis band.
- Analyze and design a Schmitt trigger to meet certain specifications.

PRE-LAB ASSIGNMENT

Read on *Op-Amp Schmitt Triggers* (e.g., Rashid's Sections 17.6: Schmitt Triggers).

DESIGN SPECIFICATIONS

Using comparator LM111, design the Schmitt trigger shown in Fig. 45-1 to meet the following specifications:

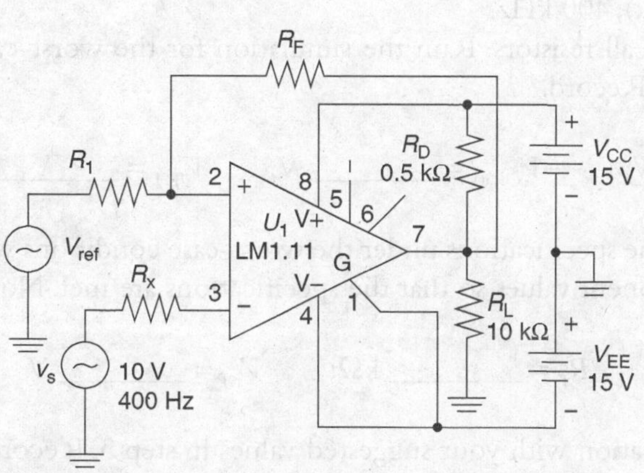

Figure 45-1 Schmitt trigger using comparator

- High threshold voltage, $V_{TH} = 8\,V \pm 5\%$
- Low threshold voltage, $V_{TL} = 2\,V \pm 5\%$
- Load resistance, $R_L = 10\,k\Omega$
- Assume dc supply voltages, $V_{CC} = -V_{EE} = 15\,V$

PAPER–PENCIL DESIGN

Note: Select the passive component values closest to the practical values.

1. After completing your design, write the circuit values and complete the calculated values in Table 45-1.

   $R_1 =$ ________ kΩ; $R_F =$ ________ kΩ; $R_x =$ ________ kΩ

   $V_{ref} =$ ________ V

2. Complete the calculated values in Table 45-1.

Table 45-1 Schmitt trigger

	$+V_{O(sat)}$ (V)	$-V_{O(sat)}$ (V)	V_{TH} (V)	V_{TL} (V)	HB = $V_{TH} - V_{TH}$ (V)
Calculated					
Simulated					
Experimental					

COMPUTER SIMULATION

Software Tools: PSpice, OrCAD, Multisim, LTSpice, or any electronic circuit simulator.

1. Simulate the amplifier shown in Fig. 45-1 by using computer simulation with an input signal voltage, $v_s = 10\,V$ (sinusoidal peak), 400 kHz.
2. Assign ±5% tolerance to all resistors. Run the simulation for the worst-case maximum output voltage. Plot both $v_S(t)$ and $v_O(t)$. Record.

   $+V_{O(sat)} =$ ________ V; $-V_{O(sat)} =$ ________ V; $V_{TH} =$ ________ V; $V_{TL} =$ ________ V

3. Does your design meet the specifications under the worst-case conditions with 5% tolerance for resistors? If not, change the component values so that the specifications are met. Note these values.

   $R_1 =$ ________ kΩ; $R_F =$ ________ kΩ; $V_{ref} =$ ________ V

4. Run the computer simulation with your suggested values in step 3. Record these values.

   $+V_{O(sat)} =$ ________ V; $-V_{O(sat)} =$ ________ V; $V_{TH} =$ ________ V; $V_{TL} =$ ________ V

5. Use computer simulation to plot the hysteresis characteristic for v_O versus v_S.

$+V_{O(sat)}$ = ________V; $-V_{O(sat)}$ = ________V; V_{TH} = ________V; V_{TL} = ________V

Does these values differ from those in step 4? If so, why? Explain.

____

____

6. Complete the simulated values in Table 45-1.
7. Replace the comparator LM111 by op-amp μA741 as shown in Fig. 45-2. Run the simulation and plot the hysteresis characteristic.
8. Compare the characteristic with that in step 5. Explain any differences or deviations. Why?

____

____

____

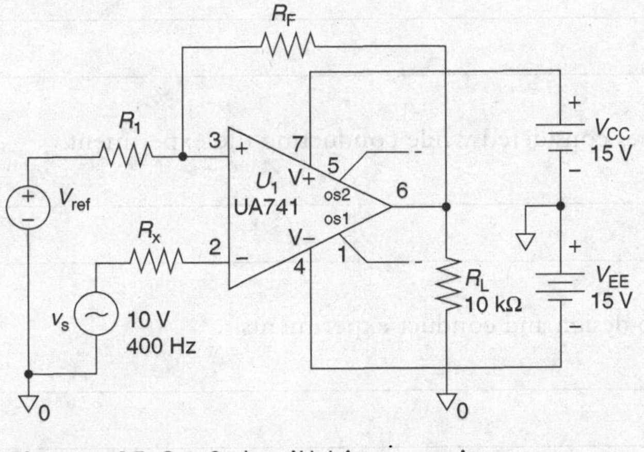

Figure 45-2 Schmitt trigger using op-amp

EXPERIMENTS

The students are strongly encouraged and recommended to build and test the amplifier circuit to validate the theoretical and computer simulation results.

1. Set up your final circuit shown in Fig. 45-1. Observe the input voltage $v_S(t)$ and the output voltage $v_O(t)$.
2. Complete the experimental values in Table 45-1.

REPORT

1. Compare the results from the computer simulation and experiment. Comment on any discrepancies.

2. Does the design meet the specifications? If not, explain the reasons.

3. What are the parameters that influence the Schmitt trigger parameters? Explain.

4. What is the estimated cost of the limiter?

5. Analyze and interpret the data due to any variations and practical limitations.

6. Describe the safety issues considered while conducting the experiment.

7. Describe the process to design and conduct experiments.

8. Conclusion and comment on achieving goals or objectives of this experiment.

ATTACH ALL PLOTS/GRAPHS TO YOUR REPORT

CHAPTER 46

Design of an Op-Amp Square-Wave Generator

Learning Objectives

To design a square-wave generator to operate at a specified frequency. We will use computer simulation to verify the design and evaluate the performance of a square-wave generator.

After the end of this experiment, you should be able to

- Describe the characteristic and operation of a square-wave generator.
- Analyze and design a square-wave generator to meet certain specifications.

PRE-LAB ASSIGNMENT

Read on *Op-Amp Square-Wave Generators* (e.g., Rashid's Sections 17.7: Square-Wave Generators).

DESIGN SPECIFICATIONS

Using comparator LM111, design the square-wave generator shown in Fig. 46-1 to meet the following specifications:

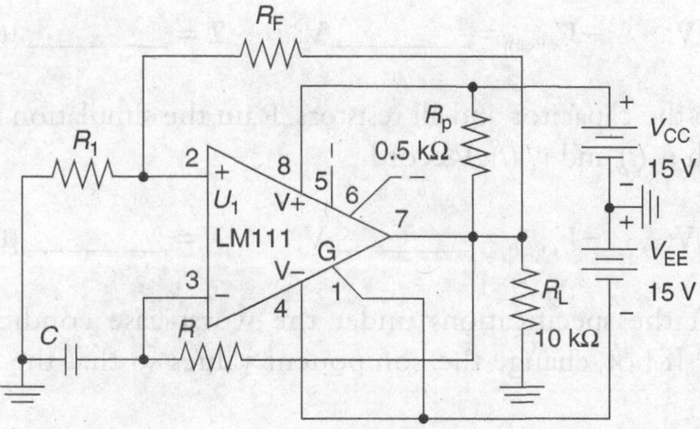

Figure 46-1 Square-wave generator

- High output voltage, $+V_{O(sat)} = 14\text{ V} \pm 5\%$
- Low output voltage, $-V_{o(sat)} = -14\text{ V} \pm 5\%$
- Output frequency, $f_o = 2.5$ kHz
- Load resistance, $R_L = 10$ kΩ
- Assume dc supply voltages, $V_{CC} = -V_{EE} = 15\text{ V}$

PAPER–PENCIL DESIGN

Note: Select the passive component values closest to the practical values.

1. After completing your design, write the circuit values.

   $R_1 =$ ________ kΩ; $R_F =$ ________ kΩ; $R =$ ________ kΩ; $C =$ ________ μF

2. Find the high and low values of the output voltage, and also its period and frequency.
3. Complete the calculated values in Table 46-1.

Table 46-1 Square-wave generator

	$+V_{O(sat)}$ (V)	$-V_{O(sat)}$ (V)	t_{on} (μs)	t_{off} (μs)	$T = t_{on} + t_{off}$ (μs)	f_o (kHz)
Calculated						
Simulated						
Experimental						

COMPUTER SIMULATION

Software tools: PSpice, OrCAD, Multisim, LTSpice, or any electronic circuit simulator.

1. Simulate the circuit shown in Fig. 46-1 by using computer simulation. Run transient analysis to plot the output voltage $v_O(t)$ and the capacitor voltage $v_C(t)$. You will need to assign an initial voltage (say 2 V) to the capacitor to start the circuit.

   $+V_{O(sat)} =$ ________ V; $-V_{O(sat)} =$ ________ V; $T =$ ________ μs; $f_o =$ ________ kHz

2. Assign ±5% tolerance to the capacitor and all resistors. Run the simulation for the worst-case maximum output voltage. Plot both $v_C(t)$ and $v_O(t)$. Record

   $+V_{O(sat)} =$ ________ V; $-V_{O(sat)} =$ ________ V; $T =$ ________ μs; $f_o =$ ________ kHz

3. Does your design meet the specifications under the worst-case conditions with 5% tolerance for capacitors and resistors? If not, change the component values so that the specifications are met. Note these values.

   $R_1 =$ ________ kΩ; $R_F =$ ________ kΩ; $R =$ ________ kΩ; $C =$ ________ μF

4. Run the computer simulation simulation with your suggested values in step 3. Record

$+V_{O(sat)} =$ ________V; $-V_{O(sat)} =$ ________V; $T =$ ________ μs; $f_o =$ ________ kHz

5. Complete the simulated values in Table 46-1.

EXPERIMENTS

The students are strongly encouraged and recommended to build and test the amplifier circuit to validate the theoretical and computer simulation results.

1. Set up your final circuit as shown in Fig. 46-1. Observe the capacitor voltage $v_C(t)$ and the output voltage $v_O(t)$.
2. Complete the experimental values in Table 46-1.

REPORT

1. Compare the results from the computer simulation and experiment. Comment on any discrepancies.

____

____

2. Does the design meet the specifications? If not, explain the reasons.

____

____

3. What are the parameters that influence the square-wave generator parameters? Explain.

____

____

4. What is the estimated cost of the limiter?

____

____

5. Analyze and interpret the data due to any variations and practical limitations.

____

____

6. Describe the safety issues considered while conducting the experiment.

____

____

7. Describe the process to design and conduct experiments.

8. Conclusion and comment on achieving goals or objectives of this experiment.

ATTACH ALL PLOTS/GRAPHS TO YOUR REPORT

CHAPTER

47

Design of an Op-Amp Stable Multivibrator

Learning Objectives

To design an astable multivibrator to operate at a specified frequency and duty cycle. We will use computer simulation to verify the design and evaluate the performance of a multivibrator.

After the end of this experiment, you should be able to

- Describe the characteristics and operation of an astable multivibrator.
- Analyze and design an astable multivibrator to meet certain specifications.

PRE-LAB ASSIGNMENT

Read on *Op-Amp Multivibrators* (e.g., Rashid's Sections 17.11.4: Astable Multivibrators).

DESIGN SPECIFICATIONS

Using the 555 timer, design the astable multivibrator shown in Fig. 47-1 to meet the following specifications:

- Output frequency, f_o = 4 kHz ± 5%
- Load resistance, R_L = 10 kΩ
- Assume dc supply voltages, V_{CC} = 12V

PAPER–PENCIL DESIGN

Note: Select the passive component values closest to the practical values.

1. After completing your design, write the circuit values.

   R_A = ________ kΩ; R_B = ________ kΩ; C = ________ μF

2. Complete the calculated values in Table 47-1.

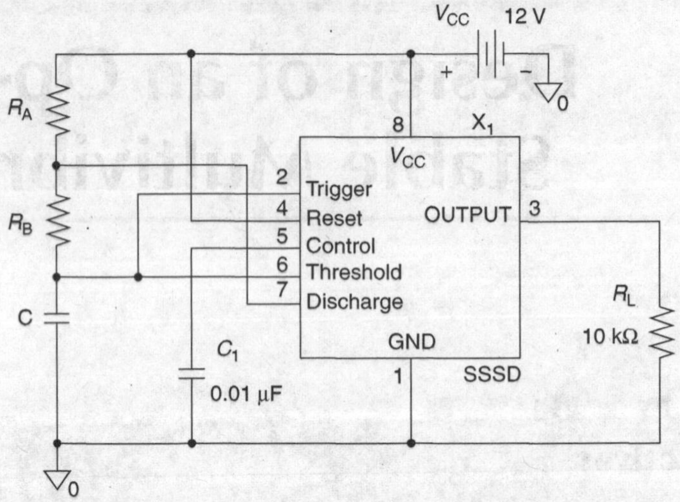

Figure 47-1 Astable multivibrator

Table 47-1 Astable multivibrator

	$+V_{O(sat)}$ (V)	$-V_{O(sat)}$ (V)	t_{on} (μs)	t_{off} (μs)	$T = t_{on} + t_{off}$ (μs)	$k = t_{on}/T\%$	f_o (kHz)
Calculated							
Simulated							
Experimental							

COMPUTER SIMULATION

Software Tools: PSpice, OrCAD, Multisim, LTSpice, or any electronic circuit simulator.

1. Simulate the multivibrator shown in Fig. 47-1 by using computer simulation. Run transient analysis and plot the output voltage $v_O(t)$. Record.

   $+V_{O(sat)}$ = ________ V; $-V_{O(sat)}$ = ________ V

   t_{on} = ________ μs; t_{off} = ________ μs; T = ________ μs; f_o = ________ kHz

2. Assign ±5% tolerance to all capacitors and resistors. Run the simulation for the worst-case maximum output voltage. Plot $v_O(t)$. Record.

   $+V_{O(sat)}$ = ________ V; $-V_{O(sat)}$ = ________ V

   t_{on} = ________ μs; t_{off} = ________ μs; T = ________ μs; f_o = ________ kHz

3. Does your design meet the specifications under the worst-case conditions with 5% tolerance for resistors? If not, change the component values so that the specifications are met. Note these values.

$R_A =$ ________ kΩ; $R_B =$ ________ kΩ; $C =$ ________ μF

4. Run the computer simulation with your suggested values in step 3. Record

$+V_{O(sat)} =$ ________ V; $-V_{O(sat)} =$ ________ V

$t_{on} =$ ________ μs; $t_{off} =$ ________ μs; $T =$ ________ μs; $f_o =$ ________ kHz

Are the values of t_{on} and t_{off} for the first cycle same as those of the subsequent cycle? If not, why? Explain.

____

____

____

5. Complete the simulated values in Table 47-1.

EXPERIMENTS

The students are strongly encouraged and recommended to build and test the amplifier circuit to validate the theoretical and computer simulation results.

1. Set up your final circuit shown in Fig. 47-1. Observe the output voltage $v_O(t)$. Record.

$+V_{O(sat)} =$ ________ V; $-V_{O(sat)} =$ ________ V

$t_{on} =$ ________ μs; $t_{off} =$ ________ μs; $T =$ ________ μs; $f_o =$ ________ kHz

2. Complete the experimental values in Table 47-1.

REPORT

1. Compare the results from the computer simulation and experiment. Comment on any discrepancies

____

____

2. Does the design meet the specifications? If not, explain the reasons.

____

____

3. What are the parameters that influence the astable multivibrator parameters? Explain.

____

____

4. What is the estimated cost of the multivibrator?

5. Analyze and interpret the data due to any variations and practical limitations.

6. Describe the safety issues considered while conducting the experiment.

7. Describe the process to design and conduct experiments.

8. Conclusion and comment on achieving goals or objectives of this experiment.

ATTACH ALL PLOTS/GRAPHS TO YOUR REPORT

Appendix

Instructions for Using the Accompanied Software

INSTALLING THE SOFTWARE

The instructions for installing the OrCAD software are printed on the Cengage Digital App. The software can be downloaded from the Cadence website at http://www.cadence.com/products/orcad/Pages/downloads.aspx.

The following steps, which pertain to OrCAD Version 9.2, are also applicable to other versions:

1. Place the schematics on the computer drive.
2. From Windows, enter the File Manager and click the left mouse button on the software.
3. Click on setup.exe, File, Run, and OK.
4. Click on OK to select the products to install Capture and PSpice.
5. Click on OK to select the default C: OrCADLite.
6. Click on Yes to choose Program Folder: OrCAD Family Release 9.2 Lite Edition.
7. Create the OrCAD Capture Lite and PSpice A/D icons from the Start menu; then go to Programs, OrCAD Family, and Capture Lite menu.
8. Click the left mouse button on the Capture Lite icon once, and the window of Capture Lite will open.

For PSpice Schematics, download version 9.1 and follow the same steps.

Note: Although there are later versions of OrCAD, the 9.2 version has proven to work well. If you have a schematic in lower version, you can run at a higher version, not vice versa. Thus, the circuit files were drawn in lower versions 9.1 and 9.2 so that these files can be run on higher versions of PSpice.

FOR USING PSpice SCHEMATICS AND OrCAD FILES IN THE BOOK

Step 1: Create a folder in the hard drive of your computer.

Step 2: Copy all the PSpice schematics and OrCAD files from Cengage Digital App to the folder in the hard drive of your computer.

Step 3: Open the window of PSpice schematics as shown in Figure 1(a) or the OrCAD Capture Lite as shown in Figure 1(b).

Step 4: Open the PSpice schematic files or the OrCAD files from your computer. For OrCAD files, select the project menu as shown in window Figure 1(b).

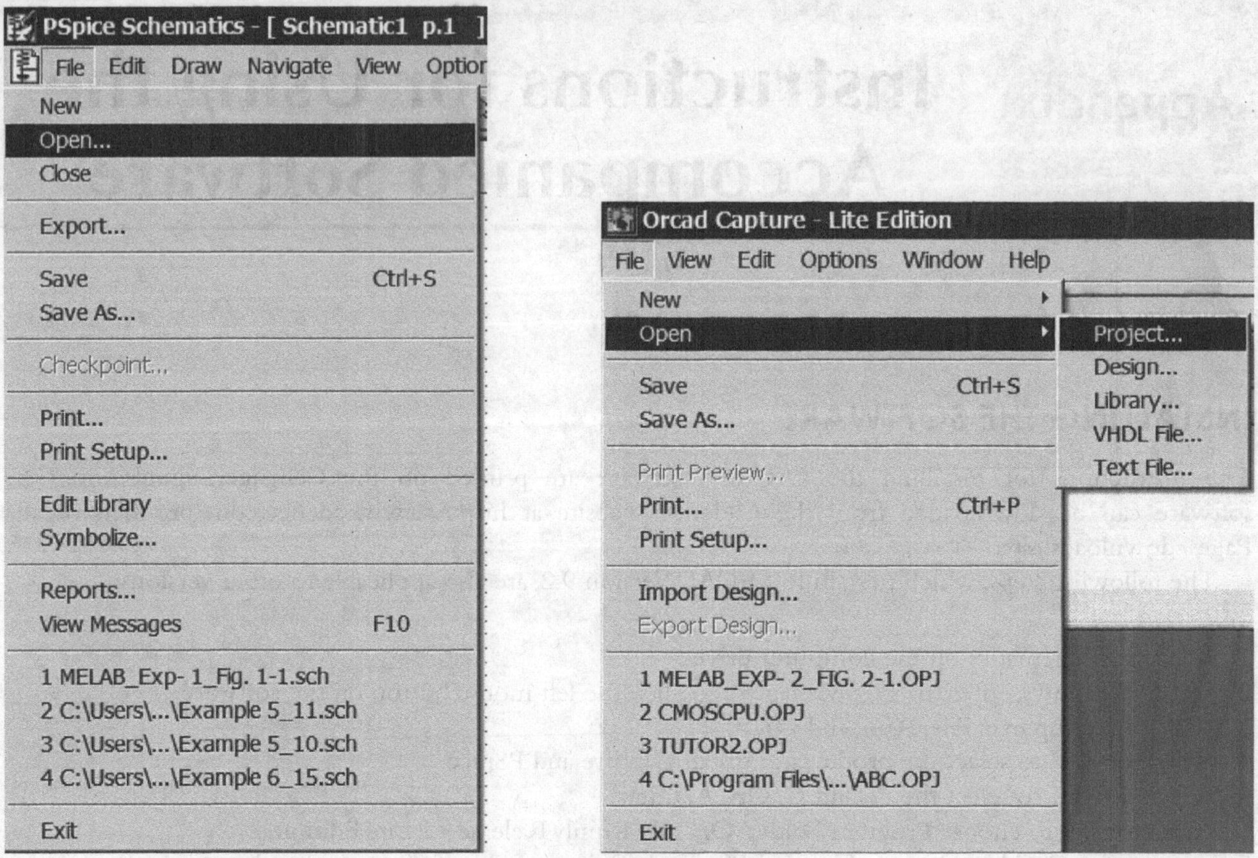

(a) PSpice Schematics (b) OrCAD Capture

Figure 1 PSpice schematics and OrCAD windows

RUNNING THE SIMULATION IN MULTISIM OR LTSpice

The schematics in text were drawn in PSpice Schematics and OrCAD captures. However, the schematics can be drawn and run in Multisim or LTSpice or any electronic circuit simulator. Running the simulation in Multisim or LTSpice would need some changes and adjustment to the files.

- **LT-Spice:** PSpice and OrCAD schematics generate LTSpice netlist. LTspice can import this netlist file and run the simulation. Download free version of LTSpice from: http://www.linear.com/LTspice
- **Multisim:** It can import OrCAD files (*.dsn) and SPICE netlist files (.cir) to run the simulation. It is not a free software.

INTRODUCTION TO OrCAD

For drawing schematics and running the simulation files, refer to Appendix A of reference book: Rashid, M.H., *Microelectronic Circuits: Analysis and Design*. Boston, MA: Cengage Publishing, 3/e, 2017, or 2/e, 2011.

USER-DEFINED MODEL PARAMETERS

1. You must include the text file (Rashid_Models_Microelectronics_3e with .txt extension) for the user-defined model parameters for diodes and transistors in the Edit Simulation Profile menu. You can edit the model parameters of the devices. But, you must change the name of the device in the schematic to match the name in the model file.
2. The text file Rashid_Models_Microelectronics_3e is included with the software.
3. This is the only user-defined file you will need to include in the library menu.
4. If there is any other file, you need to delete it from the libraries under Edit Simulation Profile.
5. But you need PSpice and OrCAD files (e.g., nom.lib) that are generally included by the PSpice or OrCAD software.